Reading Chaucer

READING CHAUCER

Selected Essays

PETER BROWN

PETER LANG
Oxford • Bern • Berlin • Bruxelles • Frankfurt am Main • New York • Wien

Bibliographic information published by Die Deutsche Nationalbibliothek.
Die Deutsche Nationalbibliothek lists this publication in the Deutsche National-
bibliografie; detailed bibliographic data is available on the Internet at http://dnb.d-nb.de.

A catalogue record for this book is available from the British Library.

Library of Congress Control Number: 2013945475

Cover image: 'Approaching Dawn', a wood engraving by Eric Gill from his illustrations to *Troilus and Criseyde* (1927).

ISBN 978-3-0343-0933-2

© Peter Lang AG, International Academic Publishers, Bern 2013
Hochfeldstrasse 32, CH-3012 Bern, Switzerland
info@peterlang.com, www.peterlang.com, www.peterlang.net

All rights reserved.
All parts of this publication are protected by copyright.
Any utilisation outside the strict limits of the copyright law, without the
permission of the publisher, is forbidden and liable to prosecution.
This applies in particular to reproductions, translations, microfilming,
and storage and processing in electronic retrieval systems.

This publication has been peer reviewed.

Printed in Germany

Contents

Abbreviations	vii
Illustrations	ix
Introduction	xi
PART ONE Borderlands	1
Higden's Britain	5
On the Borders of Middle English Dream Visions	23
Towards a Bohemian Reading of *Troilus and Criseyde*	57
PART TWO Interiors	85
The Prison of Theseus and the Castle of *Jalousie*	89
Shot wyndowe (Miller's Tale, I. 3358 and 3695): An Open and Shut Case?	97
The Containment of Symkyn: The Function of Space in the Reeve's Tale	109
An Optical Theme in the Merchant's Tale	123

PART THREE	After-Images	139
	Is the Canon's Yeoman's Tale Apocryphal?	143
	Images	157
	Journey's End: The Prologue to the *Tale of Beryn*	179

| Bibliography | 219 |
| Index | 247 |

Abbreviations

Chaucer's Works

BD	*Book of the Duchess*
CkP	Cook's Prologue
ClPT	Clerk's Prologue and Tale
GP	General Prologue
HF	*House of Fame*
KnT	Knight's Tale
LGW	*Legend of Good Women*
MerT	Merchant's Tale
MilT	Miller's Tale
PardP	Pardoner's Prologue
PardT	Pardoner's Tale
RvT	Reeve's Tale
SNPT	Second Nun's Prologue and Tale
SqT	Squire's Tale
TC	*Troilus and Criseyde*
WBP	Wife of Bath's Prologue

Other Abbreviations

EETS	Early English Text Society
ELH	*English Literary History*
IMEV	Carleton Brown and Rossell Hope Robbins, *The Index of Middle English Verse* (New York: Columbia University Press for the Index Society, 1943).
Lewis and Short	Charlton T. Lewis and Charles Short, *A Latin Dictionary*, rev. edn (Oxford: Clarendon Press, 1966).
MED	*Middle English Dictionary*, ed. Hans Kurath, Sherman M. Kuhn, Robert E. Lewis et al., 13 vols (Ann Arbor: University of Michigan Press, 1952–2001).
OED	*The Oxford English Dictionary*, 2nd edn, ed. John Simpson and Edmund Weiner, 20 vols (Oxford: Oxford University Press, 1989).
PMLA	*Publications of the Modern Language Association [of America]*
SATF	Société des Anciens Textes Français

Illustrations

Figure 1　The castle of *Jalousie*, from the *Roman de la rose* (London, British Library, MS Egerton 1069, f. 30). 93

Figure 2　Portrait of Geoffrey Chaucer, from the *Regement of Princes* by Thomas Hoccleve (London, British Library, MS Harley 4866, f. 88). 168

Introduction

This volume brings together nine essays published since 1980. They have featured in a range of journals and edited collections and so are scattered and in some cases difficult to obtain. Whatever its other merits, the present collection has the advantages of convenience and usefulness. It also includes one new essay, 'Towards a Bohemian Reading of *Troilus and Criseyde*'.

The contents are not arranged chronologically but in three groups or subsections that represent the principles of selection: 'Borderlands', 'Interiors' and 'After-Images'. The intention is to suggest how individual pieces might speak to a larger theme. The essays in 'Borderlands' explore the geographical status of Britain, Chaucer's social status as an outsider, and the sense of liminality expressed through the genre of dream vision. 'Interiors' applies to domestic space, especially in connection with privacy and imprisonment, but also to ways of describing subjectivity. The concerns of 'After-Images' are with the reputation of Chaucer, imitations of his work and its critical evaluation. More detailed synopses of the contents of the essays appear in the opening pages of each subsection.

A number of topics recur throughout the book and so provide further coherence. Chief among them are visual culture, especially as manifested through iconography and processes of ocular perception; manuscript study as a way of deepening and modifying critical interpretation; and the reception of Chaucer's works. The approach is broadly cross-disciplinary and benefits from the labours of scholars working in palaeography and the histories of art, science, politics and society. Each of the essays is committed, in its different ways, to using contextual materials as a means of reading Chaucer with a fuller understanding. His dream visions, *Troilus and Criseyde* and *Canterbury Tales* all receive significant coverage. Extensive reference is also made to a range of other authors, including Ranulph Higden, John Gower and Thomas Hoccleve.

The content of the reprinted material is unrevised, although for ease of reading and use spelling has been regularized according to British conventions and footnotes standardized and keyed to a bibliography. A full reference to the original of an essay occurs on its first page. Editors and publishers have been generous in providing the necessary permissions. Acknowledgements are due as follows to: Palgrave Macmillan for 'Higden's Britain'; Oxford University Press for 'On the Borders of Medieval Dream Visions'; Pennsylvania State University Press for 'The Prison of Theseus and the Castle of *Jalousie*' and 'The Containment of Symkyn'; the Society for the Study of Mediaeval Languages and Literature for '*Shot wyndowe* (Miller's Tale I. 3558 and 3695): An Open and Shut Case?'; the New Chaucer Society for 'An Optical Theme in the Merchant's Tale'; Taylor & Francis Ltd. for 'Is the Canon's Yeoman's Tale Apocryphal?'; Wiley-Blackwell for 'Images'; and King's College, London, for 'Journey's End: The Prologue to the *Tale of Beryn*'. The illustrations appear by kind permission of the British Library Board. Unless otherwise stated, Chaucer's works are quoted from *The Riverside Chaucer*, 3rd edn, ed. Benson et al. (1987).

In the process of writing the items in this book I have incurred many debts to individuals and groups of people who have answered queries, listened to papers based on my research and raised questions. Specific acknowledgements appear in the footnotes, but I should also like to single out Andrew Butcher, Katie Sokolowska and Alison Wiggins and audiences at the Centre for Medieval Studies, University of Reading; Emmanuel College, Cambridge; the University of Auckland, New Zealand; and Charles University, Prague; and staff and students at the Canterbury Centre for Medieval and Tudor [now Early Modern] Studies at the University of Kent. Without the help of Mary Critchley, Andrea Griffith, David Rudeforth and Christabel Scaife the book would not exist.

PART ONE

Borderlands

Higden's Britain

The *Polychronicon* is a chronicle written by the Benedictine monk Ranulph Higden (1299–1363) and translated *c.*1387 from Latin into English by John Trevisa. Higden's Britain is Chaucer's Britain: Chaucer travelled the length and breadth of the Britain Higden describes. Higden depicts an edgy country, an archipelago on the rim of the known world populated by different ethnic groups who create a pervasive instability. Britain's liminality is both a weakness and a strength, making it at once vulnerable and influential. Characterized by strong central government, it is also a country of vigorous regional identity and historical complexity.

On the Borders of Middle English Dream Visions

At the court of Edward III, where Higden acted as adviser, Chaucer won his literary spurs. His first major composition was a dream vision, closely associated with French courtly poetry but also with pilgrimage (another liminal activity) and rapidly becoming the genre of choice for a new generation of English writers, including William Langland and the *Gawain*-poet, seeking to explore social conflict, religious turmoil, self-doubt and the formation of personal identity. In the *Book of the Duchess*, commissioned by John of Gaunt on the death of his wife, Blanche, Chaucer uses the dream vision to represent the altered psychological state of being on the edge: Gaunt's grief has made him isolated and introspective and Chaucer himself, the son of a wine merchant, is a social outsider.

Towards a Bohemian Reading of *Troilus and Criseyde*

Troilus, from the mid-point of Chaucer's poetic career, shows him to all intents and purposes as an insider. Yet he represents himself, as narrator, as different from the rest of the court. Now serving Richard II, he responds to the presence of another outsider, the queen, Anne of Bohemia, and produces a poem celebrating Trojan culture. That choice refers to Anne's own sense of belonging since her father, the Holy Roman Emperor Charles IV, traced his dynasty in Prague to mythic origins in Troy. But the city is also a code for London, then known as New Troy, and one through which Chaucer represents his audience's own experiences of textual culture and piety.

Higden's Britain*

On 21 August 1352 Ranulph Higden, a monk of the Benedictine abbey of St Werburgh's, Chester, stood before the king's council at Westminster. He had been summoned to appear 'una cum omnibus cronicis vestris et que sunt in custodia vestra ad loquendum et tractandum cum dicto consilio nostro super aliquibus que vobis tunc exponentur ex parte nostra' ('with all your chronicles and those in your charge to speak and treat with our council concerning matters to be explained to you on our behalf'). This wording suggested to Edwards that Higden was probably at that time 'the official custodian of the abbey's library and the head of the *scriptorium*'.[1] However, Higden was not at court merely in his official capacity, but also as an authority on the subject of chronicles. In particular, he was the author of the well-known *Polychronicon* in seven books. The term 'cronicis vestris' in the council's summons probably refers to it.

The subject of Higden's discussion with the king's council we do not know, but we can identify at least one area of common interest. At this time Edward III was actively appropriating images of national identity for political and propaganda purposes. His deliberate revival of Arthurian mythology, proposal to establish a new 'Round Table', and founding of

---

* First published in *Medieval Europeans: Studies in Ethnic Identity and National Perspectives in Medieval Europe*, ed. Alfred P. Smyth (Houndmills: Macmillan, 1998), 103–18.

1 J. G. Edwards, 'Ranulph, Monk of Chester', *English Historical Review*, 47 (1932), 94, quoting from the Close Rolls of Edward III for 8 August 1352. For the sparse details of Higden's biography see J. Taylor, *The 'Universal Chronicle' of Ranulf Higden* (Oxford: Clarendon Press, 1966), 1–2; and A. Gransden, *Historical Writing in England*, ii: *c.1307 to the Early Sixteenth Century* (London: Routledge and Kegan Paul, 1982), 43.

the Order of the Garter in 1348, illustrate this process.² Higden also had a professed interest, expressed through the *Polychronicon*, in the origins and identity of Britain. To understand the specific nature of that interest we must first turn to the general matters of composition, genre, structure and readership.

According to his own account, Higden's first objective was to write a treatise solely on Britain, which he describes as 'tractatum aliquem, ex variis auctorum decerptum laboribus, de statu insulae Britannicae ad notitiam cudere futurorum' ('a tretes i-gadered of dyuerse bookes, of the staat of the ylonde of Britayne, to knowleche of men that cometh after vs'). He was then prevailed upon by friends to write a history of the world, to which he agreed, but without losing sight of his original intention.³ Higden completed the first version of his history about 1327. He continued working on it, expanding and revising, until 1340, then periodically added brief entries from 1341 to 1352. It survives in three versions (short, intermediate and long), which represent the different stages of its composition. An autograph manuscript of the intermediate version, which formerly belonged to St Werburgh's and which is now in the Huntington Library (HM 132), reveals much about Higden's synthetic, additive way of working.⁴

2 M. H. Keen, *England in the Later Middle Ages: A Political History* (London: Routledge, 1973), 145–6; J. Vale, *Edward III and Chivalry: Chivalric Society and Its Context 1270–1350* (Woodbridge: Boydell Press, 1982), 68–9, 70 and ch. 5; W. M. Ormrod, *The Reign of Edward III: Crown and Political Society in England 1327–1377* (New Haven: Yale University Press, 1990), 45; and C. Dean, *Arthur of England: English Attitudes to King Arthur and the Knights of the Round Table in the Middle Ages and the Renaissance* (Toronto: University of Toronto Press, 1987), 55–6.
3 Higden, *Polychronicon*, I. i; in C. Babington and J. R. Lumby (eds), *Polychronicon Ranulphi Higden Monachi Cestrensis; together with the English Translations of John Trevisa and of an Unknown Writer of the Fifteenth Century*, Rolls series 41(1865–86), i (1865), 6–9, adding here and subsequently Trevisa's translation (with thorns and yoghs transliterated).
4 Taylor, 'Universal Chronicle', ch. 6; his *English Historical Literature in the Fourteenth Century* (Oxford: Clarendon Press, 1987), 101; and V. H. Galbraith, 'An Autograph MS of Ranulph Higden's *Polychronicon*', *Huntington Library Quarterly* 23 (1959–60), 1–18.

Higden's Britain

The *Polychronicon* ('the cronicle of meny tymes')[5] belongs to a particular species of medieval historiography, 'universal history', the origins of which are in St Augustine's *City of God*. Traditionally ordered according to the six days of creation, or the six ages of history, with a seventh, sabbatical age existing beyond time, it attempted to reveal the hand of God, the structures of divine planning, in the divagations of human history. Its underlying assumptions are that the Bible is the most significant historical work ever written, and that history is exemplary: rightly considered, the past can teach its students how to act and live in accordance with God's laws. So universal history is providential history, as much concerned with the miraculous, the marvellous, the mythic and the prophetic as with what might now pass for reality.[6]

To this genre Higden introduced some significant variations, slanting his structure and content in order to emphasize Britain's place in the development of world history. The subjects represented by each book are: (1) a prefatory book on world geography, ending with Britain, followed by six books which correspond to the six ages of the world; (2) from the creation of the world to the destruction of the Jewish temple; (3) from the Babylonian captivity to the coming of Christ; (4) from the Incarnation to the Anglo-Saxon invasion of England; (5) the history of Britain from the Saxons to the Danish invasion; (6) British history from then until the Norman invasion; and (7) British history since then.[7] Regarding history as 'testis temporum, memoria vitae, nuncio vetustatis' ('wytnesse of tyme,

---

5 Higden, *Polychronicon*, I. iii, ed. Babington, i, 26 and 27.
6 M. Keen, 'Mediaeval Ideas of History' in *The Mediaeval World: Literature and Civilization*, ed. D. Daiches and A. Thorlby (London: Aldus, 1973), ii, 285–314; Taylor, '*Universal Chronicle*', 33–9; his *English Historical Literature*, 40; R. G. Collingwood, *The Idea of History* (Oxford: Clarendon Press, 1946), 52–6; R. W. Southern, 'Aspects of the European Tradition of Historical Writing: 2. Hugh of St Victor and the Idea of Historical Development', *Transactions of the Royal Historical Society*, 5th ser., 21 (1971), 159–79; and V. H. Galbraith, *Historical Research in Medieval England*, The Creighton Lecture in History, 1949 (London: Athlone Press, 1951), 9–11.
7 Higden, *Polychronicon*, I. iii; ed. Babington, i, 26–9; see also A. Gransden, 'Silent Meanings in Ranulf Higden's *Polychronicon* and in Thomas Elmham's *Liber Metricus de Henrico Quinto*', *Medium Ævum* 46 (1977), 232–3.

mynde of lyf, messager of eldnesse'), Higden packed each book with anecdotes, exempla, folk stories and personal observations, drawing on a wide variety of sources so that the *Polychronicon* resembles nothing so much as a great encyclopedia, one laced with a new interest in antiquity.[8]

One of Higden's most effective transformations of the genre is in the form of the transition which he engineers between the first book, on geography, and what follows. The link is made through the ancient idea of the microcosm, applied here in an unexpected context. Having described the physical appearance of the greater world, he turns to the little world of man, plotting their resemblances in proportion, disposition, composition, function, energies and subjection to time. Thus the history of mankind is the history of the world and the history of the world is the history of mankind.[9] Within this conception, Higden is above all concerned to understand the place, function, nature and identity of Britain.

The *Polychronicon*, in spite of its bulk, was a great success, and survives in over 120 manuscripts.[10] Many, as might be expected, belonged to Benedictine houses, but copies were also owned by the secular clergy, colleges and hospitals, by individual clerics, and even a few laymen.[11] The extent to which Higden's work was embedded in the historical consciousness of a national audience is also indicated by its frequent use as the basis for supplementary chronicles by diverse authors, in the form of continuations and reworkings, especially in the later fourteenth century, as well as by its effect on vernacular and devotional literature.[12] The intermediate version of the *Polychronicon* was translated into English by John Trevisa by

---

8   Higden, *Polychronicon*, I. i, ed. Babington, i, 6 and 7; see also Taylor, *English Historical Literature*, 96–8.
9   Higden, *Polychronicon*, II. i, ed. Babington, ii (1869), 175–201. See Gransden, *Historical Writing*, ii, 45–6; and Taylor, 'Universal Chronicle', 68–71.
10 Taylor, 'Universal Chronicle', ch. 6.
11 Taylor, *English Historical Literature*, 56, n. 87.
12 Taylor, 'Universal Chronicle', ch. 7; his *English Historical Literature*, 55–6, ch. 4 and 100–7; Gransden, *Historical Writing*, ii, 55–7; and A. S. G. Edwards, 'The Influence and Audience of the *Polychronicon*: Some Observations', *Proceedings of the Leeds Philosophical and Literary Society* (Literary and Historical Section) 17:6 (1980), 113–19.

1387, who added his own interpolations.[13] Trevisa's translation is known to exist in complete form in fourteen manuscripts.[14] There is a further English translation by a person unknown, which survives in only one manuscript. Trevisa's *Polychronicon* was printed by Caxton in 1482, with a continuation by him, and there were two further editions by 1527.[15] The only available modern edition is that begun by Babington and continued by Lumby (1865–86), which runs to nine volumes in the Rolls series.[16] It uses the intermediate version of the Latin text printed alongside Trevisa's translation and the anonymous fifteenth-century translation.

The *Polychronicon* has been the subject of studies which, understandably, have been predominantly historical in orientation. Gransden has tended to emphasize in Higden what there is of use, in the way of verifiable information, to modern, positivist researchers.[17] Taylor, on the other hand, has placed Higden firmly and centrally in relation to the genres of historiography current in the fourteenth century.[18] Each kind of approach is valuable in showing just how precocious and significant Higden's writing was. But there is another line of enquiry which merits consideration. It is more literary in orientation, but it nevertheless seeks to uncover data of historical value, namely the attitudes of mind, the mental constructs, the preconceptions which shaped both Higden's understanding of his

---

13   A. S. G. Edwards, 'John Trevisa', in *Middle English Prose: A Critical Guide to Major Authors and Genres*, ed. A. S. G. Edwards (New Brunswick, NJ: Rutgers University Press, 1984), 133–46. See also Ralph Hanna III, 'Producing Manuscripts and Editions', in *Crux and Controversy in Middle English Textual Criticism*, ed. A. J. Minnis and C. Brewer (Cambridge: Brewer, 1992), 112–19; Taylor, *'Universal Chronicle'*, ch. 8; and D. C. Fowler, *John Trevisa*, Authors of the Middle Ages, 2: English Writers of the Late Middle Ages (Aldershot: Variorum, 1993).
14   R. Waldron, 'The Manuscripts of Trevisa's Translation of the *Polychronicon*: Towards a New Edition', *Modern Language Quarterly* 51 (1990), 281–317.
15   Taylor, *'Universal Chronicle'*, ch. 8; and Lister M. Matheson, 'Printer and Scribe: The *Polychronicon*, and the *Brut*', *Speculum* 60 (1985), 593–614.
16   See n. 3, above.
17   Gransden, *Historical Writing*, ii, 50–1.
18   Taylor, *English Historical Literature*, ch. 5.

own culture and, by extension, that of his readers.[19] Such an approach is of particular value in the case of an intellectual concept such as 'national identity' which is not readily susceptible to the straightforward analysis of dates and events.

How did Higden think about Britain? How, if at all, did he construct its national identity? If we can answer such questions in relation to this well-known and influential work, we will have made considerable progress in entering the mind-set of a particularly influential set of people – especially among the educated clergy – in the middle of the fourteenth century, and therefore of understanding what, if anything, the concept of national identity might have meant in such circles at that time.[20] To the extent that the influence of the *Polychronicon* soon extended, through Trevisa's translation, to an equally influential set of lay people, we will have gained access to a highly significant aspect of their collective psychology.[21]

The evidence suggests that the geographical section of Higden's work was of especial importance and interest both to Higden and to his fourteenth-century readers. However much his original plan mushroomed, it appears both that Higden set out to write a defining account of Britain, and that his efforts were recognized for just that reason. Thus, in providing a rationale for his *magnum opus*, he makes Britain its driving force, and gives the subject pride of place. Referring to the first book, he comments:

19 Cf. G. M. Spiegel, *Romancing the Past: The Rise of Vernacular Prose Historiography in Thirteenth-Century France*, The New Historicism: Studies in Cultural Poetics, 23 (Berkeley: University of California Press, 1993), 5, 8 and 9; A. Gurevich, *Historical Anthropology of the Middle Ages*, ed. J. Howlett (Cambridge: Polity Press, 1992), 10 and 14; and for the general approach P. Burke, *The French Historical Revolution: The Annales School, 1929–89* (Cambridge: Polity Press, 1990), 67–74; and R. A. Albano, *Middle English Historiography*, American University Studies, ser. 4; English Language and Literature, 168 (New York: Lang, 1993), ch. 1.

20 On the availability of the concept see V. H. Galbraith, 'Nationality and Language in Medieval England', *Transactions of the Royal Historical Society*, 4th ser., 23 (1941), 113–28.

21 Taylor, *English Historical Literature*, 55–6; Gransden, *Historical Writing*, ii, 51–2. On the general receptivity of Higden's audience see B. Smalley, *English Friars and Antiquity in the Early Fourteenth Century* (Oxford: Blackwell, 1960), ch. 1.

[...] provincia quaeque partialis percurritur, donec perveniatur ad omnium novissimam Britanniam, tanquam ad speciem specialissimam, cujus gratia tota praesens lucubrata est historia.

[...] and for this storie is bytrauailled by cause of Brytayne, eueriche prouince and londe is descryued for to me come to Britayne the laste of alle, as most special.[22]

As for audience recognition of Higden's emphasis on Britain, this may in some part be gauged by the circulation as a separate entity of the geographical section of the *Polychronicon*, in which Britain is given such prominence.[23]

Higden's Britain may indeed have hit his readers with the force of novelty because it is deliberately presented as a viable alternative to two widespread myths of national identity then current. These Higden downplays, opting instead for a more factual, ratiocinative, less imaginative but no less fascinating account. The legend of Brutus, scion of Troy and founder of Britain, was the subject of *Brut*, a work which vied with the *Polychronicon* for popularity. With its immediate origins in a mid-thirteenth-century Anglo-Norman text, and its deeper roots in Geoffrey of Monmouth, it had proved a durable and adaptable account of Britain with particular appeal to the nobility.[24] The Brutus myth is credited in passing by Higden, but in general he quietly ignores it. Associated with it was the legend of Arthur which, again, does not make much headway in Higden's scheme of things. Instead, he is prone to adopt a sceptical attitude. For example, he comments with some incredulity on the supposed links between Arthurian

22 Higden, *Polychronicon*, I. iii, ed. Babington, i, 26–7.
23 See Edwards, 'Influence and Audience', 113; Taylor, *'Universal Chronicle'*, 58; and his *English Historical Literature*, 99. On the story of England in other chronicles circulating in the early fourteenth century, see T. Turville-Petre, *England the Nation: Language, Literature, and National Identity, 1290–1340* (Oxford: Clarendon Press, 1996), ch. 3.
24 See Taylor, *English Historical Literature*, ch. 6; his *'Universal Chronicle'*, 13–16; and L. M. Matheson, 'Historical Prose', in *Middle English Prose*, ed. Edwards, 210–14. For a recent account of the importance of Troy in medieval historiography see F. Ingledew, 'The Book of Troy and the Genealogical Construction of History: The Case of Geoffrey of Monmouth's *Historia regum Britanniae*', *Speculum* 69 (1994), 665–704.

and Roman chronologies: 'Hic magni Arthuri, si fas sit credere, magnam cunam legati adiere Romani.' ('There the messangers of Rome come to the grete Arthurus curt, if it is leeful for to trowe.')[25]

It may be objected that, in spite of his distance from familiar and long-standing myths of national identity, Higden himself was actually doing nothing new, but rather recycling well-known and durable materials, acting merely as a relatively passive *compilator*.[26] But perhaps enough has already been said to indicate that the traditional medieval practice of collecting, collating and re-presenting authoritative excerpts did not rule out originality.[27] In Higden's case it enabled him to endorse aspects of earlier versions of 'Britain', such as that by Bede, but also to be deliberately selective, making certain emphases, introducing interpolations and first-hand observations, and to compare and evaluate the validity of existing evidence.[28] The end-result was a genuinely new synthesis of what, in the mid-fourteenth century, Britain meant to a monastic chronicler and his audience.

There are two tendencies, two determining, structural motifs, which underlie Higden's account of Britain. On the one hand there are the forces which produce unity, continuity, reassurance and security, and on the other those which produce diversity, change, doubt and instability. This is no easy balance, but a fragile, volatile and potentially disastrous tension between opposites. The quality of betweenness which Higden thus perceives as characteristic of Britain's condition is explained in part by its geographical identity.

---

25   Higden, *Polychronicon*, I. xlviii, ed. Babington, ii, 76 and 77; see also J. E. Housman, 'Higden, Trevisa, Caxton and the Beginnings of Arthurian Criticism', *Review of English Studies* 23 (1947), 209–17.

26   Cf. Albano, *Middle English Historiography*, ch. 1; Taylor, *English Historical Literature*, 39, 48–9 and 97; Gransden, *Historical Writing*, ii, 47–9. The most extensive account of Higden's sources is in Taylor, *'Universal Chronicle'*, ch. 5.

27   See A. J. Minnis, *Medieval Theory of Authorship: Scholastic Literary Attitudes in the Later Middle Ages*, 2nd edn (London: Scolar Press, 1988), 113, 193–4, 200 and 205; and Albano, *Middle English Historiography*, 20–1.

28   Cf. Higden, *Polychronicon*, I. xlviii, ed. Babington, ii, 66 and 67. On Higden's editorial procedures see Galbraith, 'Autograph'; and Taylor, *'Universal Chronicle'*, ch. 6.

Higden's Britain

Britain is an island, or rather a collection of islands large and small. It is therefore crucially different from the more landlocked countries of continental Europe. Having combed a number of different sources, Higden makes these points with some insistence:

> *Alfridus.* Anglia Britannica alter orbis apellatur [...] *Solinus.* Ora Gallici littoris finis foret orbis, nisi Britannia insula nomen pene alterius orbis mereretur. *Alfridus.* Et dicta est insula eo quod in salo sit posita, crebrisque undarum jactibus adversariorumque incursibus tundatur [...] *Plinius* [...] Haec Brittannia clara Graecis nostrisque monumentis, Germaniae, Galliae, Hispaniae adversa inter septentrionem et occidentem jacet interjecto mari [...] *Isidorus* [...] Brittania intra oceanum quasi extra orbem posita, adversa Galliis ad prospectum Hispaniae sita est.
>
> *Alfr.* The Bryghtische Anglia is i-cleped the other world [...] *Solinus.* The egge of the Frensche clif were the ende of the world, nere that the ilond of Bretayne is nyh worthy to haue the name of another world. *Alfr.* This ilond is i-cleped insula, for hit is in salo, that is the see, and is often i-bete with dyuers cours of wateres and stremes and with wawes of the see. *Plinius* [...] This Britayne is acounted an holy lond bothe in oure stories and also in stories of Grees, and is i-sette aforn aye Germania, Gallia, Fraunce, and Spayne bytwene the north and the west and the see bytwene. *Isidorus* [...] Britayne is i-sette with ynne occean, as it were with oute the world, and is i-sette agenst Fraunce and Spayne.[29]

Britain's insularity, liminality and otherness can be the cause of isolation. On the other hand, there are advantages. It gives Britain a quality of holiness, and may even account for its disproportionate share of well-preserved saints.[30]

Within this context, what are the positive features which Higden discerns in the identity of Britain – those which tend towards unity and continuity? They range from topographic features, such as roads and rivers, which provide common strands linking diverse places,[31] to the natural productivity of the place and its potential for economic prosperity,[32] to the

---

29   Higden, *Polychronicon*, I. xxxix and I. xl, ed. Babington, ii, 6, 7, 10 and 11.
30   Ibid., I. xlii, 28–31.
31   Ibid., I. xlv, 44 and 45; and I. xlvi, 48–53.
32   Ibid., I. xii, 12–21.

man-made institutions of church and state and their networks of laws. Thus, as might be expected of a monastic chronicler, the history of the church in Britain, the evolution of its organization, its key personalities, receive much attention. In giving almost equal weight to the history of the monarchy, Higden stresses the influence of kings and queens in establishing cities, guaranteeing freedoms, fostering piety, encouraging agriculture and trade and controlling strife. For example, following Geoffrey of Monmouth, he credits Molmutius with the introduction of the law of sanctuary:

> Statuit Molinutius rex Britonum vicesimus tertius et primus eorum legifer, ut aratra colonum, templa deorum, viaeque ad civitates ducentes, immunitate confugii gauderunt, ita ut nullus reus ad aliquod istorum trium confugiens pro tuitione ab aliquo invaderetur.

> Molinicius, kyng of Britouns, was the thridde and twenty of hem, and the firste that gaf hem lawe. He ordeyned that plowghmen solowes, goddes temples, and highe weies, that ledeth to citees and townes, schulde haue the fredom of socour; so that eueriche man that fley to eny of the thre for socour for trespas that he hadde i-doo schulde be safe for pursuyt of alle his enemyes.[33]

This is not to suggest that Higden seeks to efface difference and diversity, or to reduce Britain to a false homogeneity. On the contrary, he rejoices in the variety of natural phenomena and identifies with relish the distinctive parts of Britain and the distinguishing features of different places: the whirlpool of the Menai Straits,[34] Hadrian's Wall,[35] the English shires,[36] ancient cities and especially London,[37] the hot springs at Bath,[38] the Roman remains near York,[39] all receive due mention. In some cases Higden hits a note of wonder and admiration, as in his account of Stonehenge:

---

33   Ibid., I. xlv, 42–5. Cf. I. i, 90–7.
34   Ibid., I. xliv, 40 and 41.
35   Ibid., I. xlviii, 68–71.
36   Ibid., I. xlix, 84–91.
37   Ibid., I. xlvii, 52–7.
38   Ibid., I. xlvii, 58 and 59.
39   Ibid., I. xlviii, 70–3.

Higden's Britain 15

> [...] apud Stanhenges juxta Sarum lapides mirae magnitudinis in modum portarum elevantur, ita ut portae portis superpositae videantur; nec tamen liquido perpenditur qualiter aut quare ibi sunt constructi.
>
> [...] at Stonhenge by sides Salisbury there beeth grete stones and wonder huge, and beeth arered an high as it were gates i-sett vppon other gates; notheles hit is nought clereliche i-knowe nother perceyued how and wherfore they beeth so arered and so wonder-liche i-honged.[40]

At its best, then, Britain is cohesive, blessed, well ordered and ruled, wondrous, and with great potential for sanctity. Higden resorts to lyric quotation in order to say how it is also, ideally, fertile, peaceful, prosperous, free and better than its neighbours:

> *Alfridus.* Ceterum Britannia omnia materia affluit, quae pretio ambitiosa seu usu necessaria est ferrariis, et salinus nunquam deficit. Unde et quidam metricus in laudem ejus sic prorupit.
> *Henricus de Praerogativis Angliae: Versus:*
> Anglia terra ferax et fertilis angulus orbis,
> Anglia plena jocis, gens libera digna jocari;
> Libera gens, cui libera mens et libera lingua,
> Sed lingua melior liberiorque manus.
> Anglia, terrarum decus et flos finitimarum,
> Est contenta sui fertilitate boni.
>
> *Alfridus.* Bretayne hath i-now of alle matire that there nedeth begge and selle, other that is nedeful to manis vse; there lakketh neither salt ne iren. Therfore a versifioure in his metre preyseth the lond in this manere: Engelond is good lond, fruytful of the wolle, but a corner; Engelond ful of pley, fremen well worthy to pleye; fre men, fre tonges, hert fre; free beeth al the leden; here hond is more fre, more better than here tonge. Also Henricus: Engelond hight of lond, floure of londes al aboute; that londe is ful payde with fruyte and corn of his owne.[41]

Yet the very qualities which make Britain a cause of celebration are also a source of anxiety. Higden cannot ignore the other consequences of

---

40 Ibid., I. xlii, 22 and 23.
41 Ibid., I. xli, 18 and 19.

Britain's liminality, its otherness, its being on the edge of the world, which make it in some sense strange and unpredictable. For if its unity depends upon the assimilation of diverse parts, those parts, the inner differences of Britain, also have potential for divisiveness.

In the first place Britain is not a single country, but a congeries of countries, or peoples, held in uncertain alliance. Its three main parts are England, Wales and Scotland, but the borders between them are not always clear. One of Higden's own interjections reads: 'Volunt tamen quidam Loegriam apud flumen Humbrae terminari, nec ulterius versus boream debere extendi.' ('Som men wolde mene that Loegria endeth at Homber, and streccheth no yonder northward.')[42] The situation is made more complex because this tripartite Britain is itself a palimpsest. Beneath it are still discernible the roughly effaced outlines of ancient kingdoms, whether of Northumberland, Kent or Mercia.[43] Furthermore, the history of both ancient and medieval kingdoms is one founded upon contention, upon ethnic difference and strife among the inhabitants of Britain, as when the Scots betrayed and destroyed the Picts.[44] Hostile incursions by foreign peoples are a further cause of cultural fragmentation and diversity: thus Romans, Danes, Saxons, Normans, have all been the cause of disruptive invasions, each bringing in its wake a new superimposition of territorial divisions and alien cultural values.[45]

There are two enduring legacies of these manifold cultural upheavals. One is the division between north and south, a division that is linguistic, geographic and economic:

> Tota lingua Northimbrorum, maxime in Eboraco, ita stridet incondita, quod nos australes eam vix intelligere possumus; quod puto propter viciniam barbarorum contigisse, et etiam proper jugem remotionen regum Anglorum ab illis partibus, qui magis ad austrum diversati, si quando boreales partes adeunt, non nisi magno auxiliatorum manu pergunt. *Ranulphus*. Frequentioris autem morae in austrinis

---

42 Ibid., I. xliii, 32 and 33.
43 Ibid., I. li, 97–109.
44 Ibid., I. lviii, 153–7.
45 Ibid., I. lviii, 153–5.

Higden's Britain

partibus quam in borealibus causa potest esse gleba feracior, plebs numerosior, urbes insigniores, portus accomodatiores.

Al the longage of the Northumbres, and speciallliche at York, is so scharp, slitting, and frotynge and vnschape, that we southerne men may that longage vnnethe vnderstonde. I trowe that that is bycause that they beeth nyh to straunge men and naciouns that speketh strongliche, and also bycause that the kynges of Engelond woneth alwey fer from that cuntrey; for they beeth more i-torned to the south contray, and yif they gooth to the north contray they gooth with greet help and strengthe. The cause why they beeth more in the south contrey than in the north, is for hit may be better corne londe, more peple, more noble citees, and more profitable hauenes.[46]

The second legacy concerns the national characteristics of the English. Many are mighty and strong in conflict and in battle, but others are the product of multi-cultural amalgamation and inter-marriage. They therefore participate in that ambivalence and edginess which, as we saw earlier, is also a feature of Britain's geographical position. Higden's own comment on this topic is as follows:

Reliqua vero gens Anglorum Loegriam inhabitans, utpote insulana, permixta, et a primitivis scatebris longius derivata, proprio motu etiam sine alieno hortatu facile flectitur ad opposita; adeo quoque quietis impatiens, curae aemula, otium nauseat; (*Willelmus de Pontificibus, libro tertio;*) ut cum hostes externos funditus depresserit, ipsa mutuo se conterat, et more vacui stomachi agat in seipsam.

But the Englische men that woneth in Engelond, that beeth i-medled in the ilond, that beth fer i-spronge from the welles that they spronge of first, wel lightliche with oute entisynge of eny other men, by here owne assent tornen to contrary deedes. And so vnesy, also ful vnpacient of pees, enemy of besynesse, and wlatful of sleuthe, (*Willelmus de Pontificibus, libro tertio,*) that whan they haueth destroyed here enemyes al to the grounde, thanne they fighteth with hem self, and sleeth eueriche other, as a voyde stomak and a clene worcheth in hit self.[47]

Later, Higden indicates that the impact of Britain's ethnic history has been so profound as to corrupt and denature the national character beyond recognition, and with dire consequences for the state of the country:

46   Ibid., I. lix, 162 and 163. Cf. 156–9.
47   Ibid., I. lx, 164–7.

Henricus, libro sexto. Angli quia proditioni, ebrietati, et negligentiae domus Dei dediti sunt, primo per Danos, deinde per Normannos, tertio per Scotos, quos vilissimos reputant, erunt conterendi; adeoque tunc varium erit saeculum, ut varietas mentium multimoda vestium variation designetur.

Englisshe men for they woneth hem to dronkelewnesse, to tresoun, and to rechelesnesse of Goddes hous, first by Danes and thane by Normans, and at the thridde tyme by Scottes, that they holdeth most wrecches and lest worth of alle, they schulleth be ouercome; than the worlde schal be so vnstable and so dyuers and variable that the vnstabilnesse of thoughtes schal be bytokened by many manere dyuersite of clothinge.[48]

When Higden wrote, there were sufficient indications of ethnic and cultural fragmentation, as well as of threats from hostile, foreign countries, for his account of British national identity to be of considerable interest.[49] Contemporary readers would also have been keen to detect any remedies which he proposed.[50] At one level Higden might be seen as advocating the virtues of strong government by church and state, and a return to a purer form of 'Englishness'. But, as many commentators have noted, he was curiously reticent about events within his own lifetime, and is not obviously proposing a political programme.[51] At the same time there is implicit in his version of Britain a deeper, more searching, less conservative response to its complexities and difficulties.

The nature of that response is discernible in the ways in which Higden goes about the activity in which he is engaged. His insistence on cultivating a sense of the past, in all its detail, and all its complexity, is one of the

---

48 Ibid., I. lx, 172–5.
49 The Franco-Scottish alliance against England, *c.*1334, is one such context. See M. McKisack, *The Fourteenth Century, 1307–1399*, The Oxford History of England, 5 (Oxford: Clarendon Press, 1959), 117–19. The subject is treated at greater length in Keen, *England*, 106–16. On the background to the disturbed state of relations between England and Scotland, see R. Nicholson, *Edward III and the Scots: The Formative Years of a Military Career, 1327–1335* (London: Oxford University Press, 1965).
50 Cf. Albano, *Middle English Historiography*, 127.
51 Taylor, 'Universal Chronicle', 45.

Higden's Britain 19

remarkable features of the *Polychronicon*. Indeed, Higden's sense of Britain's identity is intimately bound up with his sense of its history. So the activities of Higden as historian, ordering the evidence, establishing chronologies, compiling quotations, interjecting personal views, are in themselves highly significant. But he also constructs national identity by more direct, engaged methods, as in his well-known fascination with folk custom and belief[52] and, more remarkably, in a long interpolation on his own city of Chester, which includes his own eyewitness evidence.[53] The city's Roman remains, destruction by Northumbrians and prosperity under Effled queen of Mercia, as well as its borderland existence between England and Wales, make it a microcosm of British history as understood by Higden. The lively quality of his observations, as well as the suggestiveness of his interpretation, reveal the extent to which his sense of history is capable of penetrating the carapace of received ideas in order to make the present, as well as the past, more intelligible, more interesting and more problematic. Thus, Higden's personal understanding of the past is given greater depth, and linked to larger cultural ideas. In the process, place is provided with an identity:

> In hac urbe [...] sunt viae subterraneae, lapideo opere mirabiliter testudinatae, triclinia concamerata, insculpti lapides pergrandes antiquorum nomina praeferentes. Numismata quoque, Julii Caesaris aliorumque illustrium inscriptione insignita, aliquando sunt effossa.
>
> In this citee beeth weies vnder erthe, with vawtes of stoonwerk wonderliche i-wrought, thre chambres workes, greet stones i-graued with olde men names there ynne. There is also Iulius Cesar his money wonderliche in stones i-graued, and othere noble mennes also with the writynge aboute.[54]

It is appropriate that Higden the monastic scholar should have been fascinated by the ancient words found in inscriptions. Elsewhere he lists,

---

52   Cf. Higden, *Polychronicon*, I. i, ed. Babington, i, 14–17.
53   On the interest in locality among fourteenth-century monastic chroniclers see Taylor, *English Historical Literature*, 8–9. Cf. J. Fentress and C. Wickham, *Social Memory* (Oxford: Blackwell, 1992), 153.
54   Higden, *Polychronicon*, I. xlviii, 78–81.

defines and glosses the specialist Anglo-French words of legal parlance.[55] But there is more to Higden's approach than antiquarian curiosity. Time and again, etymology holds the key to identity, and forms a defining link between present and past. The changes which a word undergoes over time are symptomatic of deeper cultural transformations and may also be rooted in decisive, formative events. Perhaps the most appropriate example with which to conclude occurs at the outset of his section on Britain, immediately after a brief summary of its contents. *'De varia insulae nuncapatione'* touches on geology, a founding myth, foreign invasion, the liminality of the country and its Christian connections. The truth of the definition resides not so much in verifiable fact, as in the extent to which it reflects Higden's understanding of the complex significance of 'Britain':

> Primitus haec insula vocabatur Albion ab albis rupibus circa littoral maris a longe apparentibus; tandem a Bruto eam acquirente dicta est Britannia. Deinde a Saxonibus sive Anglis eam conquirentibus vocata est Anglia; sive ab Angela regina, clarissimi ducis Saxonum filia, quae post multa temora eam possedit; sive, ut vult Isidorus, Etymolog., quinto decimo, Anglia dicitur ab angulo orbis; vel secundum Bedam, libro primo, beatus Gregorius videns Anglorum pueros Romae venales, alludens patriae vocabulo ait: Vere Angli, quia vultu nitent ut angeli. Nam terrae nobilitas in vultibus puerorum relucebat.

> Firste this ilond highte Albion, as it were the white lond, of white rokkes aboute the clyues of the see that were i-seie wide. Aftirward Bruyt conquered this lond and cleped hit Bretayne after his owne name; thanne Saxons other Englische conquered that lond, and cleped hit Anglia, that is Engelond; other it hatte Anglia, and hath that name of a quene that owed this lond that heet Angela, and was a noble dukes doughter of Saxouns. Othere as Isidre saith, Eth. 15, Anglia hath that name, as hit were an angul and a corner of the world; other, as Beda seith, libro primo: Seint Gregorie seih Englische children to selle at Rome, and he accorded to the name of the lond, and seide: Sotheliche aungelis, for hir face schyneth as aungelis; for the nobilte of the lond schone in the children face.[56]

55 Ibid., I. i, 92–7.
56 Ibid., I. xxxix, 4–7.

Would Higden's version of national identity have been palatable to the king's council? Probably not. It poured cold water on one of Edward III's cherished myths, the Arthurian legend. It emphasized the value of region, locality and diversity, and did so with particular force for an area of the country that was part of the Lancastrian palatinate.[57] It refused to provide easy or obvious answers to contemporary domestic and foreign problems. It provided its predominantly ecclesiastical readership with an historical rationale quite different from that which prevailed in aristocratic circles through the *Brut*. It emphasized the validity of folklore, oral history and popular wisdom, as well as that of institutionalized authority. It condoned personal observation, experience and interpretation as sources of knowledge as well as officially sanctioned texts. Above all, it insisted that historical explanation is complex, and subject to critical revision and evaluation, and is not easily reducible to propaganda.

It is hardly surprising that Higden was not asked to return for further discussions with the king's council. Instead, he resumed his monastic vocation, completed 64 years in the religious life, and died at St Werburgh's on the feast of St Gregory, 1363. His tomb is in Chester cathedral.

---

57 P. Morgan, *War and Society in Medieval Cheshire, 1277–1403*, Remains Historical and Literary Connected with the Palatine Counties of Lancashire and Cheshire, 3rd ser., 34 (Manchester: Chetham Society, 1987), 63–6; and S. Walker, *The Lancastrian Affinity, 1361–1399* (Oxford: Clarendon Press, 1990), 141–81.

On the Borders of Middle English Dream Visions*

There is an extraordinary concentration of English dream visions in the second half of the fourteenth century. Of the thirty or so major English poems composed between 1350 and 1400, no fewer than a third are dream visions while others, such as Gower's *Confessio Amantis* and the *Canterbury Tales*, have strong links with the genre.[1] Poets of the alliterative revival, including their chief representatives, Langland and the *Pearl*-poet, no less than Chaucer, regarded the dream vision as an essential medium for what they had to say. Why should this have been so? What did the genre offer to poets that they found particularly useful and attractive? It cannot have been novelty. For a century and more, the *Roman de la rose* had been available as an influential model, demonstrating the genre's wide variety of applications. Within and behind it lay the enduring effects of Macrobius and the Bible.[2]

---

* First published in *Reading Dreams: The Interpretation of Dreams from Chaucer to Shakespeare*, ed. Peter Brown (Oxford: Oxford University Press, 1999), 22–50.

1 D. Pearsall, *Old English and Middle English Poetry*, Routledge History of English Poetry, 1 (London: Routledge and Kegan Paul, 1977), 296–7; J. V. Cunningham, 'The Literary Form of the Prologue to the *Canterbury Tales*', *Modern Philology* 49 (1952), 172–81.

2 On the literary tradition see A. C. Loftin, 'Visions', in J. R. Strayer (ed.), *Dictionary of the Middle Ages*, vol. 12 (New York: Scribner's, 1989), 475–8; K. L. Lynch, *The High Medieval Dream Vision: Poetry, Philosophy and Literary Form* (Stanford: Stanford University Press, 1988), 1 and 46; C. Erickson, *The Medieval Vision: Essays in History and Perception* (New York: Oxford University Press, 1976). On the influence of Macrobius see C. H. L. Bodenham, 'The Nature of the Dream in Late Mediaeval French Literature', *Medium Ævum* 54 (1985), 74–86; A. M. Peden, 'Macrobius and Mediaeval Dream Literature', *Medium Ævum* 54 (1985), 59–73; J. S. Russell, *The English Dream Vision: Anatomy of a Form* (Columbus: Ohio State University Press, 1988), 60.

Some immediate stimulus to reconsider the dream vision as a viable and useful genre may have derived from its mid-century revival in French courtly poetry, but this explanation would be restricted largely to Chaucer. In any case, Machaut and his followers were not so much reinventing the dream vision as continuing a French tradition rooted in the *Rose*.[3] In England it was otherwise. From about 1350 until the end of the century, the long-existing and familiar literary currents expressed through the dream vision became revitalized, charged with new possibilities, and the stimulus to original compositions. This phenomenon cannot be attributed to the chance cross-pollination of literary ideas. Instead, we need to ask (*a*) What was so distinctive, attractive, and different about the dream vision? (*b*) What was special in the circumstances of the writers that made them regard this genre as particularly relevant, to the point of giving it preferential treatment? and (*c*) Which theoretical approach might enable further exploration of the dream vision within its historical context?

Recent studies of the genre have begun to map out some explanatory hypotheses. Kruger relates the dream vision in its late medieval phase to the then current theories of dreaming. He finds in the productions of Langland, Chaucer and others a distinct kind of 'middle vision' corresponding to a theoretical category of dream. As Macrobius' *somnium* is half-way between dreams caused by divine inspiration and those caused by physical or mental disorder, so its literary counterpart is situated in a similarly ambiguous position. Positing a 'growing distance between humanity and divinity' in the later medieval period, Kruger sees the late medieval English dream vision as a means of negotiating the increasingly tenuous connections between mundane reality and the transcendent world. Its ability to respond to an acute sense of 'betweenness' helps to account for its popularity.[4]

Russell attributes the late medieval flowering of the genre to a 'confluence of literary and philosophical currents'.[5] Lynch is more confident

---

3 See M. M. Pelen, 'Machaut's Court of Love Narratives and Chaucer's *Book of the Duchess*', *Chaucer Review* 11 (1976), 128–55.
4 S. F. Kruger, *Dreaming in the Middle Ages*, Cambridge Studies in Medieval Literature, 14 (Cambridge: Cambridge University Press, 1992), 129–30.
5 Russell, *English Dream Vision*, 195.

about the way in which the genre responds to historical change. She quotes Jauss and Fowler to the effect that 'genres are not instruments for prescribing meaning after the fact or classifying it afterward, but for interpreting and producing meaning in the moment, for a specific work and for a specific historical time'. She adds: 'it is now more crucial than ever to try to rehistoricize genres, to recover not just their internal laws but the mechanics by which historical developments exert pressures on those laws'. And yet hers remains, like Russell's, a history (and mechanics) of ideas: the 'extraliterary historical conditions' turn out to be 'synchronically [...] the context of contemporary philosophical discourse' and 'diachronically [...] how philosophical change influenced the reception of the late classical visionary dialogue into the medieval tradition and how that dialogue in its turn sought to speak to its own time'.[6]

It is that last phrase, 'its own time', which begs the question. What was special, distinctive, characteristic, about the time when the authors of these dream visions wrote that might have made them (and philosophers too) want to speak to it in particular ways? For there is surely something unsatisfactory (though not wrong) about the historical contexts proposed by Kruger, Russell and Lynch, in that each is represented in causative, monolithic and general terms. To be convincing the historical context needs to be more specific, more complex, more circumstantial, embracing economic factors as well as philosophical discourse, and social and political history as much as religious matters.

By building on the work of Kruger, Russell and Lynch, how might it be possible to produce a more satisfactory historical account of the dream vision as it appears in English literature of the second half of the fourteenth century? In the first place, by describing and analysing what is, after all, crucial and distinctive about the genre, namely the illusion that, prior to writing his poem, the author has made a transition into, and out of, a dream. Such a procedure might help to root Kruger's theory of betweenness more securely in literary evidence. In this respect, Lynch is surely right to suggest that, in order to understand the historical context more fully, we first

6   Lynch, *High Medieval Dream Vision*, 5–6, 8, 9–10.

need to pay closer attention to the phenomenon which it produced. Much of what follows is therefore descriptive in nature, the data deriving from a range of English writers, but with reference to the French context, particularly as it affected Chaucer.[7] Largely excluded from the discussion are visions – religious or otherwise – which do not involve a dream, although, as we shall see, it is sometimes useful and necessary to take these undreamed visions into account.[8] Much of the material will be familiar, but it builds into a detailed picture of the key literary mechanism, and shows how it functioned as a powerful device for signalling a state of altered consciousness. Thus the first part of this chapter attempts to answer question (*a*) above. The second, shorter, part, in answer to questions (*b*) and (*c*), is more speculative in nature. It argues for the suitability of theories of liminality in attempting to root the Middle English dream vision more securely in its historical context.

It is not difficult to see why, a priori, later medieval poets found the dream such a useful means of framing their narratives. As a rhetorical device it has numerous advantages. It intrigues and engages the interest of an audience by appealing to a common experience and by inviting its members to become analysts or interpreters. It allows for the introduction of disparate and apparently incongruous material. It encourages and facilitates the use of memorable images. It permits the author to disavow responsibility for what follows. It invokes an authoritative and impressive tradition of visionary literature. It provides a way of dealing with a wide variety of subjects: divine prophecy; erotic adventure; political or philosophical speculation; apocalyptic vision. It offers a point of entry into a representational mode

---

[7] I have taken as my guide B. A. Windeatt, ed. and trans., *Chaucer's Dream Poetry: Sources and Analogues*, Chaucer Studies, 8 (Woodbridge: Boydell and Brewer, 1982). Cf. J. M. Davidoff, *Beginning Well: Framing Fictions in Late Middle English Poetry* (London: Associated University Presses, 1988), ch. 3.
[8] Peden, 'Macrobius', 63; cf. Russell, *English Dream Vision*, 45, and Lynch, *High Medieval Dream Vision*, 15.

(sometimes allegorical) which is less restrictive than, say, the conventions of realist narrative.[9]

But the aesthetic or functional capabilities of the dream vision are not my immediate interest. Instead my topic is the significance of the boundary between waking and sleeping. I wish to ask what this genre can disclose about the meaning of the dream experience as understood by the authors concerned, and therefore by their audiences. To this end my focus narrows to the moment when the narrator falls asleep to enter a dream. What is the significance of this moment within the 'richly developed register of expression' which dream-vision poets commanded?[10] Any attempt at an answer must pay attention both to the preconditions of dreaming, and to the afterlife of the dream, as well as to the dream threshold itself.

The external circumstances of the dream are sometimes given with a remarkable degree of specificity.[11] In *Pearl*, the poet is emphatic about the place and time: 'þat spot' in 'þat erber grene | In Auguste' (37–9).[12] Chaucer gives 'The tenthe day now of Decembre' as the date of his dream at the beginning of the *House of Fame* (63). There are precedents for this specificity of time and place in the book of Ezekiel: 'Now it came to pass in the thirtieth year, in the fourth month, on the fifth day of the month, when I was in the midst of the captives by the river Chobar, the heavens were opened, and I saw the visions of God' (I:1: 'Et factum est in trigesimo anno, in quarto, in quinta mensis, cum essem in medio captivorum iuxta fluvium Chobar, aperti sunt caeli, et vidi visiones Dei'), as well as in Apocalypse, where St John has his revelation 'on the Lord's day' (1:10: 'in

---

9   Cf. S. Delany, *Chaucer's House of Fame: The Poetics of Skeptical Fideism* (Chicago: University of Chicago Press, 1972), 37–8.
10   R. R. Edwards, *The Dream of Chaucer: Representation and Reflection in the Early Narratives* (Durham, NC: Duke University Press 1989), xv.
11   B. Nolan, *The Gothic Visionary Perspective* (Princeton: Princeton University Press, 1977), 146–8.
12   *The Poems of the Pearl Manuscript: Pearl, Cleanness, Patience, Sir Gawain and the Green Knight*, ed. Malcolm Andrew and Ronald Waldron (London: Arnold, 1978).

dominica die').[13] Such details authenticate the dream or vision which follows, but they also invest it with an air of significance.[14] The time and place may have profound personal associations, or they may represent a fateful or divinely ordained conjunction.

Not unusually the setting is a natural one, and the time spring or summer.[15] The C-text of *Piers Plowman* begins 'In a somur sesoun whan softe was þe sonne', while the prelude to a subsequent dream finds the dreamer lingering by a wood to hear birdsong, 'Blisse of þe briddes'. He lies down under a lime-tree and 'Murthe of here mouthes' lulls him to sleep (C. X. 61–7).[16] For Chaucer in the *Legend of Good Women* it is spring, especially the month of May, when 'fowles synge, | And [...] floures gynnen for to sprynge' (37–8), which lures him from his books and makes him a prey to dream experiences. It is May, 'when mirthes bene fele' and 'softe bene the wedres' when the poet of the *Parlement of the Thre Ages* begins his dream adventure (1–2).[17] Similarly, the narrator of *Wynnere and Wastoure* is wandering in bright sunshine along the bank of a stream near an impressive wood, by a pleasant meadow, as his experience begins (1–46).[18] In the later fourteenth century, the English spring countryside seems to have been full of dreaming poets. One wonders why they never met.

13 This and subsequent quotations from the Bible are taken from the Vulgate, using *Biblia sacra iuxta vulgatam Clementinam*, ed. A. Colunga and L. Turnado, 4th edn, Biblioteca de Autores Cristianos 14. 1 (Madrid: Editorial Catolica, 1965); with translations from *The Holy Bible: Douay Version Translated from the Latin Vulgate (Douay A.D. 1609: Rheims, A.D. 1582)* (London: Catholic Truth Society, 1956).

14 Cf. E. Baumgartner, 'The Play of Temporalities; or, The Reported Dream of Guillaume de Lorris', in *Rethinking the 'Romance of the Rose': Text, Image, Reception*, ed. K. Brownlee and S. Huot (Philadelphia: University of Pennsylvania Press, 1992), 23–4.

15 R. Tuve, *Seasons and Months: Studies in a Tradition of Middle English Poetry* (Paris: 1933; repr. Cambridge: Brewer, 1974), 99–122.

16 W. Langland, *Piers Plowman: An Edition of the C-Text*, ed. D. Pearsall, York Medieval Texts, 2nd ser. (London: Arnold, 1978). Subsequent citations from the C-text are from this edition.

17 *The Parlement of the Thre Ages*, ed. M. Y. Offord, EETS os 246 (1959).

18 *Wynnere and Wastoure*, ed. S. Trigg, EETS os 297 (1990).

The landscapes through which they move, and which so beguile them, have a marked tendency to be idealized, to resemble paradise.[19] After the *Wynnere and Wastoure* poet has wandered, sunlit, by his stream, forest and meadow, he finds many flowers unfolding beneath his feet. As he lies down beside a hawthorn bush, the thrushes vie with each other in song, woodpeckers hop among the hazel bushes, wild geese peck at the bark, jays jangle and other birds twitter. The noise of birds and the rushing stream keep the narrator awake until dusk (36–44). The landscape of the *Parlement of the Thre Ages* is brimming with natural life. There are, again, a wood, a stream and flowers – 'The primrose, the pervynke, and piliole þe riche' (9), dew-drenched daisies, and burgeoning blossom swathed in pleasant dawn mists – and birds (cuckoos, wood-pigeon, thrushes), but other beasts too: as day breaks, harts and hinds make their way to the hills, foxes and polecats go to earth, hares crouch by hedges, then go quickly to their forms (1–20). Another dawn scene, in the F-version of the *Legend of Good Women*, finds Geoffrey Chaucer, or his narrative persona, enthralled by the beauty of the daisy, kneeling and waiting for one to unclose 'Upon the smale, softe, swote gras' (F 118), the flower being an epitome of ideal natural beauty, 'For yt surmounteth pleynly alle odoures, | And of riche beaute alle floures' (F 123–4). The birds meanwhile, glad that winter is past and that they have escaped the hunter, sing in defiance of the fowler, and croon love-songs to each other. Especially in the case of Chaucer, the influence of the *Rose* – part of which he may have translated as the *Romaunt of the Rose* – is everywhere apparent, with its opening in May, a 'tyme of love and jolite', burgeoning nature, and birdsong (49–95).

What are we to make of such preludes to dreaming? However specific, however detailed, they are not novelistic descriptions designed to give each composition a sense of uniqueness. Were that so, we would not find similar details across several poems by different authors. We are, of course, in the presence of a set of conventions which a poet might invoke in order to prepare an audience for a dream.[20] But that should not be taken to imply that

---

19 Nolan, *Gothic Visionary Perspective*, 136–9.
20 A. C. Spearing, *Medieval Dream-Poetry* (Cambridge: Cambridge University Press, 1976), 17–18.

the poet is himself a somnambulist, reaching absent-mindedly for hand-me-down details once the beginning of a dream vision is in prospect.[21] The stream, the forest, the sound of birds, a paradisal landscape are all signifiers to be deliberately deployed, in various kinds of combination and in varying degrees of elaboration, to create particular kinds of meaning.[22]

There is a notable alternative setting – one which, again, is not restricted to an individual writer. It is that of the bedchamber. Jean Froissart's *Paradys d'Amours* begins there (1–32), as does Chaucer's *Book of the Duchess*, influenced by the *Paradys*.[23] Chaucer's insomniac narrator, sitting up in bed, calls for a book 'To rede and drive the night away' (49). In it he finds Ovid's tale of Ceyx and Alcyone. Impressed by the discovery, within that narrative, of a God of Sleep, he resolves to give Morpheus some gorgeous, if imaginary, gifts: a feather-bed stuffed with white doves' down, striped with gold, and clad in fine black foreign satin; and many pillows, covered in soft French linen from Rennes and 'al that falles | To a chambre' (238–58). Such an opening – and this is part of its point – belies expectation and contrasts with the familiar landscape opening, creating a world which is confined rather than free, and artificial rather than natural.

A dreamer is by definition alone, solitary, separated from social activity.[24] Langland's dreamer is 'walkynge myn one' (C. X. 61), while Nicole de Margival reports in his *Dit de la panthère d'Amours* (*c.*1300) that he was

---

21   Lynch, *High Medieval Dream Vision*, 3–4. Cf. Davidoff, *Beginning Well*, 73.
22   P. Piehler, *The Visionary Landscape: A Study in Medieval Allegory* (London: Arnold, 1971), 13. Most of these signifiers are conveniently illustrated by the opening lines of Sir John Clanvowe's *Boke of Cupid*, ed. V. J. Scattergood, in *The Works of Sir John Clanvowe* (Cambridge: Brewer, 1965), lines 1–90. Cf. J. Gower, *Vox Clamantis*, ed. G. C. Macaulay, in *The Complete Works of John Gower*, iv: *The Latin Works* (Oxford: Clarendon Press, 1902), 20; *The Major Latin Works of John Gower: The Voice of One Crying and The Tripartite Chronicles*, trans. E. W. Stockton (Seattle: University of Washington Press, 1962), 49.
23   J. Froissart, *Le Paradis d'Amour; L'Orloge amoureus*, ed. P. Dembowski (Geneva: Droz, 1986); Windeatt, *Chaucer's Dream Poetry*, 41–2.
24   Russell, *English Dream Vision*, 116.

'loing de mon païs' (53: 'far from my own country').[25] Solitude may be an expression of being lost. Langland's dreamer wanders aimlessly 'wondres to here' (C. Prol. 4), an activity which later finds him by 'a wilde wildernesse' (C. X. 62). *The Wynnere and Wastoure* dreamer is 'in the weste wandrynge myn one' (32) before his encounter with the paradisal landscape. In the *House of Fame* 'Geffrey' falls asleep like someone exhausted after a pilgrimage (111–18). Here, as elsewhere with the image of the lost and errant dreamer, there may be an allusion to the idea current in ancient literature and traditional tribal culture that, during sleep, the soul steps out of its bodily boundaries and wanders in other, no less real, worlds.[26]

Insomnia is another circumstance which dreamers must endure before the dream begins. In the *Book of the Duchess*, Chaucer's luxurious bedding is invented as a propitiatory gift to the God of Sleep, for the narrator begins by complaining:

> I have gret wonder, be this lyght,
> How that I lyve, for day ne nyght
> I may nat slepe wel nygh noght.
> (1–3)

– sentiments which Froissart would have recognized. Not unexpectedly, it is often in the limbo-land between sleeping (or trying to sleep) and waking that dreams begin, as in Guillaume de Machaut's *Dit de la fonteinne amoureuse*[27] and Clanvowe's *Boke of Cupide* (86–90).

---

25 N. de Margival, *Le Dit de la panthère d'Amours*, ed. H. A. Todd, SATF (1883); Windeatt, *Chaucer's Dream Poetry*, 127.
26 See. J. S. Lincoln, *The Dream in Primitive Cultures* (London: Cresset Press, 1935), 27; W. Wolff, *The Dream – Mirror of Conscience: A History of Dream Interpretation from 2000 B.C. and a New Theory of Dream Synthesis* (New York: Grune and Stratton, 1952), 8 and see 24; see also Spearing, *Medieval Dream-Poetry*, 8; Lynch, *High Medieval Dream Vision*, 49–50; B. Tedlock, 'Zuni and Quiché Dream Sharing and Interpreting', in *Dreaming: Anthropological and Psychological Interpretations*, ed. Tedlock (Cambridge: Cambridge University Press, 1987), 113–16.
27 G. de Machaut, *The Fountain of Love (La Fonteinne amoureuse) and Two Other Love Vision Poems*, ed. and trans. R. B. Palmer, Garland Library of Medieval Literature 54, ser. A (New York: Garland, 1993) lines 61–71 and 1563–8.

More sombrely, but inevitably, given the implications of sleep, the dreamer can seemingly be on the brink of death.[28] The *Pearl*-poet slips into a heavy sleep, a 'slepyng-sla3te' where 'sla3te' can mean 'slaughter' or 'death by violence' as well as 'stroke' and 'blow'. Langland's narrator, before one dream, has grown, 'wery of the world' (C. XX. 4), while the dreamer of the *Book of the Duchess* declares with fear: 'drede I have for to dye' (24). This state of inertia should be contrasted with the heightened sensual awareness of the narrator before his dream in poems like *Wynnere and Wastoure*, the *Parlement of the Thre Ages*, and Chaucer's *Legend of Good Women*.

Solitude, insomnia, wandering, a sense of death, are each expressive of the dreamer's mental and emotional condition. He tends to be preoccupied, in a state of inwardness and anxiety, an anxiety which derives from loss of confidence as well as uncertainty about the nature, sources, truth and application of dreams. St John was 'in the spirit on the Lord's day' (Apocalypse 1:10: 'in spiritu in dominica die') before experiencing his vision.[29] One recalls Dante's state of dislocation at the beginning of *Inferno*, alone in the dark wood, 'pieno di sonno' (1. 11: 'full of sleep').[30] The dreamer of the *Book of the Duchess* is numb, 'mased' (lost in a maze) with preoccupation:

> Al is ylyche good to me –
> Joye or sorowe, whereso hyt be –
> For I have felynge in nothing,
> But as yt were a mased thyng,
> Alway in poynt to falle a-doun [...]
> (9–13)

---

28   Russell, *English Dream Vision*, 55.
29   Russell, *English Dream Vision*, 36, 40 and 79; D. G. Hale, 'Dreams, Stress, and Interpretation in Chaucer and his Contemporaries', *Journal of the Rocky Mountain Medieval and Renaissace Association* 9 (1988), 47. See also Nolan, *Gothic Visionary Perspective*, 139–42.
30   D. Alighieri, *The Divine Comedy*, i: *Inferno*, ed. and trans. J. D. Sinclair, rev. edn. (London: Oxford University Press, 1948); and see Russell, *English Dream Vision*, 17; Lynch, *High Medieval Dream Vision*, 147.

More playfully, the narrator of the *House of Fame* is in a state of confusion about the alleged causes, and terminology, of dreams (7–58), although his counterpart in the *Parliament of Fowls* is more sombre: 'to my bed I gan me for to dresse, | Fulfyld of thought and busy hevynesse' (88–9). At the beginning of the *Consolation of Philosophy*, influential on later dream visions although not strictly one itself, Boethius describes a contemplative and introverted condition (using Chaucer's translation, *Boece*): 'I, stille, recordede these thynges with myself' (I. prosa 1. 1–2),[31] while de Margival is 'du cuer pensif' (49: 'extremely pensive') before his dream occurs.[32]

There is a certain homogeneity among highly personalized accounts of the narrator's state prior to the onset of dreaming, but the inwardness of the narrator is ascribed to a wide variety of causes. That of the *Pearl*-poet is caused by grief. He stands before the grave of his young daughter:

> Bifore þat spot my honde I spennd
> For care ful colde þat to me caȝt;
> A deuelly dele in my hert denned [...]
> (49–51)

The poet of *Wynnere and Wastoure* broods on the political and social state of Britain, recalling its origins in heroism and treachery, and describing his own mixed perception of the wit and trickery which obtains, wise words contending with sly, deceptive ones (1–30). In a prophetic mode, and apocalyptic mood, he sees the world turned upside-down, with the wisdom and experience of mature men despised in favour of the callow jabbering of the young. The sad contemplations of Boethius, too, are brought about by political circumstances: head of the civil service under the Gothic emperor Theodoric, he fell from favour and was imprisoned in Pavia – the occasion for his *Consolatio* – before being executed. The beginning of Chaucer's translation reads: 'Allas! I wepynge, am constreyned to bygynnen vers of

---

31 See Russell, *English Dream Vision*, 11. The *Consolation* is used as a model in T. Usk, *The Testament of Love*, ed. W. W. Skeat, in his *The Complete Works of Geoffrey Chaucer*, vol. 7: *Chaucerian and Other Pieces* (London: Oxford University Press, 1897), Prol. 26.
32 Windeatt, *Chaucer's Dream Poetry*, 127.

sorwful matere, that whilom in florysschyng studie made delitable ditees'
(I. metrum 1. 1–3).

The desires and frustrations of erotic love prompt numerous literary dreams. Guillaume de Machaut, in order to console himself and to fix his thoughts on the object of his affections, makes a determined resolve in the *Fonteinne amoureuse* to compose a cheerful and optimistic poem (1–12). The author of *Li Fablel dou Dieu d'amors* (mid-thirteenth century) describes the onset of his dream in these terms:

> Par i matin me gisoie en mon lit;
> D'amors pensoie, n'avoie autre delit;
> Quant el penser in'endormi i petit,
> Songai un songe dont tos li cuers me rist.
> (9–12)

(One morning I was lying in my bed – I was thinking of love and had no other pleasure – when I fell asleep a little with my thoughts. I dreamed a dream which delighted my heart.)[33]

Jean de Condé (d. 1345) begins his *Messe des oisiaus:*

> En pensant a la douche joie
> Dont amans en espoir s'esjoie,
> Fui couchié une nuit de may
> Tout sans pesance et sans esmay.
> Si m'endormi sans point d'arrest
> Et songai [...]
> (1–6)

(While thinking of the sweet joy with which a lover cheers himself in his hope, I went to bed one May evening, quite free from sorrow and care. I then went straight off to sleep and I dreamed [...]).[34]

---

33 Ed. C. Oulmont, in *Les Débats du clerc et du chevalier dans la littéraire poétique du moyen-âge* (Paris: Champion, 1911); Windeatt, *Chaucer's Dream Poetry*, 85.

34 J. de Condé, '*La Messe des oiseaux*' et' '*Le Dit des Jacobins et des Fremeneurs*', ed. J. Ribard (Geneva: Droz, 1970); Windeatt, *Chaucer's Dream Poetry*, 104.

All too easily, though, the darker side of love breaks through, and melancholy, that plague of the despondent lover, replaces forced cheerfulness. It is melancholy, rather than what le Goff calls 'the Christian intellectual's feeling of guilt', which breeds these dreams.[35] As Kruger demonstrates, Chaucer provides an anatomy of it in the *Book of the Duchess*. There, the dreamer is afflicted by the depressing images which flood his brain: 'sorwful ymagynacioun | Ys alway hooly in my mynde' (14–15). He is denatured, alienated from his own nature and from the natural world: 'agaynes kynde | Hyt were to lyven in thys wyse' (16–17); he has lost his vitality through 'melancolye', a sickness which has 'sleyn my spirit of quyknesse' and prompted disturbing fantasies (23–9). The narrator of the *House of Fame* identifies the 'melancolyous' (30) man as one prone to dream, a prognosis confirmed by Machaut in the *Fonteinne amoureuse* (61–8) and the tormented Froissart of the *Paradys d'Amours* (5–8).[36]

In dealing with the immediate cause of a narrator's preoccupation, we are in effect discussing his receptivity.[37] Whether brooding on a personal grief or a political crisis, or in a state of spiritual elevation or frustrated love, his inwardness predisposes him to the experience of dreaming. He has become susceptible and sensitized by intense preoccupation. This receptivity, crucial to the onset of dreaming, is embodied in Langland's narrator, who 'In a somur sesoun whan softe was þe sonne [...] Wente forth in þe world wondres to here' (C. Prol. 1 and 4). Another way of thinking of the narrator's anxiety is as a route to the dream threshold, a kind of searching or wandering which is then represented in his physical circumstances:

---

35 J. le Goff, 'Dreams in the Culture and Collective Psychology of the Medieval West', in his *Time, Work, and Culture in the Middle Ages*, trans. A. Goldhammer (Chicago: University of Chicago Press, 1980), 201.

36 Steven Kruger, 'Medical and Moral Authority in the Late-Medieval Dream', in *Reading Dreams: The Interpretation of Dreams from Chaucer to Shakespeare*, ed. Peter Brown (Oxford: Oxford University Press, 1999), 51–83. See W. Calin, *A Poet at the Fountain: Essays on the Narrative Verse of Guillaume de Machaut* (Lexington: University Press of Kentucky, 1974), 148–9; Edwards, *Dream of Chaucer*, 68–9.

37 Lynch, *High Medieval Dream Vision*, 69 and 148. Cf. Erickson, *Medieval Vision*, 33–5.

wandering through the countryside, sleepless in his bedchamber, walking by a forest or stream.

What difference, then, does it make when a narrator crosses the boundary from wakefulness to sleep? What is the significance of that moment? The first point to be made is that the boundary is not an absolute division but a party wall within the same house, a wall with a connecting door. One thinks here of the lover's moment of entry into the garden of delight in the *Rose* – through a door which connects an excluded, if idealized, world with a privileged one (*Romaunt*, 509–644). Which is to say that the dream world is not to be thought of as wholly different from waking experience, but in some measure a different account of it, although the connections are not always immediately obvious. They were clear enough to Macrobius, who found in that portion of Cicero's *De republica* on which he wrote his commentary the following statement: 'it frequently happens that our thoughts and conversations react upon us in dreams' ('fit enim fere ut cogitations sermonesque nostri pariant aliquid in somno').[38] The idea resurfaces in, say, *Dives and Pauper*, written between 1405 and 1410, as well as in late fourteenth-century poetry.[39] In *Pearl*, the 'slepyng-slaȝte' of the dreamer reflects Pearl's death and resurrection, and foreshadows his own spiritual death and rebirth.[40] In the *Book of the Duchess*, Chaucer assumes the existence of a door connecting the rooms of wakefulness and sleep, while leaving the reader to puzzle out the nature of the relationship between the story of Ceyx and Alcyone (which the dreamer was reading before he dozed off)

---

38 Cicero, *Somnium Scipionis*, I. 4, in Macrobius, *Ambrosii Theodosii Macrobii Commentarii in Somnium Scipionis*, ed. J. Willis, Bibliotheca Scriptorum Graecorum et Romanorum Teubneriana (Leipzig: Teubner, 1963), 156; trans. W. H. Stahl in Macrobius, *Commentary on the Dream of Scipio*, Records of Civilization: Sources and Studies, 48 (New York: Columbia University Press, 1952), 70. See also Russell, *English Dream Vision*, 39.
39 *Dives and Pauper*, I. xliii; ed. P. H. Barnum, vol. 1, pt. 1, EETS os 275 (Oxford, 1976), 175, lines 12–16. This aspect of medieval dream theory endured: see Sir Thomas Browne, 'On Dreams' (before 1682), in *The Works of Sir Thomas Browne*, ed. G. Keynes, new edn (London: Faber, 1964), iii, 230.
40 Piehler, *Visionary Landscape*, 146.

and the story of the Black Knight, which forms the subject of the dream (1324–34). In the *Parliament of Fowls* he is more forthright:

> The wery huntere, slepynge in his bed,
> To wode ayeyn his mynde goth anon;
> The juge dremeth how his plees been sped;
> The cartere dremeth how his cart is gon;
> The riche, of gold; the knyght fyght with his fon;
> The syke met he drynketh of the tonne;
> The lovere met he hath his lady wonne.
>
> (99–105)

To insist too much on the interconnectedness of waking experience and the dream world might give the impression that the boundary between them is, after all, relatively insignificant. That is far from being the case.[41] Continuity there may be between the preoccupations of waking life and the dream content, but the latter is not simply an extension of the former: the dream, which by definition always has the dreamer at its centre, allows for a confrontation with the self and its preoccupations such that a process of self-realization may be achieved.[42] To put it another way: the boundary between wakefulness and sleeping divides us from ourselves. *Piers Plowman* is perhaps the most notable late medieval English example of a literary dream used to explore individual identity: once the narrator has fallen asleep, it is not long before the 'I' of the poem is being accused by Holy Church of being a 'dotede daffe' (C. 1. 138) for failing to understand the rudiments of Christian doctrine.[43]

---

41 For the orthodox Freudian view see H. Nagera et al., *Basic Psychoanalytic Concepts on the Theory of Dreams*, Hampstead Clinic Psychoanalytic Library, 2 (London: George, Allen and Unwin, 1969), 15 and 40–2; but cf. R. de Becker, *The Understanding of Dreams, or the Machinations of the Night*, trans. M. Heron (London: Allen and Unwin, 1968), 8 and 9.

42 Spearing *Medieval Dream-Poetry*, 5; Russell, *English Dream Vision*, 115; Browne, 'On Dreams', ed. Keynes, 232.

43 Cf. J. H. Anderson, *The Growth of a Personal Voice: 'Piers Plowman' and 'The Faerie Queene'* (New Haven: Yale University Press, 1976), 3; K. Brownlee, *Poetic Identity in Guillaume de Machaut* (Madison: University of Wisconsin Press, 1984), *passim*.

As in the case of *Piers Plowman*, to cross the boundary into the dream world is to enter territory which is authorized – authorized in the sense that it is populated by figures, like Holy Church, who have authority, who understand where they are, and authorized also because of the dream's sense of import. The narrator's existence, prior ro the dream, may have lost its meaning, but within the dream it is full of enigmatic significance. The latent significance of dreams is sometimes reinforced by reference to appropriate authors. The *Rose* begins with a tribute to Macrobius, who took Scipio's dream seriously, and an affirmation of the prophetic nature of dreams (*Romaunt*, 1–20). The divine origin of biblical dreams gave this idea credence and currency.[44] Was it not to the prophets themselves that God spoke, in visions and dreams? 'If there be among you a prophet of the Lord, I will appear to him in a vision, or I will speak to him in a dream' (Numbers 12:6 'Si quis fuerit inter vos propheta Domini, in visione apparebo ei, vel per somnium loquar ad illum').[45] Chaucer uses such precedents playfully to authorize the dream of the *Book of the Duchess*. His dream was so wonderful, says the narrator, that no one has the wit to interpret it:

> No, not Joseph, withoute drede,
> Of Egipte, he that redde so
> The Kynges metynge Pharao.
> (280–2)

Paradoxically, the constraints of authority within the dream world coincide with a loss of personal control and a sense of liberation. No longer responsible for his own actions (or inaction), the dreamer comes under

---

[44] C. B. Hieatt, *The Realism of Dream Visions: The Poetic Exploitation of the Dream-Experience in Chaucer and his Contemporaries*, De Proprieraribus Litterarum, series practica, 2 (The Hague: Mouton, 1967), 24; D. F. Hult, *Self-Fulfilling Prophecies: Readership and Authority in the First 'Roman de la rose'* (Cambridge: Cambridge University Press, 1986), 114–26. Cf. Lynn Thorndike, *A History of Magic and Experimental Science*, ii: *During the First Thirteen Centuries of Our Era* (New York: Columbia University Press, 1923), 154, 161–4 and 575–7.

[45] Peden, 'Macrobius', 59–60; Russell, *English Dream Vision*, ch. 2; Wolff, *Mirror of Conscience*, 13.

the influence of powers beyond himself, to which he has no choice but to abandon himself. This is as true of the religious vision as it is of the secular dream: 'The word of the Lord came to Ezechiel the priest [...] and the hand of the Lord was there upon him' (Ezekiel 1:3: 'factum est verbum Domini ad Ezechielem [...] et facta est super eum ibi manus Domini'). This signals the exertion of divine authority. As a result, the prophet is released into a privileged but autonomous world. The *Pearl*-poet, on falling asleep, has the sense of his soul's escaping from his body. His body remains on his daughter's grave-mound, but 'my spyryt þer sprang in space' (61). By means of the dream his spirit is released for adventure, but consequently he has lost his bearings: 'I ne wyste in þis worlde quere þat hit wace' (65). One critic sees this kind of surrender as a response to, or compensation for, the preoccupations of waking life.[46] That this is not always the case is intimated in the vision of Boethius, where his confrontation and dialogue with Lady Philosophy lead to a sense of existential liberation, however much he remains incarcerated in Theodric's prison. One thinks also of the *Book of the Duchess*, where a claustrophobic bedchamber is transformed in the dream to one engulfed in spring birdsong, set with dazzling, sun-filled windows, from which the dreamer is soon transported to join in a bustling hunt. In this he has no choice, but the sense of relief, of vitality, and sociability after his denatured, alienated and claustrophobic waking existence is almost palpable.

Perhaps one of the most significant features of the boundary between waking and dreaming is its offer of a point of entry into new levels of perception otherwise inaccessible. According to Macrobius, who quotes Porphyry, 'All truth is concealed. Nevertheless, the soul, when it is partially disengaged from bodily functions during sleep, at times gazes and at times peers intently at the truth, but does not apprehend it' ('latet [...] omne verum. hoc tamen anima cum ab officiis corporis somno eius paululum libera est interdum aspicit, non numquam tendit aciem nec tamen pervenit').[47]

---

46 Piehler, *Visionary Landscape*, 3.
47 Macrobius, *Commentary on the Dream of Scipio*, 1. 3, 18; ed. Willis, ii, 12; trans. Stahl, 92.

Before the inner eye of Langland's dreamer there unfolds a vision of the universe – Tower of Truth, field full of folk, dale of death – which is nothing short of a marvel: 'merueylousliche me mette' (C. Prol. 8). He sees things normally hidden, and the sense of having broken through to a fundamental level of understanding is very strong. The dream makes possible perceptions which, while anchored in the dreamer's spiritual self, are also moral, social and political.[48]

The dream threshold also transforms reality: the other world which the dreamer enters is both like and unlike the familiar one of waking experience. Having pondered social and political divisiveness, and having walked through an attractive landscape, the poet of *Wynnere and Wastoure* falls asleep to dream of a place – 'Me thoghte I was in the werlde' (47) – which is a pleasant green expanse a mile wide where two opposing armies face each other. The transformation of reality can mean an intensification of natural effects to the point where they become altogether different. The *Pearl*-poet finds himself walking among hills set with crystal cliffs, past trees with leaves like burnished silver, and grinding beneath his feet gravel made of pearls (73–84).

The grammar and syntax of the world beyond the borderland of sleep are also different.[49] The everyday is both transformed and laden with tantalizing meanings. With his eyes closed, the dreamer enters a world where meaning is nevertheless relayed in visual terms, but ones which may lack apparent coherence and stability.[50] Its language is symbolic: ideas are represented in associated images, in a more or less complex systematic way, to the point where the dream may become an allegory in its own right.[51] To the extent that a dream represents ideas, part of its function in providing

---

48 Cf. *Mum and the Sothsegger*, ed. M. Day and R. Steele, EETS os 199 (1936), lines 871 ff.
49 Spearing, *Medieval Dream-Poetry*, 10.
50 Wolff, *Mirror of Conscience*, 303.
51 Cf. M. Zink, 'The Allegorical Poem as Interior Memoir', in *Images of Power: Medieval History/Discourse/Literature*, ed. K. Brownlee and S. G. Nichols, Yale French Studies, 70 (New Haven: Yale University Press, 1986), 100–26.

a new level of understanding should be called analytical.[52] Whatever the subject-matter, the content of medieval literary dreams signals a turning inwards, accelerating and intensifying a process that may have begun before the dream. Dreams can only happen inside the mind. But they certainly do not reflect the kind of analysis which is entirely cerebral. Their processes include feeling as much as thought, free association as much as logic, images more than abstractions.

What do all these differences, either side of the dream boundary, add up to? One general answer might be that the onset of dreaming indicates a state of altered consciousness.[53] The state of altered consciousness which the dream boundary encloses is sometimes suggested by a quickening of the spirits or a sharpening and intensifying of sensual experience, as if the narrator, once inside the dream, is more fully alive, however inert his body may be. Guillaume de Lorris's lover dreams of taking an intense pleasure in the May birdsong (*Romaunt*, 100–8), and of being 'Joly and gay, ful of gladnesse' (109) as he walks by a stream, delighting in its appearance (110–31). Similarly, and as already noted, the narrator of the *Book of the Duchess*, who complains that 'Defaute of slep and hevynesse | Hath sleyn my spirit of quyknesse' (25–6), is seemingly regenerated by his dream, with its celestial May birdsong (291–320), flowery meadow and burgeoning trees which harbour numerous deer, squirrels and other animals (397–42).[54] In de Margival's *Dit de la panthère* (47–90) the immediate effect of the dream is, again, a sudden arrival in an idealized landscape full of wild vitality which contrasts with the civilized but withdrawn state of the narrator.[55]

Yet such evidence of the exciting of physical awareness is not confined to the far side of the dream boundary. As we have seen in, say, the case of the *Parlement of the Thre Ages*, and in numerous other examples, the May setting, the birds, stream, forest, flowers, are almost *de rigueur* as a prelude

---

52 Piehler, *Visionary Landscape*, 20; cf. Edwards, *Dream of Chaucer*, 2.
53 Cf. W. C. Curry, *Chaucer and the Mediaeval Sciences*, rev. edn (New York: Barnes and Noble, 1960), 208, quoting Averroes.
54 J. A. W. Bennett, *Chaucer's 'Book of Fame': An Exposition of the 'House of Fame'* (Oxford: Clarendon Press, 1968), 8–9.
55 Windeatt, *Chaucer's Dream Poetry*, 127–8.

to dreaming. In which case, are we to think of the dream boundary as a cause, or merely as a symptom, of altered consciousness?

Certainly in a number of cases the existence of the dream is crucial and important. Scipio's account of the universe is given credibility by Macrobius precisely because it derives from a dream – dreams being, on certain occasions such as this one, divinely inspired. A similar sense of authenticity attaches to the experience of the *Pearl*-poet's dreamer, not least because his revelation of another world (and of the continued existence in it of his beloved daughter) has biblical precedent, in Apocalypse itself. Langland, too, clearly attaches, and wants his audience to attach, great importance to the idea that dreams can be of divine origin.

In such cases, the dream is both cause *and* symptom: it provokes a special, intense kind of altered consciousness, in which the dreamer is made the recipient of God's word, while at the same time telling us that state of altered consciousness has been achieved.[56] There may be an analogy here with another indicator of altered consciousness: enchantment. The departure of a hero or heroine for faery (and their eventual return) similarly shows both that he or she has entered an altered state and that the altered state has been caused by the intervention of powers beyond the individual's immediate control. This, perhaps, is the secular equivalent of the causative dream, for the experiences reserved for faery are to do with the social order. One thinks of the seizing by faery forces of Herodis in the Middle English romance *Orfeo* (before 1330), when her adventure in the other world is a means of representing social response to mental disorder, or madness.[57] Other instances of literary dreams are more ambiguous as to whether the dream is to be seen as a cause or an effect of altered consciousness. Chaucer is notorious for keeping in play that very question: *are*

---

56 Cf. Lynch, *High Medieval Dream Vision*, 55–6.
57 *Sir Orfeo*, ed. A. J. Bliss, 2nd edn (Oxford: Clarendon Press, 1966), lines 57–194. N. Frye, *The Secular Scripture: A Study of the Structure of Romance* (Cambridge, Mass.: Harvard University Press, 1976), 102, and see pp. 53, 99, and 102–4. Note also how resistant the dream vision is to the exploration of serious mental disturbance in Thomas Hoccleve, *The Regiment of Princes*, ed. M. C. Seymour, in his *Selections from Hoccleve* (Oxford: Clarendon Press, 1981), lines 109–11.

dreams divinely inspired, or merely caused by bad digestion? But in many cases – perhaps the majority – the casual use, arbitrary placing, or indeed the absence of a dream boundary where one might be expected suggest that it should be read as a symptom of an altered state and nothing more, that the existence of a dream boundary is not in itself crucial to the meaning of the poem. It follows that the genre 'dream vision' is perhaps not as watertight as some writers have suggested.[58]

Let me illustrate this from some examples. Machaut's *Dit dou lyon* begins with the familiar spring setting: nature is in full throat. In a neat reversal of the usual scenario, the narrator wakes to birdsong, and recollects his lady-love. Prompted by the fine weather, music and the beauty of nature, he rises from his bed to walk by a river which encloses a garden. Finding a boat, he crosses the river and so enters the garden. There are shades here of the *Rose*, and a dream-like quality to the events which unfold, but Machaut has dispensed with the dream boundary which might have marked the point of transition to a state of altered consciousness.[59] The *Dit dou lyon* might be compared with the anonymous *Fablel dou Dieu d'amors*, the opening of which contains many of the same elements, but with the inclusion of a dream boundary. The sequence is: lying in bed with thoughts of love, falls asleep and dreams; within dream arises in May to the sound of birdsong; walks in flowery meadow, through which runs a delightful stream; walks by the river until a garden, enclosed by a moat, comes into view; enters garden; observes that the garden belongs to Love and is accessible only to those of high birth (9–74).[60] It is diffcult to see quite what Machaut lost by excluding the dream boundary, or what the author of the *Fablel* gained by including it.[61] In another poem, *Le Lay de franchise*, Deschamps

---

58 Cf. Russell, *English Dream Vision*, 2 and 5.
59 G. de Machaut, *Le Dit dou lyon*, ed. E. Hoepffner, in his *Œuvres de Guillaume de Machaut*, ii, SATF (1911), lines 1–188; Windeatt, *Chaucer's Dream Poetry*, 65–6. See C. B. Hieatt, 'Un Autre Forme: Guillaume de Machaut and the Dream Vision Form', *Chaucer Review* 14 (1979), 97–115.
60 Windeatt, *Chaucer's Dream Poetry*, 85.
61 Calin, *Poet at the Fountain*, 160; cf. G. de Machaut, *The Judgment of the King of Navarre*, ed. and trans. R. B. Palmer, Garland Library of Medieval Literature 45, ser. A (New York: Garland, 1988), lines 1–547.

studiously avoids a dream boundary when he might have been expected to include one: on a glorious May day the narrator dresses in green and sets off to the wood to gather blossom – a ritual which betokens his state of amorous sorrow. Thinking of his lady in terms of a flower, he crosses a heath to a manor, surrounded by a moat, where he observes other May rituals performed by aristocratic people.[62]

I am not suggesting that the dream boundary has become redundant, or been reduced to the status of an outworn convention, but that for certain poets it is one option among many for signifying a state of altered consciousness, and is probably reserved for signalling an intensification or deepening of that state. The dream vision is thus distinguished from the *chanson d'aventure*, with which it shares a number of generic markers: birdsong, the stream, the forest, the garden.[63] Many are by their nature images of threshold. Entry into the garden, as already noted, is crucial; so is crossing the stream or river; or being at the edge of the forest; or leaving a bedchamber.[64]

Earlier in this chapter, such situations were seen as preparatory to the experience of dreaming, signalling a state of readiness or receptivity before a state of altered consciousness should develop. It may be more accurate to see them as representing a series of boundaries, marking progressive stages of penetration of an altered state. They may culminate in the dream boundary, or the dream boundary may be an early indicator of altered consciousness, followed by others, or it may be entirely absent. That all depends on the priorities and choices of the author.

---

62 E. Deschamps, *Le Lay de franchise*, ed. le marquis de Queux de Saint-Hilaire, in Œuvres complètes de *Eustache Deschamps*, ed. Saint-Hilaire and G. Raynaud, ii, SATF (1880), lines 1–130; Windeatt, *Chaucer's Dream Poetry*, 152–4. Cf. J. Gower, *Confessio Amantis*, ed. J. A. W. Bennett, in his *Selections from John Gower* (Oxford: Clarendon Press, 1968), lines 93–137, where the onset of dreaming is again withheld, despite the usual indicators.
63 Davidoff, *Beginning Well*, 36–46.
64 At least one of these images, that of a river, was taken by medieval dream interpreters to indicate a range of meanings, from security to anxiety and impending danger. See S. R. Fischer, *The Complete Medieval Dreambook: A Multilingual, Alphabetical 'Somnia Danielis' Collation* (Bern: Lang, 1982), 122–3.

To see the dream boundary in this way, as one device among many for signifying a state of altered consciousness, helps to explain the apparently casual treatment of dreaming sometimes found in writers like Chaucer and Langland who might be expected to have been more careful. The F-version of Chaucer's Prologue to the *Legend of Good Women* describes the narrator worshipping the daisy in a paradisal spring landscape, before falling asleep in an arbour and dreaming of the God of Love (F 197–209). In the revised G-version, the account of falling asleep in the arbour is advanced so that it precedes the description of the landscape (G 89–103). This may be evidence not of revision for the sake of it, but of an awareness of the respective potency of the dream boundary and idealized nature as indicators of a changed state, and of the different effects and meanings to be achieved by virtue of their relative positions. In the G-version, there follows a further intensification of other-worldly perceptions as the arrival of the God of Love is heralded by signifiers – flowers, birdsong – which almost suggest that the poet is experiencing a dream within a dream (G 104–43).[65]

Then again there is the notorious case of one of Langland's dreams within a dream. In the B-version of *Piers Plowman* (XVI. 18–167), his account of the tree of Charity is enclosed by a dream boundary within an already existing dream. Whether this is credible or not is beside the point: the episode is a moment of intense visionary experience, vouchsafed by no less a person than Piers himself, a figure for Christ. It culminates in an account of Christ's suffering, death and eventual triumph which brings tears to the eyes of the dreamer.[66] In the revised C-version, Langland's account of the personal effects of the Christian story is dropped. According to one editor, he decided to postpone the impression that the dreamer was, by this stage, 'fully prepared for the full revelation of Christ's sacrifice'.[67]

---

65 Cf. J. M. Gellrich, *The Idea of the Book in the Middle Ages: Language Theory, Mythology, and Fiction* (Ithaca, NY: Cornell University Press, 1985), 215.
66 W. Langland, *The Vision of Piers Plowman: A Critical Edition of the B-Text*, ed. A. V. C. Schmidt (London: Dent, 1978). Subsequent citations from the B-text are from this edition. The complexities of effect are rehearsed in A. V. C. Schmidt, 'The Inner Dreams in *Piers Plowman*', *Medium Ævum* 55 (1986), 24–33.
67 Ed. Pearsall, 301, note to XVIII. 179.

Consequently, in the C-version Langland deleted the onset of an inner dream because the vision of the tree of Charity does not lead to an intensification of personal consciousness (although he inadvertently preserves the moment of waking from the inner dream). Here again, what might appear to be an arbitrary or even a muddled decision may point instead to a clear sense of the uses and effects of the dream boundary.[68]

A few words remain to be said about the boundary on the other side of the literary dream, beyond which lies the return to waking reality – but waking reality of a particular kind, because it is marked by a reflecting back on the content and meaning of the dream. The sense that dreams need to be composed (or reconstituted) before they can be understood is, naturally, an appealing idea to the authors of literary dreams, in that it provides them with a role to which they are eminently suited. The dependence of dream survival upon literary reconstruction is clear from Apocalypse onwards, when John is enjoined by God: 'What thou seest, write in a book and send to the seven churches which are in Asia' (Apocalypse 1:11: 'Quod vides, scribe in libro: et mitte septem Ecclesiis, quae sunt in Asia'). On waking from *his* dream Langland reaches for his writing implements: 'And y wakned þerwith and wroet as me mette' (C. XXI. 481). Chaucer's narrator is more self-conscious about the literary possibilities of a dream. At the end of the *Book of the Duchess* he resolves, over time, to 'put this sweven in ryme' (1332).

The afterlife of a dream is, naturally enough, a time when the validity or otherwise of the experience is opened to debate. This allows the author a considerable amount of latitude, or margin for error. It is an occasion when the latent ambiguities about the significance of dreams can be fully exploited.[69] Authors, it might be thought, have a vested interest in suggesting that 'their' dream was authentic and significant. This is certainly the case with Macrobius' commentary on the dream of Scipio, for in the third

---

68 See S. Kruger, 'Mirrors and the Trajectory of Vision in *Piers Plowman*', *Speculum* 66 (1991), 78–9 and 93–5.
69 See Russell, *English Dream Vision*, 51 and ch. 2. For an additional anatomy of dream types see *Dives and Pauper*, I. xliii; ed Barnum, i, pt. 1, pp. 74–7.

chapter he erects an extremely influential theory of dreams on the basis of what Scipio saw, and proceeds to evaluate the dream according to his various categories.[70] Langland, for his part, wants to muddy the water, to mingle the categories of personal and divine dreams in order to encourage his audience to take dreams seriously. Awaking on Malvern hills, he rehearses the stories of Daniel, Nebuchadnezzar and Joseph (C. IX. 304–18). 'Sowngewarie', the interpretation of dreams, is not therefore something to be dismissed out of hand as superstitious nonsense, although it may be this, as the author of *Dives and Pauper* stresses (I. xliii–xlvi). Biblical precedent suggests that 'on meteles to stodie' is an instructive and crucial activity. Chaucer, as already noted, can leave his audience more room for manoeuvre – reminding it of various theories but leaving to them an assessment of the dream in the light of those possibilities of interpretation (see *HF* 12–58), or he might, as in the *Parliament of Fowls* (31) invoke a recognized authority such as Macrobius on which to pattern his own 'recalled' dream.

But the afterlife of a dream is not merely an arena in which an author can more or less conspicuously display his wealth of literary strategies. It is also a time when, without beating about the bush and rehearsing dream theory, he can register the impact of the dream as a revelation of truth, a clarification of perplexing thoughts. De Margival's narrator, in his *Panthère d'Amours*, awakes from a painful dream, reconsiders it, and finds 'Riens [...] qui fust mensonge' (2197: 'nothing in it which was untrue').[71] What is more, it gives him new volition to labour faithfully in pursuit of his lady, in the hope of winning mercy. Oton de Grandson's dreamer in *Le Songe Saint Valentin* awakes with a more radical conviction: that love is not wrong (as he had formerly thought) but a fundamental bond between people and among animals, in short a natural thing, a God-given good. As experienced by human beings it can cause sorrow, but here the dreamer maintains his new-found perspective by expressing sympathy and compassion for those

---

70 Macrobius, *Commentary*, I. 3, 1–11; ed. Willis, ii, 8–11; trans. Stahl, 87–90.
71 Windeatt, *Chaucer's Dream Poetry*, 132.

who suffer through love. He ends with a prayer to the God of Love that the hope, fidelity, and loyalty of lovers should be rewarded (314–449).[72]

It is not always thus.[73] Far from waking with a new sense of calm understanding, Langland's dreamer is prone to awake more puzzled and agitated then when he began. The *visio* ends with him troubled and worried by the concluding scene of his second dream, when Piers receives a controversial and enigmatic pardon from Truth. It causes an argument between Piers and a priest and, in two versions of the poem, is torn up by Piers himself. The sound of their argument wakes Langland's dreamer, who finds himself 'Meteles and moneyles on Maluerne hulles | Musynge on this meteles' (C. IX. 297–8). Similarly, the effect of a later dream is to drive him further into himself, ever more preoccupied and distracted with problems which, at the outset, he had not dreamt of, and which now appear to control his form of life:

> And I awakede þerwith, wittetes ner-hande,
> And as a freke þat fay were forth can y walken
> In manere of a mendenaunt mony ȝer aftur.
> And many tymes of this meteles moche thouhte y hadde [...]
> (C. XV. 2–5)

Langland's narrator cannot always escape the therapeutic effects of dreams. Having witnessed in sleep the defeat of Satan by Christ with triumphant commentary by Righteousness, Peace, Truth, Mercy and Love, he awakes from the carolling of these damsels to the ringing of bells on Easter morning, and calls Kit his wife and Calote his daughter so that they might go to church and honour the cross on which Christ died (C. XX. 470–8). Thus can the afterlife of a dream see doubted values reaffirmed, or readjusted, if only after a tortuous process of self-examination. Here, as in other cases, the dreamer is changed from the state he was in before the

---

72 Ed. A. Piaget, in his *Oton de Grandson: sa vie et ses poésies*, Mémoires et Documents Publiés par la Société d'Histoire de la Suisse Romande, ser. 3, vol. 1 (Lausanne: Payot, 1941); Windeatt, *Chaucer's Dream Poetry*, 123–4.
73 Hale, 'Dreams, Stress, and Interpretation', 53.

dream began.[74] He is put back in touch with himself or (as it might be) with nature. He is no longer alienated but integrated and resocialized. If formerly lost, he now has a sense of direction. In short his identity in relation to society has been reconstructed. In his dream he suffers a sense of dislocation, and his surroundings are de-familiarized, so that he emerges with a fresh acuity of perception.[75]

If the dream framework was one device among many for indicating a state of altered consciousness, it was nevertheless strongly favoured by English poets in the second half of the fourteenth century. It provided them with an instrument of radical analysis and evaluation. For, unlike other, less potent, indicators of transition, the dream enabled writers to explore the roots both of the self and of society. In some measure, the literary dream is the meeting-place of both, being at once intensely private and expansively public, providing a means whereby the outer world can be read through the inner. Dreams, by their nature, are able to express a sense of fragmentation, a loss of continuity between the self and the outer world, since they operate through striking juxtaposition, distortion, displacement, condensation and apparent incoherence.[76] A dream is therefore well suited to the representation and analysis of alienation, of a sense of lost authority, or of a searching for connections that have become hidden, tenuous or problematic.

Into what explanatory historical framework might we put the literary mechanism of the dream vision? From the evidence so far adduced, it would be plausible to see the remarkable concentration of literary dreams in the second half of the fourteenth century as a response to those economic, social, political and religious conditions which were likely to produce a sense of fragmentation, of lost identity, of questionable authority. One might speculate on the social impact of severe depopulation caused by

---

74   Cf. Russell, *English Dream Vision*, 136.
75   Cf. Froissart, *Paradis d'Amours*, ed. Dembowski, lines 1696–1723; Windeatt, *Chaucer's Dream Poetry*, 56–7.
76   See D. Brewer, 'Escape from the Mimetic Fallacy', in *Studies in Medieval English Romances: Some New Approaches*, ed. Brewer (Cambridge: Brewer, 1988), 6–7; Nagera, *Basic Psychoanalytic Concepts*, 54–5.

recurrent plague, of prolonged war, of schism, revolt and heresy, and their likely effects on the sensibilities of poets.[77] We might therefore understand the widespread use of the dream vision in these terms: society itself was in a state where boundaries were breaking down under the pressure of severe, recurrent and frequent crisis. What the dream vision provided was a radical means of representing, and reflecting upon, both those experiences and the pervasive sense thereby produced of being in a state of transition.[78]

To proceed further, in an unquestioning manner, along this speculative path, runs the risk of recreating precisely that kind of inadequate historicizing pinpointed in the opening paragraphs of this essay. For instance, it would be tempting, especially in the case of a writer like Langland, to take an issue such as authority and demonstrate the closeness of its social, religious and literary manifestations. But to do so would privilege one kind of text at the expense of others, and the conclusions reached would not necessarily fit other dream visions by his contemporaries.[79] Nor would it advance an answer to the present question: why this genre at this time? The subject of authority is hardly one that depended for its poetic treatment on the dream vision.

We must return, therefore, to what is distinctive about the genre, namely its capacity, as identified earlier, to indicate a state of altered consciousness. Is it possible to clarify or redefine that general term? It would be difficult to improve upon the word used by Kruger: the state of altered consciousness which the dream vision signals and explores is precisely that of 'betweenness'. It is as if the author of a dream vision is saying: 'I want to focus on the state of being between sleep and wakefulness, death and life, inertia and excitation, natural and artificial states, experience and authority, salvation and damnation, being lost and finding direction, solitude

---

77 Cf. C. Muscatine, *Poetry and Crisis in the Age of Chaucer*, University of Notre Dame Ward-Phillips Lectures in English Language and Literature, 4 (Notre Dame, Ind.: University of Notre Dame Press, 1972), ch. 1.
78 Cf. P. E. Dutton, *The Politics of Dreaming in the Carolingian Empire* (Lincoln, Nebr.: University of Nebraska Press, 1994).
79 On Chaucer's more elliptical approach in *HF* and *LGW* see Gellrich, *Idea of the Book*, chs. 5 and 6; cf. Delany, *Skeptical Fideism*, 46–7 and 118–22.

and sociability, private and public, male and female, health and sickness, constraint and liberation, alienation and integration.' Of course, the middle ground which the dream vision thus opens up is by its nature constantly shifting, elusive, open to renegotiation.

The experience of betweenness is what the dream vision, distinctively, allows poets to express and explore. That experience, we might reasonably assume, derives from the extraordinary circumstances found in English society in the second half of the fourteenth century. What we now need is a subtle instrument of analysis, founded in a theoretical approach, in order to test that assumption – one which will provide the fullest possible historical context for differing representations of betweenness across a wide range of texts. Now the condition of betweenness, or liminality, is a cultural phenomenon well known to anthropologists, and it is in their discipline, as Lynch has recognized, that the theoretical structure exists for a more thorough historicizing of the dream vision. There are various theories of liminality, but one particularly appropriate to the present enquiry was developed by Victor and Edith Turner.[80] Its focus was pilgrimage – a cultural practice well known in the Middle Ages, but also one which not infrequently appears as a motif within the dream vision.[81]

---

80   See J. R. Andreas, 'Festive Limitiality in Chaucerian Comedy', *Chaucer Newsletter* 1.1 (1979), 3–6:3; E. Turner, 'The Literary Roots of Victor Turner's Anthropology', in K. M. Ashley (ed,), *Victor Turner and the Construction of Cultural Criticism: Between Literature and Anthropology* (Bloomington: Indiana University Press, 1990), 163–9; T. Pison, 'Liminality in *The Canterbury Tales*', *Genre* 10 (1977), 157–71; F. B. Jonassen, 'The Inn, the Cathedral, and the Pilgrimage of *The Canterbury Tales*', in *Rebels and Rivals: The Contestive Spirit in the 'Canterbury Tales'*, ed. S. G. Fein, D. Raybin and P. C. Braeger, Studies in Medieval Culture, 29 (Kalamazoo, Mich.: Medieval Institute Publications, 1991), 4–8; and also B. Geremek, 'The Marginal Man', in *Medieval Callings*, ed. J. le Goff, trans. L. G. Cochrane (Chicago: University of Chicago Press, 1987), 347–73.

81   *Piers Plowman* is one notable, if complex, example. See also G. de Deguileville, *The Pilgrimage of the Lyfe of the Manhode: Translated Anonymously into Prose from the First Recension of Guillaume de Deguileville's Poem 'Le Pèlerinage de la vie humaine'*, ed. A. Henry, i, EETS os 288 (1985), pt. 1, lines 1–146, 1–4; and for commentary L. R. Muir, *Literature and Society in Medieval France: The Mirror and Its Image 1100–1500*

The recurrent representation of pilgrimage within dream visions is due in part to the complex figurative status which pilgrimage enjoyed in the Western Christian tradition. It signalled the alienation of the soul from God, and its desire to progress towards salvation.[82] The dream vision, on the other hand, given its biblical status as a mode of communication with God, is an appropriate context in which to address such matters. Conversely, the practice of pilgrimage is not infrequently bound up with visionary experiences, notably when a saint appears in a dream to perform a miracle far removed from his or her shrine, or when a vision of the saint itself prompts a pilgrimage.[83] Thus pilgrimage and dream have complementary potentials: the one, pilgrimage, is ideally an exteriorized mysticism; the other, dream vision, may be an interiorized pilgrimage, with an urge to mirror and effect spiritual transformation through self-examination.[84]

(Basingstoke: Macmillan, 1985), 172–5; S. K. Hagen, *Allegorical Remembrance: A Study of 'The Pilgrimage of the Life of Man' as a Medieval Treatise on Seeing and Remembering* (Athens, Ga.: University of Georgia Press, 1990), 112–17; S. Wright, 'Deguileville's Pèlerinage de Vie Humaine as "Contrepartie Edifiante" of the *Roman de la Rose*', *Philological Quarterly* 68 (1989), 399–422. See also the beginning of *The Pilgrimage of the Soul: A Critical Edition of the Middle English Dream Vision*, ed. R. P. McGerr, i, Garland Medieval Texts, 16 (New York: Garland, 1990), bk. 1, lines 1–20, from a Middle English translation (*c*.1413) of the second part of Guillaume's trilogy, written in 1355. For a brief discussion of other dream pilgrimages in the French tradition, see S. A. Barney, 'Allegorical Visions', in *A Companion to 'Piers Plowman'*, ed J. A. Alford (Berkeley and Los Angeles: University of California Press, 1988), 126–8.

82   G. B. Ladner, '*Homo Viator*: Mediaeval Ideas on Alienation and Order', *Speculum* 42 (1967), 233–59; F. C. Gardiner, *The Pilgrimage of Desire: A Study of Theme and Genre in Medieval Literature* (Leiden: Brill, 1971), ch. 1.

83   Cf. B. Ward, *Miracles and the Medieval Mind: Theory, Record and Event 1000–1215* (London: Scolar Press, 1982), 97; and see J. Sumption, *Pilgrimage: An Image of Mediaeval Religion* (London: Faber, 1975), 16–17 and 26–7.

84   V. and E. Turner, *Image and Pilgrimage in Christian Culture: Anthropological Perspectives*, Lectures on the History of Religions Sponsored by the American Council of Learned Societies, NS 11 (New York: Columbia University Press, 1978), 7; Lynch, *High Medieval Dream Vision*, 48; Nolan, *Gothic Visionary Perspective*, ch. 4; S. Stanbury, *Seeing the Gawain-Poet: Description and the Act of Perception*

Given the possible, generic, interpenetrations of pilgrimage and dream vision, the anthropological approach developed by Turner and Turner would seem to provide a promising model for analysing both cultural phenomena. Drawing on the work of van Gennep, they describe how liminality is experienced in the course of a rite of passage.[85] The rite has three phases: separation; limen, or margin; and aggregation:

> The first phase comprises symbolic behavior signifying the detachment of the individual or group, either from an earlier fixed point in the social structure or from a relatively stable set of cultural conditions [...] during the intervening liminal phase, the state of the ritual subject [...] becomes ambiguous, he passes through a realm or dimension that has few or none of the attributes of the past or the coming state, he is betwixt and between all familiar lines of classification; in the third phase the passage is consummated, and the subject returns to classified secular or mundane social life.[86]

The application of a liminoid structure to the dream vision would seem fairly straightforward.[87] Separation would correspond with the alienated and solitary state of the dreamer; limen to the dream experience itself; aggregation to the afterlife of dreaming. This order of analysis has been proposed by Lynch.[88] But the correspondences are more subtle. For the dream vision, like the pilgrimage, is from the anthropological viewpoint initiation to, not through, a threshold. In other words, what appeared to be

---

(Philadelphia: University of Pennsylvania Press, 1991), 12–13; S. Stakel, 'Structural Convergence of Pilgrimage and Dream-Vision in Christine de Pizan', in *Journeys Toward God: Pilgrimage and Crusade*, ed. B. N. Sargent-Baur, Studies in Medieval Culture, 30 (Kalamazoo, Mich.: Medieval Institute Publications, 1992), 195–203.

85 A. van Gennep, *The Rites of Passage* [1908], trans. M. B. Vizedom and G. L. Caffee (Chicago: University of Chicago Press, 1960).

86 Turner and Turner, *Image and Pilgrimage*, 2. See also E. Leach, *Culture and Communication. The Logic by which Symbols are Connected: An Introduction to the Use of Structuralist Analysis in Social Anthropology* (Cambridge: Cambridge University Press, 1976), 77–9.

87 See V. Turner, 'Liminal to Liminoid, in Play, Flow, and Ritual: An Essay in Comparative Symbology', in his *From Ritual to Theatre: The Human Seriousness of Play* (New York: Performing Arts Journal Publications, 1982), 20–60.

88 Lynch, *High Medieval Dream Vision*, 47–8.

marginal, peripheral, a state of transition, both into and out of the dream, is on reflection central, essential. An acceptance of the state of being liminal, between heaven and hell, is a crucial movement towards spiritual enlightenment; the realization that one occupies disputed territory, between the conflicting claims of individual identity and those of society at large, is a step in the direction of both intellectual expansion and social reintegration.

According to Turner's account, the pilgrim is an initiand who experiences a new and more profound mode of existence.[89] Pilgrimage frees the participants from the secular world, and intensifies their piety. The act of piety expressed through pilgrimage reaches its apogee at the pilgrim's destination, usually a shrine within a holy place, which represents in a particularly powerful way the basic components of the faith. Although the pilgrim then returns to everyday life, the belief remains that he or she has made a significant spiritual advance.

Pilgrimage has many features in common with the liminality attributed more generally to rites of passage. First, there is a deliberate rejection of social norms and structures. Differences of status are ignored or inverted, anonymity is preferred, dress and behaviour tend towards simplicity, possessions count for little. Within the pilgrimage group a sense of *communitas* develops which itself levels social difference and offers an alternative to conventional structures. This is especially marked when the impulse to pilgrimage is a response to crisis, to an impending or perceived fracturing of the social structure. The reconfiguration of normal social relations leads to a novel, challenging, and sometimes playful and comic, juxtaposition of incongruous components.

Second, not only the group but also the individual embraces self-awareness and reconstruction. That process may be associated with death

---

89 What follows is based on Turner and Turner, *Image and Pilgrimage*, 8, 9, 14, 15 and 34; V. Turner, *The Forest of Symbols: Aspects of Ndembu Ritual* (Ithaca, NY: Cornell University Press, 1967), ch. 4; his *The Ritual Process: Structure and Anti-Structure*, The Lewis Henry Morgan Lectures, 1966 (Chicago: Aldine, 1969), chs 3 and 4; his 'Liminal to Liminoid', 24–30; his *Dramas, Fields, and Metaphors: Symbolic Action in Human Society* (Ithaca, NY: Cornell University Press, 1974), ch. 5; and his 'Pilgrimage and Communitas', *Studia Missionalia* 23 (1974), 305–27.

and rebirth, with entering darkness and emerging into light, with anonymity, with a sense of freedom, with deliberate privation, which may include poverty, nakedness, ordeal, submissiveness and humility. The initiand is also driven inwards to consider the general meaning but also the personal significance of those religious and cultural values normally taken for granted. As a result the individual, through personal learning and transformation, evaluates subjective experience within its institutionalized context, to the point of becoming critical of both. What eventually emerges is an integral person and purpose from the multiple personae and roles which formerly obtained. Finally, there are dislocations of place and space. The leaving of familiar territory is characterized as a departure for the unknown, for a wilderness, which itself figures spiritual and intellectual waywardness. At the same time, stasis is exchanged for movement, which in turn reflects the whole process of self-realization.

Such categories of analysis have tremendous potential for describing and understanding the workings and priorities of the dream vision, but they also have limitations, and it is therefore important to proceed with some caution. Attractive and applicable though Turner's theory may be, its abstracting, generalizing and universalizing tendencies need to be resisted, and are open to question and qualification. For instance, if one thinks of later fourteenth-century England, then the ideal model of pilgrimage advanced by Turner would seem to be in retreat, either through its incorporation into institutional practices, or through its abuse, or by virtue of the attacks made upon pilgrimage by reformers such as the Lollards. Again, it would be difficult to demonstrate that a pilgrimage narrative like the unfinished *Canterbury Tales*, with its affinity to the dream vision, or the perpetually self-examining *Piers Plowman*, ever arrive, through the motif of pilgrimage, at a stable, transcendent moment of personal and social reintegration. Each work is more adequately characterized as offering a pluralism, a variety of unreconciled points of view, subsumed under the common experience of pilgrimage. The nature, intention and objective of that pilgrimage vary from voice to voice and from persona to persona and from character to character so that there are as many Canterburys, or Truths, as there are pilgrims. What both works offer in their representation of pilgrimage is – and here I quote from a recent critique of Turner's thesis – '*a realm of competing discourses*'.[90]

On the other hand, Turner's theory of liminality, precisely because it is so wide-ranging, provides a means of studying the 'betweenness' so extensively and subtly represented by dream visions in a wider social and historical context. For liminality cannot be studied in isolation from its social context. It is seen by anthropologists to apply to all phases of decisive cultural change, in which the previous orderings of thought and behaviour are subject to revision and criticism; when hitherto unprecedented modes of ordering relations between ideas and people become possible and desirable.[91] Theories of liminality thus have great potential for understanding the nature of the English dream vision in the later fourteenth century and for plotting its affiliations with the cultural moment from which it sprang.[92] It offers a framework within which to consider decisive cultural changes and responses to it, be they social, political, religious or literary.

90 J. Eade and M. J. Sallnow, Introduction to *Contesting the Sacred: The Anthropology of Christian Pilgrimage*, ed Eade and Sallnow (London: Routledge, 1991); but cf. Turner, *Dramas, Fields, and Metaphors*, 198, quoting Lewis.
91 Turner and Turner, *Image and Pilgrimage*, 2; Turner, *Ritual Process*, 148 and 153–4.
92 Turner, *Ritual Process*, 42, offers a brief comment on the importance of dream symbolism to the instigators of communitas, using the example of St Francis.

Towards a Bohemian Reading of *Troilus and Criseyde*

Geoffrey Chaucer never went to Bohemia but Bohemia came to him, a consequence of international negotiations to secure a bride for the boy king, Richard II. Chaucer had visited Milan in 1378 with Sir Edward de Berkeley to discuss with Bernabó Visconti, duke of Milan, and the powerful English mercenary who served him, Sir John Hawkwood, certain needs of the king concerning the propagation of war ('pur ascunes busignes touchantes lexploit de nostre guerre').[1] Hard on the heels of that mission, a second delegation visited Bernabó whose daughter, Caterina, was of eligible age. It included Sir Simon Burley, a member of the so-called Chaucer circle.[2] Whether or not the English diplomats exchanged information about their impressions of the Milanese court, Chaucer later styled Bernabó 'scourge of Lombardye',[3] the discussions in Milan foundered, and English attention switched to Prague and Anne of Bohemia, daughter of the holy Roman emperor, Charles IV (reigned 1346–78). It was hoped that an alliance with Bohemia might also help English efforts in the war against France. On this occasion also Burley was a key player in the discussions. An Anglo-Bohemian treaty was secured and Anne, then aged sixteen, was dispatched to England with her entourage.[4]

---

1   Martin C. Crow and Clair C. Olson, eds, *Chaucer Life-Records* (Oxford: Clarendon Press, 1966), 54.
2   Derek Pearsall, *The Life of Geoffrey Chaucer: A Critical Biography*, Blackwell Critical Biographies, 1 (Oxford: Blackwell, 1992), 105.
3   Monk's Tale, line 2400. Cf. David Wallace, '"Whan She Translated Was": A Chaucerian Critique of the Petrarchan Academy', in *Literary Practice and Social Change in Britain, 1380–1530*, ed. Lee Patterson (Berkeley: University of California Press, 1990), 171–6, 190–207.
4   Anthony Tuck, 'Richard II and the House of Luxembourg', in *Richard II: The Art of Kingship*, ed. Anthony Goodman and James Gillespie (Oxford: Clarendon Press,

The Bohemians arrived in Dover in December 1381, proceeded via Canterbury to Leeds Castle, near Maidstone, where they spent Christmas, and arrived in London in January. Richard was enjoying some new-found prestige for having faced down the rebels at Mile End the preceding June. Most of the chroniclers, for their part, took a cursory if not superstitious approach to the arrival of Anne and other Bohemians. Thomas Walsingham opined that Bernabó Visconti's daughter would have been a better match. Soon after Anne disembarked at Dover her ship sank in the harbour and Walsingham took the event as an ambiguous one that either 'showed the favour of God and presaged future happiness for the land' or was a dreadful portent, 'a dark, perplexing omen of doubtful meaning'.[5] The author of the Westminster chronicler deplored the impoverished state of the courtiers who arrived with her and Anne's lack of a dowry:

> About this Queen somebody wrote the verse: 'Worthy to enjoy manna, | To Englishmen is given the noble Anna'; but to those with an eye for the facts it seemed that she represented a purchase rather than a gift, since the English king laid out no small sum to secure this tiny scrap of humanity.[6]

Others would comment disparagingly on the extravagance of the Bohemians or their outlandish fashions that included long, pointed shoes. Walsingham complained about the expense of maintaining Anne and her Bohemians, not least when they visited English monasteries (like his) in excessive numbers.[7]

1999), 216–21; Nigel Saul, *Richard II* (New Haven: Yale University Press, 1997), 84–95.

5 Thomas Walsingham, *Chronicon Angliae 1328–1388*, ed. E. M. Thompson, Rolls series 64 (1874), 331; *The Chronica maiora of Thomas Walsingham 1376–1422*, trans. David Preest, ed. James G. Clark (Woodbridge: Boydell Press, 2005), 170–1. For a less gloomy account see *The Brut, or the Chronicles of England*, ed. Friedrich W. D. Brie, ii, EETS os 136 (1908), 338–9.

6 *The Westminster Chronicle*, ed. and trans. L. C. Hector and Barbara F. Harvey (Oxford: Clarendon Press, 1982), 22–5; quoted by Andrew Taylor, 'Anne of Bohemia and the Making of Chaucer', *Studies in the Age of Chaucer* 19 (1997), 95, who emends the final words to 'small piece of flesh' (*carnis porcione*).

7 Taylor, 'Anne of Bohemia', 102 and n. 27; Thomas Walsingham, *Historia Anglicana*, ed. H. T. Riley, Rolls series 28 (1864), ii, 96–7.

In spite of their frosty reception, the Bohemians made themselves at home, though Walsingham even turns this to their disadvantage, noting how quickly English hospitality made them forget Bohemia and irk their hosts.[8] Some embraced their adoptive culture in more ways than one, and married into the English nobility.[9] Richard earned the Westminster chronicler's criticism because he 'at his own expense married some of the queen's countrywomen to men of rank'.[10] One such union was especially controversial. In 1387, the king's favourite, Robert de Vere, earl of Oxford, divorced his wife (a grand-daughter of Edward III) for one of Anne's ladies-in-waiting, Agnes of Lancecrona, the daughter of a saddler.[11] Such incidents helped to make the Bohemian contingent at court a focus for the critique of Richard's rule as articulated by the Appellants. One of their targets was Burley, Richard's former tutor and the negotiator of his marriage treaty. He was accused by the Westminster chronicler of causing the king

> by wicked design to have [...] in his household a great number of aliens, Bohemians, and others, and to give them great gifts out of the revenues and commodities of the realm; whereby our lord the king is greatly impoverished and the people utterly oppressed.[12]

When Burley was arraigned, the queen implored the earl of Arundel to spare his life. She remained on her knees for several hours, but her pleadings were to no avail and Burley was beheaded in 1388.[13] De Vere was exiled and the Bohemians dismissed from the queen's household.[14]

---

8   *Chronica maiora*, trans. Preest, 220.
9   Saul, *Richard II*, 92, n. 36.
10 *Westminster Chronicle*, ed. and trans. Hector and Harvey, 160–1; and *Chronica maiora*, trans. Preest, 251.
11 *Westminster Chronicle*, ed. and trans. Hector and Harvey, 188–91.
12 Ibid., 272–5; Ardis Butterfield, 'French Culture and the Ricardian Court', in *Essays on Ricardian Literature: In Honour of J. A. Burrow*, ed. A. J. Minnis, Charlotte Morse and Thorlac Turville-Petre (Oxford: Clarendon Press, 1997), 94.
13 Taylor, 'Anne of Bohemia', 103.
14 May McKisack, *The Fourteenth Century, 1307–1399*, The Oxford History of England, 5 (Oxford: Clarendon Press, 1959), 459.

Political marriage it may have been but there is a general consensus among modern historians that strong affections developed between Richard and Anne. Unusually for a queen, Anne accompanied Richard on many if not all of his frequent peregrinations and he, according to Walsingham, seldom let her leave his side. She acted as intercessor, often to better effect than in the case of Burley, securing mercy when the king's judgments might otherwise have been unduly harsh.[15] On her death in June 1394, Richard ordered the destruction of the royal manor house at Sheen, even though it was 'a most splendid one', because that is where the queen had died.[16] Richard's act was surely a token of considerable grief for the woman he loved.[17] Their tomb effigies in Westminster Abbey, commissioned by Richard at Anne's death, are the first in England to show a king and queen together. The design allowed them to hold hands.[18]

For better or worse, Anne and her Bohemians put a highly distinctive stamp on English court life, especially during the six years immediately after their arrival. It was the court culture in which Chaucer lived, moved and worked, although he cannily withdrew from it just before the events

---

15 Walsingham, *Historia Anglicana*, ed. Riley, ii, 119; Paul Strohm, *Hochon's Arrow: The Social Imagination of Fourteenth-Century Texts* (Princeton: Princeton University Press, 1992), 106–7; Michael van Dussen, 'Three Verse Eulogies for Anne of Bohemia', *Medium Ævum* 78 (2009), 256, n. 6; David Wallace, *Chaucerian Polity: Absolutist Lineages and Associational Forms in England and Italy* (Stanford: Stanford University Press), 363–4; Saul, *Richard II*, 455–7 for an overview, as also Carolyn P. Collette, *Performing Polity: Women and Agency in the Anglo-French Tradition* (Turnhout: Brepols, 2006), ch. 5.

16 *The Chronicle of Adam Usk 1377–1421*, ed. and trans. C. Given-Wilson (Oxford: Clarendon Press, 1987), 19. Cf. *Historia vitae et regni Ricardi secundi*, ed. George B. Stow, Haney Foundation series, 21 (Philadelphia: University of Pennsylvania Press, 1977), 134, contrasting the general affection towards Anne at her death with the hostile reception of the Bohemians.

17 Saul, *Richard II*, 93–4.

18 Philip Lindley, 'Absolutism and Regal Image in Ricardian Sculpture', in *The Regal Image of Richard II and the Wilton Diptych*, ed. Dillian Gordon, Lisa Monnas and Caroline Elam (London: Harvey Miller, 1997), 61–74; Eleanor Scheifele, 'Richard II and the Visual Arts', in *Richard II*, ed. Goodman and Gillespie, 262–4.

of 1388.[19] At the time of Anne's arrival he was approximately forty years old and had established himself as a trusted client of royal patronage. He had undertaken a number of diplomatic journeys to France and two to Italy, having visited Florence in 1372 as well as Milan six years later. He had enjoyed a number of prestigious offices bestowed by the Crown, most recently as customs controller in the Port of London. And he enjoyed a connection with John of Gaunt, eldest surviving son of Edward III. Chaucer's wife, Philippa Roët, served in Gaunt's household and was probably sister to Catherine Swynford, Gaunt's mistress and eventually his third wife.[20] Gaunt had, indeed, commissioned – or so it would seem – Chaucer's first major literary composition, the *Book of the Duchess*, which commemorates the death of Gaunt's first wife, Blanche.

The *Canterbury Tales* were as yet to see the light of day. What Chaucer did produce in the very middle of the Bohemian phase of English court culture was a poem some regard as his greatest achievement – *Troilus and Criseyde*, with its very strong appeal to a courtly audience. It therefore behoves us to think about the interplay between that culture and poem produced in and for it. Significantly, it is a poem much concerned with cultural relativity – especially the difference between ancient, pagan Troy and Christian, medieval present – but also with the ways in which different people in different places at different times do things differently (even if their underlying experiences and motivations are essentially the same). At the beginning of Book II the narrator reminds us that there are many alternative ways of achieving the same end, whether travelling to a foreign country or conducting a love affair; indeed what passes for normality in England might cause disaster if practised elsewhere:

> For every wight which that to Rome went
> Halt nat o path, or alwey o manere;
> Ek in som lond were al the game shent,

---

19 Paul Strohm, 'Politics and Poetics: Usk and Chaucer in the 1380s', in *Literary Practice*, ed. Patterson, 90–7.
20 Pearsall, *Life of Chaucer*, 99–109; Nicola F. McDonald, 'Chaucer's *Legend of Good Women*, Ladies at Court and the Female Reader', *Chaucer Review* 35 (2000), 25–6.

> If that they ferde in love as men don here,
> As thus, in opyn doyng or in chere,
> In visiting in forme, or seyde hire sawes;
> Forthi men seyn, 'Ecch contree hath his lawes'.
> (*TC* II. 36–42)

These words are framed by a playful admonishment to be tolerant and not dismiss practices of love in ancient Troy as outlandish: 'Ek for to wynnen love in sondry ages | In sondry londes, sondry ben usages' (*TC* II. 27–8). What follows is an attempt to put these 'postcolonial' words of advice into practice through an interpretation of some aspects of *Troilus and Criseyde*, specifically by exploring the consequences of the cultural difference associated with the Bohemian moment in English court culture. It is hoped that the end result will be a somewhat different orientation for the poem, which is more usually seen in the context of Italian literary culture (by virtue of Chaucer's main narrative source, the *Il Filostrato* of Giovanni Boccaccio), or French culture (the background for Chaucer's notions of chivalric love). The importance of such a reorientation has been stressed by David Wallace, in drawing attention to the 'congruence of cultural fields' between the Bohemians and Chaucer.[21] The main areas of focus are textual culture, the myth of Troy and attitudes to piety.

Chaucer would have had certain expectations of 'Bohemia' before he encountered its representatives at first hand and not just through reports relayed by the likes of Burley. The Luxembourgs had a reputation for literary patronage far beyond what we know Chaucer to have experienced at the Plantagenet court before 1382.[22] That patronage directly affected

---

21   Wallace, *Chaucerian Polity*, 363 and cf. 376–7. See also his 'Anne of Bohemia, Queen of England, and Chaucer's *Emperice*', *Litteraria Pragensia* 5 (1995), 8–9.

22   Nigel Wilkins, 'A Pattern of Patronage: Machaut, Froissart and the Houses of Luxembourg and Bohemia in the Fourteenth Century', *French Studies* 37 (1983), 257–84; V. J. Scattergood, 'Literary Culture at the Court of Richard II' in *English Court Culture in the Later Middle Ages*, ed. V. J. Scattergood and J. W. Sherborne (London: Duckworth, 1983), 29–43; Patricia J. Eberle, 'Richard II and the Literary Arts', in *Richard II*, ed. Goodman and Gillespie, 231–53.

two poets well-known to Chaucer either through their writing or personally. The French court poet and musician, Guillaume de Machaut (*c*.1300–77), exerted a formative influence on Chaucer's understanding of the genres of the lyric and dream vision – the constituents of his early compositions. He used a poem or *dit* by Machaut, *Le Jugement dou roy de Behaigne* (Judgement of the King of Bohemia) as an armature for the *Book of the Duchess*. For some seventeen years from *c*.1323 Guillaume served Jean d'Aveugle of Luxembourg, king of Bohemia, as secretary and clerk, accompanying him on diplomatic trips to Prague. Jean was Anne of Bohemia's grandfather and his sponsorship of Guillaume was repaid handsomely in eulogies penned by the French poet. In the *Jugement* named after him, Jean resides in his real-life castle at Durbuy and mediates a love debate. His court is a place of wealth, splendour, and magnificence. When first encountered he is described as 'faithful, brave, generous and proficient, and gentle, unassuming, and courteous to all'. He is seated on a silken carpet and a clerk is reading to him about a battle from the story of Troy.[23]

There is a possibility that Chaucer met Machaut at Rheims,[24] but he could hardly have avoided Jean Froissart (*c*.1337–*c*.1405) for they were both habitués of the court of Edward III: Froissart as resident chronicler and poet, Chaucer as a young page and esquire.[25] Froissart is primarily known today as the chronicler of the Hundred Years War but he was also a poet of distinction. His *Paradys d'Amours* is another important model for Chaucer's *Book of the Duchess*. In 1368, having left the employ of Edward and his campatriote, Queen Philippa of Hainault, Froissart went to Brussels and enjoyed the patronage of Wenceslas of Brabant (d. 1383), Anne of

---

23 Alfred Thomas, *A Blessed Shore: England and Bohemia from Chaucer to Shakespeare* (Ithaca, NY: Cornell University Press, 2007), 52. Blind though he was, Jean fought at Crécy in 1346 on the French side and died an heroic if quixotic death. Jean Froissart, *Chronicles*, ed. and trans. Geoffrey Brereton, rev. edn (Harmondsworth: Penguin, 1978), 90.
24 James I. Wimsatt, *Chaucer and His French Contemporaries: Natural Music in the Fourteenth Century* (Toronto: University of Toronto Press, 1991), 78–9.
25 Ibid., 175–81.

Bohemia's uncle, and for whom he composed *Méliador*, a long and unfinished verse romance.[26]

Chaucer's knowledge of the writings of Machaut and Froissart, and of the patronage they enjoyed, may help to explain the form in which he crafted *Troilus and Criseyde* – as a narrative with intercalated lyrics. It was a procedure he encountered in his main source, Boccaccio's *Il Filostrato*, while another source, the *Consolatio philosophiae* of Boethius, alternates discursive prose with poetry. But Chaucer more than doubled the number of lyrics found in Boccaccio's text and in so doing he may have been responding to a practice that was à la mode among other writers who influenced him and who served patrons of the house of Luxembourg. Froissart embedded in *Méliador* lyrics penned by Wenceslas of Brabant and Machaut's *Jugement dou roy de Behaigne* also mixes narrative and lyric.[27]

Evidence that Anne of Bohemia was similarly well disposed to literary compositions surfaces in *The Boke of Cupide* by Chaucer's associate, the chamber knight Sir John Clanvowe (c.1341–91). The poem borrows from Chaucer's *Parliament of Fowls* in creating a love debate between a cuckoo and a nightingale. Its resolution is deferred until St Valentine's day, when the assembled company of birds is to reconvene 'Vnder the maple that is feire and grene, | Before the chambre wyndow of the Quene | At Wodestok, upon the grene lay' (283–5).[28] Clanvowe's sense of familiarity with the queen's person was not merely fanciful. He was one of the executors of her will. There is a similar allusion in the F-Prologue to Chaucer's *Legend of Good Women* where Alceste instructs the dreaming poet to deliver the

---

26 For further literary dealings between Froissart and his patron, evidenced in the *Prison amoureuse*, see Laurence de Looze, *Pseudo-Biography in the Fourteenth Century: Juan Ruiz, Guillaume de Machaut, Jean Froissart and Geoffrey Chaucer* (Gainseville: University Press of Florida, 1997), 114–17; and Wilkins, 'Pattern of Patronage', 265–79.
27 Wimsatt, *Chaucer and His French Contemporaries*, ch. 5.
28 *The Works of Sir John Clanvowe*, ed. V. J. Scattergood (Cambridge: Brewer, 1965). For commentary, see Lee Patterson, 'Court Politics and the Invention of Literature: The Case of Sir John Clanvowe', in *Culture and History 1350–1600: Essays on English Communities, Identities and Writing*, ed. David Aers (Hemel Hempstead: Harvester Wheatsheaf, 1992), 9–13, 20–6.

legend, when it is complete, to the queen 'at Eltham or at Shene'. There were royal manor-houses for the use of the queen's household in both places – the one at Sheen, as previously mentioned, destroyed by Richard in his grief over Anne's death.[29] The reference to the queen also suggests that what the prologue represents is the commissioning of a poem.[30] And a tortuous business it seems to have been. Chaucer represents himself as the author of a number of works we know he composed and as a poet of growing reputation, but as nevertheless clumsy, obtuse, prone to give offence unwittingly, his intentions likely to be misunderstood. Faced with accusations by the God of Love he is abject, a 'worm' (F 318), and it takes the intervention of Queen Alceste to secure some leniency.[31] Commentators have seen in Alceste's action a reflection of the intercessory role habitually played by Anne of Bohemia as Richard's queen, to some extent a formal and ceremonial one.[32] Certainly the prologue, like Clanvowe's poem, is

---

29 Saul, *Richard II*, 298; Chris Given-Wilson, *The Royal Household and the King's Affinity: Service, Politics and Finance in England 1360–1413* (New Haven: Yale University Press, 1986), 29–31.

30 Julia Boffey and A. S. G. Edwards, 'Manuscripts and Audience', in *A Concise Companion to Chaucer*, ed. Corinne Saunders (Oxford: Blackwell, 2006), 34.

31 For commentary see Wallace, *Chaucerian Polity*, 53–6, 366–70; and Lisa Kiser, *Telling Classical Tales: Chaucer and the 'Legend of Good Women'* (Ithaca, NY: Cornell University Press, 1983), ch. 3 and 132–5.

32 For the identification of Anne with Alceste see William A. Quinn, *Chaucer's 'Rehersynges': The Performability of the 'Legend of Good Women'* (Washington DC: Catholic University of America Press, 1994) 31, n. 3 and 38, n. 4; the explanatory notes by M. C. E. Shaner and A. S. G. Edwards to *LGW* in the *Riverside Chaucer*, ed. Benson et al., 1061, col. 1.; Florence Percival, *Chaucer's Legendary Good Women* (Cambridge: Cambridge University Press, 1998), 47–8, 88–9; McDonald, 'Chaucer's *Legend of Good Women*', 25; Wallace, '"Whan She Translated Was"', 209–11. On Chaucer's use of the Alceste legend see V. A. Kolve, 'From Cleopatra to Alceste: An Iconographic Study of the *Legend of Good Women*', in *Signs and Symbols in Chaucer's Poetry*, ed. John P. Hermann and John J. Burke (University: University of Alabama Press, 1981), 171–4; Percival, *Chaucer's Legendary Good Women*, ch. 2; the introduction by Helen Phillips to the Prologue to *LGW* in *Chaucer's Dream Poetry*, ed. Helen Phillips and Nick Havely (London: Longman, 1997), 283–6; and Kiser, *Telling Classical Tales*, 18–19, n. 3.

energized by the role-playing and play-acting at the sort that happened in so-called courts of love, and in which the court of Richard and Anne may have participated.[33]

Of particular interest for present purposes is the nature of the treason or heresy of which Chaucer's alter ego stands accused: the translation and composition of narratives that might make people think twice about the benefits of love. One key exhibit is his writing the story of Criseyde, 'That makith men to wommen lasse triste' (F 333). The act of redress eventually negotiated, thanks to Alceste's intervention, is the composition of a palinode: a series of narratives about trustworthy, faithful, and virtuous women, what we now know as the *Legend of Good Women*. This citing of the story of Criseyde speaks volumes about the courtly milieu of *Troilus and Criseyde* and its controversial reception.[34] It seems to have stirred debate and made its author something of a celebrity.[35] In particular, Alceste's reference to Chaucer's great love narrative puts Richard and Anne – Anne, in particular, as the intended beneficiary of Chaucer's act of community service – at the heart of the audience for *Troilus*.[36]

It is possible to speak with relative confidence of Anne of Bohemia as the intended recipient of the *Legend of Good Women*. Did she also fulfil a similar role in respect of *Troilus and Criseyde*? It is impossible to determine,

---

33 Richard Firth Green, 'The *Familia Regis* and the *Familia Cupidinis*', in *English Court Culture in the Later Middle Ages*, ed. V. J. Scattergood and J. W. Sherborne (London: Duckworth, 1983), 105–6; Percival, *Chaucer's Legendary Good Women*, ch. 15.
34 The earliest witness is the *Testament of Love* by Thomas Usk, which praises the philosophical content of Chaucer's poem and may have been composed by 1385. See Thomas Usk, *Testament of Love*, ed. Gary W. Shawver (Toronto: Toronto University Press, 2002), 24–8. Usk was beheaded in 1388, a victim of the Merciless Parliament by means of which the Appellants moved also against the king's favourites, including Burley. See Strohm, 'Politics and Poetics', 85–90.
35 For an intriguing precedent, involving Machaut and, possibly, Anne's aunt (Bonne of Luxembourg), see Wimsatt, *Chaucer and His French Contemporaries*, 161–8; and Percival, *Chaucer's Legendary Good Women*, ch. 8.
36 Christopher Baswell, *Virgil in Medieval England: Figuring the 'Aeneid' from the Twelfth Century to Chaucer*, Cambridge Studies in Medieval Literature, 24 (Cambridge: Cambridge University Press, 1995), 249–55.

but there are some telling indications that Chaucer wished both her and his larger audience to know that, in writing his poem, he had Anne very much in mind. At the climactic moment in book 1, just before Troilus sees Criseyde for the first time and falls passionately in love, Chaucer describes her beauty in the following terms: 'Right as oure first letter is now an A | In beaute first so stood she, makeless' (I. 171–2). Of course, our first letter has always been an 'A': it is the qualifying 'now' that makes all the difference and which has led commentators to read the line as an allusion to Richard's 'first lady', Anne of Bohemia, also known as Alceste. They have been less forthcoming about an allusion at the end of the poem that is of equal, if not greater, significance. Recognizing that the story of a woman who betrayed her lover may not be to the taste of 'every lady bright of hewe, | And every gentil womman', the narrator asks to be excused from blame in telling Criseyde's story and begs that they do not direct their ire at him: 'for that gilt she be nat wroth with me'. His concern is not with Criseyde's guilt, for others have been sufficiently condemnatory: 'Ye may hire gilt in other bokes se'. By way of recompense, should such ladies wish it, 'yif yow leste', he offers to write of more admirable women, of 'Penelopeës trouthe and good Alceste' (V. 1772–8).

This is knowing, courteous, mischievous. Intriguingly, it anticipates the scenario of the prologue to the *Legend of Good Women*; it puts a decorous distance between Criseyde, whose beauty is so like Anne's, and Anne, who is more like Alceste; and it nods in the direction of a woman whose patronage Chaucer might very well want, even if it is not at present enjoy it.[37] And lest we should be in any doubt as to what kind of paragon Alceste was, Chaucer embeds her story in the preceding narrative. Troilus, disturbed by an ominous dream, seeks its interpretation from his sister, Cassandra, the famous soothsayer. The sooth she says is not at all to his liking: his dream of Criseyde in the arms of a wild boar portends her act of betrayal with the Greek knight, Diomede. Troilus finds the idea ludicrous and dismisses Cassandra's interpretation. For him, Criseyde is unimpeachable, and he retorts:

---

37 Cf. Percival, *Chaucer's Legendary Good Women*, 154–5.

> As well how myghtest lien on Alceste
> That was of creatures, but men lye,
> That evere weren, kindest and the beste!
> For whan hire housbonde was in jupertye
> To dye hymself but if she wolde dye,
> She ches for hym to dye and gon to helle,
> And starf anon, as us the bokes telle.
> (V. 1527–33)

As a way of referencing Anne, what more appropriate figure could there be than this devoted wife of a king beset by crisis?[38]

Troilus and Cassandra disagree about the meaning of his dream, although she is right; and just as Troilus derives his story of Alceste from 'bokes', so she draws on what 'men in bokes fynde' (V. 1463), written authority that shows how the boar signifies Diomede, son of Tideus, who slew a boar that threatened Thebes. To an extraordinary extent, even by Chaucer's standards, *Troilus and Criseyde* is about texts, intention, authorship and interpretation, whether of words or of other kinds of signs, be they dreams or something altogether more material. While Troilus may deny Cassandra's reading of the boar's embrace, in his heart he knows it to be true. On waking from the dream he is full of anxiety and foreboding, and declares to Pandarus: 'My lady bright, Criseyde, hath me bytrayed, | In whom I trusted most of ony wight' (V. 1247–8). Pandarus dismisses the interpretation as misleading, although Troilus cannot forget the disturbing mental image and its possible significance (V. 1443–9), even before Cassandra supplies her own gloss. While Troilus might be in denial about the dream, there is soon more tangible evidence of Criseyde's behaviour that he cannot but read correctly. In the course of a skirmish, Diomede's cloak is captured and brought back to Troy as a trophy of war. Troilus sees it and his eye is caught by a brooch – the very one he had given to Criseyde on the day they parted and which she had promised always to keep. Now, at last, 'ful wel he wiste, | His lady nas no lenger on to triste' (V. 1665–6). She has taken Diomede as her lover.

---

38 Cf. Strohm, *Hochon's Arrow*, 116–19; Wallace, *Chaucerian Polity*, pp. 362, 365–6.

A discussion of sign systems and their interpretation within Chaucer's poem could be extended to include reading the stars and other forms of augury, or the reading of facial expressions and other forms of body language. But it is above all on the written text, as a model, or underpinning authority, for other kinds of reading, that the emphasis falls. Troy is a highly literate place, at least in those aristocratic circles to which Chaucer's account of it gives access. The city, like London itself, must have had a thriving book trade, and a quarter full of scriveners, stationers and parchment-makers, not to mention engravers of signets for seals. In an aubade after his first night with Criseyde, Troilus chides the bright sunshine, peering in at every chink and gap, telling it to go an help those who 'smale selys grave' (III. 1462), who need bright illumination for their intricate work.

There is much familiarity with the materiality, production and appearance of texts and their modes of transition. When Pandarus first woos Criseyde on Troilus's behalf he finds her in a paved parlour, engaged in an act of communal reading. She, with other members of her household – all female – are listening to a reading from a 'romaunce' called the *Siege of Thebes*. Pandarus knows it well, and refers to its subdivisions into twelve books. Having heard about the killing of King Layus by his son, Oedipus, Criseyde points to the place they have reached in the text, which is rubricated: 'here we stynten at thise lettres reed – | How [...] as the bok kan telle, | Amphiorax fil thorough the ground to helle' (II. 103–5). The *Siege of Thebes* sounds a little austere as amusements go, but may be to Criseyde's taste as a widow and daughter of a traitor whose vulnerability makes her anxious about the outcome of a war that takes the form of a siege of her own city. That anxiety is revealed in one of the first questions to Pandarus, puzzled as she is by his irrepressible ebullience: 'is then th'assege aweye? | I am of Greeks so fered that I deye' (II. 123–4). Reading about their indomitable acts cannot have helped. What Criseyde reads, or has read to her, reflects her preoccupations but it also reflects her status. She resists Pandarus's invitation to dance on grounds of impropriety: it is not fitting behaviour for a widow. Better to sit in a cave to pray and read an even more austere text: the anachronistic 'holy seyntes lyves' (II. 118). In point of fact, the *Siege of Thebes* is more appropriate than either she or Pandarus knows. It contains the story of Tideus, who slew the boar, the father of Diomede, the Greek who will become Criseyde's lover. It is one of those 'olde bokes' that, could she but read it aright, spells out Criseyde's fate and that later enables Cassandra's correct interpretation of Troilus's dream. Nor is the story of Oedipus's blindness irrelevant to Troilus's own fate (IV. 300).

In this society the written word, as well as being a means of establishing 'true readings', is also an essential mode of communication, understanding and self-awareness, in politics or love. Not just books but documents circulate and are topics of discussion. Troilus, feigning sickness, produces from 'his beddes hed | The copie of a tretys and a letter' (II. 1697) sent to him by Hector, who wishes to know if a certain man deserves death. He gives the document to his bedside visitors: his brother Deiphebus, in whose house is lodging, and to Helena. Ostensibly, Troilus is seeking their advice, but it is a stratagem to distract them so that he might speak alone with Criseyde. The trick works like a charm. Deiphebus and Helena earnestly 'gan this letter for t'enfolde', wander outside as they read it intently, 'faste it gonne byholde', go down some stairs and out into a garden. They are preoccupied for the best part of an hour as they scrutinize the manuscript: 'Thei gonne on it to redden and to pore' (II. 1702–8). Elsewhere, Chaucer details the writing of letters, the doubts and hesitations of their authors, the folding or sewing of the parchment (II. 1201–4), the sealing of it with wax. Such information is not merely technical but closely integrated with the affective content of the trivial actions of everyday life. Having carefully composed his first letter to Criseyde, Troilus reads it over, folds it, 'and with his salte teris gan to bathe | The ruby in his signet' – an instrumental as well as an emotional act, because the moisture would prevent the signet from sticking as he 'it sette | Upon the wexe deliverliche [deftly] and rathe [quickly]' (II. 1088). Tears apart, these are practised actions by a king's son used to official procedures.

The postal or courier service is run by Pandarus although, like most postmen, he does not always get the welcome he expects, and sometimes has to leave his delivery in an unusual place. Having once again visited Criseyde, he leads her to a place in her garden where they cannot be heard and pulls out Troilus's first letter, passing on to her his greetings, and requests, when time allows, 'som goodly answere' (II. 1125). Criseyde will have none of it, being all too fearful of where an exchange of letters might lead: 'Scrit ne bille

[...] Ne bring me noon' (II. 1130–2), and she tells Pandarus to take Troilus's letter back unopened, returned to sender. Pandarus mocks her timidity and the idea that he would bring her a letter that might harm her, then abruptly 'in hire bosom the letter down he thraste' (II. 1155). As the body contact suggests, Criseyde's resistance to the intimacy of letter writing is futile. She replies – 'the firste letter | That evere I wroot' (II. 1213–14) – and so a lengthy correspondence develops, of which the narrative provides a number of full texts as examples. They mark key stages in the romance of Troilus and Criseyde, their reading usually accompanied by the recipient's withdrawal to a private space – a chamber or closet – to mull over the letter's contents.

If the reception of these letters is at all representative, the process of reading involves a careful determination of an author's tone, style and intentions. Criseyde reads Troilus's letter 'word by word in every lyne', finds nothing to object to in spite of her intital fears, and thinks what he says appropriate to their circumstances: 'he koude good' (II. 1178). Troilus, in a state of mixed hope and dread on receiving Criseyde's answer, decides on balance in favour of hope, though her precise meaning is hard to pin down:

> But finaly, he took al for the beste
> That she hym wroot, for somewhat he byheld,
> On which hym thought he myghte his herte reste
> Al covered she tho words under sheld.
> (II. 1324–7)

As their relationship deteriorates, so the letters become ever more blotted with Troilus's tears and indicative of Criseyde's ambiguities. Troilus begins to register a widening gap between her intentions and words. His mentality is decidedly textual: he declares, as part of his initial, gut response, to the infamous dream: 'God woot, I wende, O lady bright, Criseyde | That every word was gospel that ye seyde!' (V. 1264–5). Yet he does unearth a kind of unwitting truth in her final letter, written from the Greek camp where she now lives with her new lover. Evasive to a fault, she ends by excusing her poor skills in letter-writing and in particular her lack of concision, and then concludes: 'Th'entente is al, and nat the lettres space' (V. 1630). Her actual intentions behind the 'letters' are becoming all too clear, even to the besotted Troilus. He finds what she has written 'straunge', sighs deeply, and takes it 'like a kalendes of chaunge' (V. 1634). Soon afterwards, he encounters the cloak of Diomede with its tell-tale brooch.

The convolutions (material, intellectual, emotional, interpretative) involved in the production, transmission and reception of texts are also a marked feature of the narrator's take on his own activities. As in his protagonists' experiences, the process of composing words is tangled up with fluctuating emotions, to the point at which writing becomes physically difficult. Embarking on the story of the 'double sorwe of Troilus' he invokes the Fury, Thesiphone to help because, as he writes, he weeps (I. 7). Again, at the beginning of book IV, as Troilus's fortunes take a nosedive, the narrator observes that his heart 'right now' begins to bleed 'And now my penne [...] with which I write, | Quaketh for drede of that I moste endite' (IV. 12–13). Rhetorical posturing, perhaps, but consonant with the experience of Troilus and Criseyde. Like them, the narrator is caught in his own kind of inescapable destiny: he is not inventing his story but, as he would have us believe, translating it from another book written in Latin by an 'auctor' named Lollius. Not unlike Pandarus, he plays the postman, the fallible intermediary responsible for transmitting a text. And he is all too aware of the perils of reception. He assures his audience that his purpose is but to convey faithfully to them not just the 'wordes' of his source but also the 'sentence', its meaning or intention. Admitting to having added or 'in-eched' some words of his own, he recognizes that meaning is essentially a process of negotiation, a collaborative enterprise between 'auctor' and translator and narrator and audience. Those changes he does introduce he leaves to the judgement of his audience, acknowledging deferentially that everything he writes is subject to their correction and improvement for he is not, like them, familiar with love. He gives them free rein to add or subtract from his language; in fact, he beseeches them to do so:

> For myne words, here and every part,
> I speke hem alle under correccioun
> Of yow that felyng han in loves art,
> And putte it al in youre discreccioun
> To encresse or maken dymynucioun
> Of my langage, and that I yow biseche.
> (III. 1331–6)

Towards a Bohemian Reading of Troilus and Criseyde

The interactive nature of the narrator's relationship with his audience, insofar as it represents Chaucer's relationship to his, returns us again to perhaps its most significant member, Anne of Bohemia. If, as seems likely, it is she who is being indicated in the line 'Right as oure first lettre is now an "A"', than it is important to note that the statement is not just about her social pre-eminence. By comparing that with the first letter of the alphabet, Chaucer introduces a frame of reference that includes letter-forms, writing, texts and literacy. It is appropriate that he should have done so. Anne had a reputation for linguistic ability. French was a *sine qua non* at her father's court, which strove to emulate the manners and magnificence of the Anjou dynasty, but she probably also knew German, Latin and Czech.[39] Wyclif argued that, were she to have possessed bibles in those languages (a distinct possibility, since vernacular versions of the Bible circulated at her father's multilingual court) then no one would have dared condemn her as a heretic.[40] If we may trust the evidence of the *Legend of Good Women* and *Troilus* itself, Anne also acquired a sophisticated command of English. Her father encouraged the translation of the Latin Vulgate bible into Czech and she was credited with possessing the glossed gospels in English.[41] The latter claim was attributed to no less a person than Archbishop Thomas Arundel, speaking at Anne's funeral and rejoicing in the fact that 'not wiþstanding þat sche was an alien borne, sche hadde on Englische al þe foure Gospeleris wiþ þe doctoris vpon hem.'[42] Given Arundel's hostility to Bible translation, the story may be apocryphal. It dates from 1401 at the earliest and could be a Lollard attempt to provide the glossed gospels in English

---

39 For Charles IV as Francophone see Saul, *Richard II*, 349–51.
40 Taylor, 'Anne of Bohemia', 103–4. For literacy and pious reading at the Prague court, see Thomas, *Blessed Shore*, 34–7.
41 For Charles IV's translation project and encouragement of vernacular languages see Wallace, *Chaucerian Polity*, 359. On the circulation of the scriptures in English at Richard's court see A. I. Doyle, 'English Books In and Out of Court from Edward III to Henry VII', in *English Court Culture*, ed. Scattergood and Sherborne (1983), 168–9.
42 Curt F. Bühler, 'A Lollard Tract: On Translating the Bible into English', *Medium Ævum* 7 (1938), 178.

with credibility.[43] More certain is Anne's patronage of Queen's College, Oxford, home to individuals such as Nicholas Hereford and John Trevisa, who are associated with the translation of the Wycliffite Bible;[44] and her commissioning of a treatise on heraldry by Johannis de Bado Aureo.[45] If there is indeed substance to these reports of Anne's predilection for written words, languages, translation, texts and reading, the emphasis on those very topics and the reflexivity they entail, as embodied in *Troilus and Criseyde*, becomes explicable as part of Chaucer's larger engagement with the Bohemian element in his audience. One of his first set-piece descriptions, of a group of aristocratic women gathered to listen to a text being read aloud, echoes the circumstances in which Anne's own literacy would have developed.[46] The written communications of Troilus and Criseyde, and the emotions entailed, would also have had resonance for a queen who, increasingly devoted to Richard, kept in touch with him by letter during their rare separations.[47]

Chaucer's awareness of his audience's levels of textual awareness – especially, perhaps, Anne's – might also help to shed light on one of the conundrums of his rhetorical strategy in *Troilus and Criseyde*. As is well known, Chaucer's main narrative source was not a Latin text by Lollius but an Italian one by Giovanni Boccaccio, *Il Filostrato*. Precisely why Chaucer chose to cloak his 'auctor' in a pseudonym is not clear. He is not so coy elsewhere in naming his other Italian authors, Dante and Petrarch. 'Lollius' must have foxed his audience as much as it foxes modern critics, for the name is otherwise almost unknown.[48] Thus, when the narrator invites

43 Taylor, 'Anne of Bohemia', 104–6.
44 Taylor, 'Anne of Bohemia', 98, 100.
45 Taylor, 'Anne of Bohemia', 97, 99.
46 The scene may also draw indirectly on the iconography of St Anne who taught her daughter, Mary, to read. On Anne of Bohemia's devotion to the saint, see Saul, *Richard II*, 324; Thomas, *Blessed Shore*, 37–8; and Michael van Dussen, *From England to Bohemia: Heresy and Communication in the Later Middle Ages* (Cambridge: Cambridge University Press, 2012), 28–31.
47 Saul, *Richard II*, 456.
48 Cf. Richard Firth Green, *Poets and Princepleasers: Literature and the English Court in the Late Middle Ages* (Toronto: University of Toronto Press, 1980), 160–1.

Towards a Bohemian Reading of Troilus and Criseyde 75

his audience to evaluate his additions to the source-text they are not in a position to do so. He has thrown them off the scent by referring to a non-existent author. Even if, by some stretch of the imagination, a Latin text by Lollius were taken to mean an Italian ('Latin language') one by Boccaccio, there would have been few if any members of Chaucer's actual audience in a position to make textual comparisons. Italian, unlike French, was a relatively new vernacular for literary composition; Boccaccio's writings are not known to have circulated in England in the later fourteenth century; and although some associates of the English court had a command of Italian – useful as it was in diplomatic and financial transactions – it was hardly a lingua franca. The story of Troilus and Criseyde was indeed known to Chaucer's audience, but chiefly in French, through the *Roman de Troie* (c.1160) of Benoît de Saint-Maure.[49] There, by contrast with Chaucer's extended treatment, the love affair is dealt with in a relatively abbreviated fashion.

Another intriguing aspect of the Lollius attribution, as used by Chaucer's narrator, is that it is a blanket term. It is used to suggest that there is a single 'auctor' behind the work of translation, when in fact there are several: Boccaccio in the main, but also Dante, Boethius, Statius – and Petrarch. Indeed, it is directly before Chaucer's translation of one of Petrarch's *Canzoniere* that there is the first of only two allusions to Lollius. The narrator wants his audience to know that the following 'Canticus Troili' is a verbatim version that also captures the meaning of the original:

---

49 David C. Benson, *The History of Troy in Middle English Literature* (Woodbridge: Boydell and Brewer, 1980), ch. 1 on Benoît and the later (1287) Latin version, *Historia destructionis Troiae* by Guido delle Colonne. On Chaucer's debt to Guido see 138–43. See also Roberto Antonelli, 'The Birth of Criseyde – An Exemplary Triangle: "Classical" Troilus and the Question of Love at the Anglo-Norman Court', in *The European Tragedy of Troilus*, ed. Piero Boitani (Oxford: Clarendon Press, 1989), 21–48. Excerpts from Benoît are to be found in *The Story of Troilus as Told by Benoît de Saint-Maure, Giovanni Boccaccio, Geoffrey Chaucer, Robert Henryson*, trans. R. K. Gordon (New York: Dutton, 1964), 3–22.

> And of his song naught only the sentence
> As writ myn auctour called Lollius,
> But plainly, save oure tonges difference,
> I dar wel seyn, in al, that Troilus
> Seyde in his song, loo, every word right thus
> As I shal seyn [...]
> (I. 392–8)

As the very first translation of one of Petrarch's sonnets into English – predating Wyatt and Surrey by some 150 years – this is indeed a momentous event. The maniculum of Lollius's name, coupled with a reiteration of the process of translation, showcases one example of 'in-eching' that might conceivably have been properly appreciated. Francis Petrarch and Anne of Bohemia's father, Charles IV, were correspondents over a long number of years. Charles met Petrarch in Italy and Petrarch visited the court in Prague in 1356 and wrote of it in glowing terms. The archbishop of Prague, Ernest of Pardubice, and Charles's chancellor, John of Newmarket, also exchanged letters with Petrarch.[50] We do not know if Chaucer was aware of the receptivity of the court to Prague to Petrarch and his writings, nor of the extent to which Anne herself knew of her father's friendship, or was indeed knowledgeable about Petrarch's sonnets. But in the light of Petrarch's connection with Prague, Chaucer's choice of source material for Troilus's song is highly felicitous, given Anne's central presence at court.

Petrarch lauded the Bohemian court because he found in Charles IV a monarch alive to his own cultural project. Doubtless, association with Petrarch the prince-pleasing poet benefited Charles as well. More generally, he made his court at Prague congenial to poets and historians because they were vehicles who could help publicize its splendour and renown. He invested also in other kinds of cultural capital, encouraging vernacular literature (especially Czech and German); employing architects and artists to rebuild and glorify the city as a place worthy of a Holy Roman Emperor;

---

50 Wallace, *Chaucerian Polity*, 359–60; his 'Anne of Bohemia', 4–5; S. Harrison Thomson, 'Learning at the Court of Charles IV', *Speculum* 25 (1950), 8.

and founding the university that still bears his name.[51] The Luxembourgs were relative newcomers to the throne of Bohemia. In order to give the impression that the Luxembourg dynasty held its position by ancient right, he traced his lineage back to the supposed founder of chivalry, Aeneas. To buttress this myth of origins be commissioned numerous versions of the Trojan legends and adorned the walls of his castle at Karlstein with portraits of his Trojan 'ancestors'.[52] It is no accident that, when Machaut depicted Jean l'Aveugle, king of Bohemia, listening to a story, it was the story of Troy.

Thus, when Anne came to England as Richard's bride she was already saturated in the Trojan story as part of her own identity as a royal princess of the Bohemian court. In choosing Troy as the location for a narrative retold for her new court, Chaucer was working within a framework very familiar to Anne. That is not to deny the importance Troy had in the imaginary of the English as the exemplar for London, also known as New Troy, and – according to the country's own myth of origins – founded by the great-grandson of Aeneas, Brutus, who gave his name to Britain. What *Troilus and Criseyde* offers is a Troy that accommodates the Bohemian myth to its English counterpart, providing Anne and Richard with possible roles for legitimizing their own, merged, Anglo-Bohemian rule. The extent to which a Troy hybrid came to be part and parcel of the way Richard and Londoners imagined themselves is evident in a variety of sources. For instance, the first book of Gower's *Vox clamantis* represents the invasion of London during the uprising of 1381 as the fall of 'new Troy'; and Froissart records how

[51] Wallace, *Chaucerian Polity*, 357–9; Thomson, 'Learning', 6–7, 9–11, 13–16; Paul Crossley, 'Bohemia Sacra: Liturgy and History in Prague Cathedral', in *Pierre, lumière, couleur: études d'histoire de l'art du Moyen Age en l'honneur d'Anne Prache*, Cultures et Civilisations Médiévales, 20 (Paris: Presses de l'Université de Paris-Sorbonne, 1999), 341–65; and his 'The Politics of Presentation: The Architecture of Charles IV of Bohemia', in *Courts and Regions in Medieval Europe*, ed. Sarah Rees Jones, Richard Marks and A. J. Minnis (York: York Medieval Press, 2000), 99–172.

[52] Sylvia Federico, *New Troy: Fantasies of Empire in the Late Middle Ages*, Medieval Cultures, 36 (Minneapolis: University of Minnesota Press, 2003), xii–xiii; Marie Tanner, *The Last Descendant of Aeneas: The Hapsburgs and the Mythic Image of the Emperor* (New Haven: Yale University Press, 1993), 91–8; Crossley, 'Politics of Presentation', 143.

Richard welcomed participants to 'la neuf Troie' at his Smithfield tournament in 1390.[53] The myth was more durable and resilient than Federico has suggested.[54] The *Concordia* of the Carmelite friar, Richard of Maidstone, records the reception of the king and queen in the city in August, 1392. It was a scripted ceremony of reconciliation between the king and the citizens of London.[55] The latter had not, to Richard's mind, provided him with the financial support he had needed, and so he had adopted punitive measures.[56] The person acting as intermediary, bringing the two sides together, is Anne. Maidstone represents London as 'Trinovant' (12), as 'glad new Troy' (18) and 'Troy' (39). He notes how, as part of the pageant, both Anne and Richard are represented by their monograms 'A' and 'R' (93), versions of which can still be seen in the chasing on their tomb effigies.[57] He refers to Richard as Troilus (112) and praises Anne's beauty in terms that recall the first, peerless appearance of Criseyde, seen in a crowd: 'She's beautiful, with other beauties all around; | Led by such Amazons, New Troy is unsurpassed' (122–3). Anne's appearance, like Criseyde's, stands out on account of her clothes: 'Her country's fashion beautifies her all the more' (196). As Anne, kneeling before Richard, makes the case for clemency, she refers to the story of Brutus and its relevance to Britain (479). Maidstone thus brings into parallax the Ricardian present and the Trojan past, much as Chaucer had already done in *Troilus and Criseyde*.[58]

53   Federico, *New Troy*, 70.
54   Ibid., 93–4. Cf. Seth Lerer, *Chaucer and His Readers: Imagining the Author in Late-Medieval England* (Princeton: Princeton University Press, 1993), 54–5; and for background John Clark, 'Trinovantum – The Evolution of a Legend', *Journal of Medieval History*, 7 (1981), 135–51.
55   Richard of Maidstone, *Concordia: The Reconciliation of Richard II with London*, trans. A. G. Rigg, ed. David R. Carlson (Kalamazoo: Medieval Institute for TEAMS, 2003), 1–7. Line references are to this edition.
56   Caroline M. Barron, 'The Quarrel of Richard II with London 1392–7', in *The Reign of Richard II*, ed. F. R. H. DuBoulay and Caroline M. Barron (London: Athlone Press, 1971), 173–201.
57   Lindley, 'Absolutism', 69–71 and illus 36, 37, 102.
58   For further commentary, see Strohm, *Hochon's Arrow*, 107–11.

Towards a Bohemian Reading of Troilus and Criseyde 79

Whatever else it may be, Chaucer's Troy is a combustible place. Calkas knows by his 'calkulynge' of the fate that awaits the city and when its citizens discover he has defected they wish the same disaster on him and his family: 'he and al his kyn at-ones | Ben worthi for to brennen, fel and bones' (I. 9–10). Troy's fate hangs ominously over the narrative, clouding its future. Troilus's own changes in fortune are bound up with those of the city. In pleading with the Greek lords 'In consistoire' (IV. 65) for his daughter to be exchanged for the Trojan prisoner, Antenor, Calkas reminds them of what astronomy and augury have confirmed: that Troy will be burnt and razed, 'ybrend and beten down to grownde' (IV. 77), for 'the tyme is faste by | That fire and flaumbe on al the town shal sprede' (IV. 117–19). It is the same fate that befell Thebes (V. 1510), that city whose history is so intertwined with the history of Troy. As if in anticipation of the future of a city whose name he bears, Troilus imagines his own immolation in 'the fir and flaumbe[...] | In which my body brennen shal to glede' (V. 302–3).

In the last instance, Troilus has just bade farewell to Criseyde and, despairing of ever seeing her again, provides Pandarus with instructions for his funeral rites. Ever more metaphysical in his conceit, he continues by asking his friend to collect 'The poudre in which myn herte ybrend shal torne' (V. 309), to conserve it in a gold urn, and to present it to Criseyde 'for a remembraunce' (V. 315). What Troilus imagines is the logical outcome of an emotion he has been suffering ever since he fell in love with Criseyde, and that has consumed his heart: the 'fyr of love'. Of royal blood he may be, but the fire of love spares no one. It finds many different ways to affect this particular victim: it 'brende hym so in soundry wise ay newe, | That sexti tyme a day he loste his hewe' (I. 440–1). The only alleviation, 'his hote fir to cesse' (I. 445), is by seeing Criseyde. So changed are his condition and his appearance that he has to feign a 'fevere' (I. 491) in order that others do not suspect that 'the hote fir of love him brent' (I. 490).

Troilus is no doubt about what the 'fire' signifies – 'desir so brenningly me assaileth' (I. 606) – and the narrator confirms it, for 'as the fir he brende | For sharp desir of hope and of plesaunce' (III. 425–6). Yet Troilus's desire is not quenched after his first night with Criseyde. On the contrary, he asserts to Pandarus in the aftermath: 'I hadde it nevere half so hot as nowe' (III. 1650). Once Troilus's access to Criseyde is threatened by political events, the heat is generated as much by the glowing coals of frustration as by desire: 'A thousand sikes hotter than the gleede, | Out of his brest ech after other went' (IV. 337–8). Pandarus, worldly wise, counsels Troilus to 'sle with resoun al this hete' (IV. 1583) and thinks to himself that the fire will cool as time goes by (V. 507), as indeed it does (V. 1659), its energies recycled as anger when, on the battlefield, Troilus pursues Diomede 'with many a cruel hete' (V. 1761).

The association of fire with passionate love, and especially with desire, is conventional enough. But Chaucer's emphasis on the phrase 'fyr of love' at the outset of Troilus's experience, as well as some of the circumstances in which the idea of the fire of love appears, suggest a particular frame of reference. When the phrase first appears, it is coupled with a brief prayer uttered by the narrator from his Christian standpoint: 'The fyr of love – wherfro God me blesse' (I. 436), as if in recognition of what the fire can do, for better or worse. As the poem develops, the incendiary nature of love is placed in a fuller, and more reinforcing, context. Pandarus acknowledges that experiencing the fire of love is an unavoidable condition of being human. In so doing he encompasses not merely sexual desire but desire of heaven: 'Was nevere man or woman yet bigete | That was unapt to suffren loves hete, | Celestial, or elles love of kynde' (I. 977–9). At the beginning of Book 3 there is a further expansion of the discussion about the place of love within the universe. The narrator's hymn to Venus, while maintaining the pagan atmosphere, includes lines to which no Christian could object: 'God loveth, and to love wol nought were, | And in this world no lyves creature | Withouten love is worth, or may endure' (III. 12–13). Here, love is a life-force, the stuff of creation, its informing principle, and what affects the hearts of those, like Troilus, whom Venus 'wol sette a-fyre' (III. 24). Further, it is an improving force, making its recipients dread shame, flee vice and live more courteously or considerately, as the case of Troilus illustrates (III. 1777, 1805). It is the social glue that binds together kingdoms, households and friends.

Troilus internalizes this philosophy. At the end of the same book, at the centre of which is a celebration the sensuality of love, he expatiates on Love as the key ingredient of the universe. It is the principle that keeps everything in a state of harmony, whether the earth, see, peoples, communities or couples. Crucially, Troilus links love with faith, both principles emanating from God the creator, 'auctour of kynde' (III. 1765). He wishes that others might know what he knows, through the heat of love: 'And hertes colde, hem wolde I that he twiste | To make hem love' (III. 1769–70). This second *Canticus Troili* reads as an answer to the questions posed in the first: 'If no love is, O God, what fele I so? | And if love is, what thing and which is she?' (I. 400–1).

The meaning of human love, in relation to society, faith and the cosmos, is a question, if not *the* question, at the heart of Chaucer's poem. The terms of the discussion are rooted in Chaucer's reading and translation of the *Consolatio* by Boethius, but they also have affinities with writings by English religious authors of his day. In his *Incendium Amoris* (Fire of Love), Richard Rolle's focus is very much on 'love celestial', but he describes the fire of love as a physical experience. Though generated from within, rather than by external stimuli, it produces delight, sweetness, and warmth so intense the lover 'fears he may melt away' (114).[59] This love, the love of Christ, 'is a fire which sets our hearts aflame so that they glow and burn' (56), prompting desire for heaven. That longing is an extrapolation from the experience of human desire: 'For what is love but the transforming of the desire into the loved thing itself? Or if you prefer, love is a great longing for what is beautiful, and good, and lovely, with its thought ever reaching out to the object of its love. And when he has got it a man rejoices, for joy is caused only by love. Every lover is assimilated to his beloved: love makes the loving one like what he loves.' (99–100).

Rolle is nevertheless careful to differentiate between the fires of carnal and spiritual love. The former is spiritually destructive: such lovers 'are firmly earthbound by the very weight of their desires' (57). Yet it is possible for the force of divine love to offer a progression towards spiritual purification by burning up former sins (67). In spite of this duality, love for Rolle is natural, inevitable, to be welcomed: 'Nothing is better than mutual love, nothing sweeter than holy charity. To love and be loved is the

---

[59] Richard Rolle, *The Fire of Love*, trans. Clifton Walters (Harmondsworth: Penguin, 1972).

delightful purpose of all human life; the delight of angels and God, and the reward of blessedness. If then you want to be loved, love! Love gets love in return. No one has ever lost through loving good, if he has persisted in love to the end. On the other hand he does not know what it is to rejoice who has not known what it is to burn with love' (121). Sensual pleasure is a way of understanding the even more intense and exquisite delights of loving Christ: 'To be sure, the delights of loving Christ are sweeter than all the tasty pleasures of the world in the flesh. Indeed, unimaginable carnal pleasure, and abundant earthly possession, in comparison with the minutest sweetness poured by God into an elect soul are paltry and appalling!' (126). To describe the intensity of 'love celestial' Rolle uses the language and mechanisms of human sexuality as ways of figuring heavenly delight. The soul's union with Christ is described as an impregnation: 'Let him kiss me and refresh me with his sweet love; let him hold me tight and kiss me on the mouth, else I die; let him pour his grace into me, that I may grow in love' (125).

Similar statements could be identified in other religious writing of the period, but it is Rolle's metaphor of the fire of love that makes his text particularly interesting as a context for Chaucer's use of the same image in *Troilus and Criseyde*. In some respects *Troilus* might seem to be in dialogue with a text such as the *Incendium Amoris* for its hero, too undertakes a kind of pilgrimage built on love, fidelity and suffering that culminates in other-worldly rapture and the laughter of spiritual delight that Rolle elsewhere describes.[60] It is just that, unlike Rolle's, Chaucer's text insists on the indivisibility of the carnal and the spiritual. If Troilus had not fallen in love with Criseyde, and made love to her, he would not have gained the spiritual insights that lead to his apotheosis. Anne and others might well have understood such a dialogue. The Carthusians, whose asceticism

60 Some of Rolle's English lyrics also invite comparison with *Troilus* and in particular its closing stanzas, in which Chaucer contrasts earthly and heavenly love. See especially 'A Song of Love-longing to Jesus', 'A Song of the Love of Jesus', 'The Nature of Love', and 'Thy Joy Be in the Love of Jesus', in *English Writings of Richard Rolle, Hermit of Hampole*, ed. Hope Emily Allen (Oxford: Clarendon Press, 1931), 41–7, 49–51, 52–3.

forms an important context for religious attitudes at Richard's court, were readers of Rolle's works and especially the *Incendium Amoris*.[61] Moreover, Rolle's writings, including the *Incendium Amoris*, circulated in Bohemia during the fourteenth century.[62]

Such considerations in turn raise questions about the religious mindset of Anne. She was the patron of some religious institutions, such as Coventry Charterhouse and Eye Priory, although that in itself gives little away.[63] Perhaps more indicative is her choice of three of the so-called Lollard knights (Sir Lewis Clifford, Sir John Clanvowe, and Sir Richard Stury) as the executors of her will.[64] The verse eulogies, recently discovered in Prague by Michael van Dussen, and which were probably displayed at Anne's tomb soon after her funeral in August 1394, corroborate her reputation for piety.[65] One may have been by Richard of Maidstone and another occurs in the company of Hussite texts and writings by Rolle.[66] They emphasize acts of charity, compassion towards pregnant women, dedication to St Anne and the virtuous prudence that drove her intercessory acts. She might therefore have warmed to hero whose piety – though ostensibly directed at pagan deities – is conscientious to a fault. Praying to Venus is, for Troilus, an habitual activity (I. 421, I. 972, III. 715, IV. 288). In this he echoes his more famous fellow protagonist in the Troy story, Aeneas.[67] Even as his lovemaking with Criseyde gets under way he does not neglect to pause and give thanks to Venus – much to Criseyde's dismay (III. 1303–9). There are constant reminders, not only of the spiritual dimension of Troilus's apprehension

---

61 J. Anthony Tuck, 'Carthusian Monks and Lollard Knights: Religious Attitudes at the Court of Richard II', *Studies in the Age of Chaucer: Proceedings*, 1 (1984): *Reconstructing Chaucer*, ed. Paul Strohm and Thomas J. Heffernan, 149–61, esp. 159.
62 Hope Emily Allen, *Writings Ascribed to Richard Rolle, Hermit of Hampole, and Materials for His Biography*, Modern Language Association of America, Monograph series, 3 (New York: Modern Language Association of America, 1927), 47–9, 209–29; van Dussen, *From England to Bohemia*, 40–5.
63 Taylor, 'Anne of Bohemia', 98.
64 Saul, *Richard II*, 298.
65 van Dussen, 'Three Verse Eulogies', 233–4.
66 van Dussen, 'Three Verse Eulogies', 240–3.
67 Tanner, *Last Descendant*, 15.

of Criseyde – described as 'aungelik', 'inmortal', 'hevynssh' (I. 102), the means by which he is brought to heaven (III. 1204, 1251), with eyes that spell paradise (V. 817) and a face 'like of Paradys th'image' (V. 863) – but also of the devotional and quest-like nature of his search for faithful love. Once converted to love (I. 308), being a lover is like belonging to an 'ordre' (I. 336). Troilus becomes a pillar of the church of love (I. 1000), his service bringing in its wake both the avoidance of vice (III. 1805) and 'remors of conscience', 'devocioun', and 'attricioun', as well as 'holyness' (I. 554) and possible martyrdom (IV. 623, 818). Criseyde's empty and shuttered house, where Troilus formerly knew such joy, is like visiting a shrine bereft of its saint (V. 553). He later imagines himself, incongruously, seeking Criseyde in the Greek camp, dressed as a pilgrim (V. 1577).

It is in these three cultural fields of texts, the myth of Troy and piety where there are significant affinities between *Troilus and Criseyde* and what we know of Anne of Bohemia's own horizons of experience. Taken individually, Chaucer's treatment of these topics might be explained in a variety of ways. But they occur together, and the same collocation is a feature of Anne's profile. So it is reasonable to presume that *Troilus and Criseyde* was in some measure a response to expectations in an audience within which Anne was as pre-eminent as the letter A in the alphabet.

PART TWO

Interiors

The Prison of Theseus and the Castle of *Jalousie*

The *Canterbury Tales* is a work of Chaucer's mature years, showing him at the height of his poetic powers. In its blending of the new with the old, Boccaccio with Boethius, the aesthetic of the Knight's Tale is similar to that of *Troilus*, but Chaucer also reaches into the formative text of an earlier phase of his career, the *Roman de la rose*. Kolve's analysis of the tension between mimetic and symbolic aspects of the prison of Theseus is enhanced by an understanding of Jean de Meun's description of castle of *Jalousie*, a part of the *Rose* well known to Chaucer's audience. The allusion thickens the symbolic meaning of imprisonment while highlighting the effects of Arcite's jealousy of Palamon.

Shot wyndowe (Miller's Tale, I. 3358 and 3695)

Pilgrimage and imprisonment are examples of material phenomena which Chaucer used to figure psychological, emotional and social predicaments. In the Miller's Tale he plays with the idea of privacy (*pryvetee*) to explore the jealousy of an old husband and the wayward tendencies of his wife and lodger. The ethos of the Miller's Tale runs counter to that of the Knight's Tale in suggesting that the boundaries on which *pryvetee* depends are there to be joyfully transgressed – no more so than in the notorious episode at a *shot wyndowe* with which the tale concludes. Appropriately enough, it is the window of a privy.

The Containment of Symkyn: The Function of Space in the Reeve's Tale

The maintenance of privacy depends on the control of personal and social space, but such control may also be used to mask pretension and villainy. In the Reeve's Tale, Symkyn, miller of Trumpington, dominates his clientèle and, by virtue of his marriage to the bastard daughter of the village parson, he has social aspirations. The arrival of two quick-witted students, who seduce his wife and daughter, cuts him down to size. This hilarious nocturnal saga hinges on visual error and the appropriation and misappropriation of a domestic interior.

An Optical Theme in the Merchant's Tale

The successful manipulation of interiors in turn depends upon accurate vision. In the Merchant's Tale, visual deception and blindness become metaphors for the pride, jealousy and lust that govern old January's inner world. But in domestic politics his wife, May, is the more skilled practitioner. She takes advantage of her husband's blindness to arrange a tryst with her lover, his squire. Then, when January's sight is miraculously restored, she succeeds in persuading January that he has not seen what, in fact, had taken place before his eyes: her act of infidelity. May's persuasiveness derives in part from Chaucer's deployment of scientific materials taken from the medieval optical tradition.

The Prison of Theseus and the Castle of *Jalousie**

What follows is intended as a comment on one aspect of V. A. Kolve's *Chaucer and the Imagery of Narrative: The First Five Canterbury Tales*. In the concluding paragraphs Kolve acknowledges, with characteristic humility, that his book 'is finally no more than *a* reading of *The Canterbury Tales*: one reader's account of his experience'. He also recognizes that his study of those narrative images which organize the meaning of Chaucer's tales may have neglected 'images of comparative significance'.[1] Although the present writer cannot pretend to match Kolve's erudition and sophistication in the explication of texts through visual images, there are grounds for thinking that one 'image of comparable significance' has been identified.

It is an image which concerns the meaning of that most important of loci within the Knight's Tale, the prison tower of Theseus. In his chapter on that tale Kolve subjects Chaucer's representation of the prison to a brilliant analysis in support of one of his central arguments: that the major images of Chaucerian narrative exist in a state of tension between the mimetic and the symbolic. Thus the prison is the place, integral to the action, where Palamon and Arcite are incarcerated; it is described realistically, and in a way which makes it memorable. Gradually, however, the prison undergoes a series of redefinitions so that it acquires symbolic status.

At the mimetic level, Chaucer departs from his source, Boccaccio's *Teseida*, and goes to considerable lengths to represent the harsh circumstances and wretchedness of imprisonment.[2] First, there are architectural revisions. A room within Teseo's Renaissance palace, with a balcony and

---

*   First published in *Chaucer Review* 26 (1991), 147–52.
1   V. A. Kolve, *Chaucer and the Imagery of Narrative: The First Five Canterbury Tales* (London: Arnold, 1984), 360–1.
2   N. R. Havely, ed. and trans., *Chaucer's Boccaccio: Sources of 'Troilus' and the 'Knight's' and 'Franklin's Tales'*, Chaucer Studies 3 (Cambridge: Brewer, 1980), 111–14.

adjoining garden, becomes a barred dungeon within a medieval castle tower which rises high above the city, massive and impenetrable, a type of prison familiar to Chaucer and his contemporaries.[3] It is 'the grete tour, that was so thikke and stroong, | Which of the castel was the chief dongeoun' (1056–7).[4] Boccaccio's heroes are close enough to Emilia to hear her singing in the garden, and are able to put their heads out of the window in order to see her. But the prison window through which Palamon sees Emelye at a great distance (he cannot hear her sing) is 'thikke of many a barre | Of iren greet and square as any sparre' (1075–6). Second, Chaucer, unlike Boccaccio, pays attention to the restrictive experience of imprisonment, during which the goaler exercises close control over the movements of his charges (1064). The tower is where Arcite is 'yfetered' (1229) and for Palamon it is an empty, echoing interior, a place of misery, woe, and anguish: 'the grete tour | Resouneth of his youlyng and clamour' (1277–8). He seems destined 'in cheynes and in fettres to been deed' (1343), and dwells 'in derknesse and horrible and strong prisoun' (1451).

Chaucer's realism is disingenuous. He has an ulterior motive in accentuating the oppressiveness of the tower prison. He makes it memorable because he wishes to attach to it a symbolic significance germane to an understanding of the experiences which Palamon and Arcite undergo, not only in prison but also in the outside world. The symbolic dimensions of the prison do not transcend and make redundant the mimetic ones – both kinds of representation co-exist, interplay and depend on each other. As Kolve puts it, the symbolic is 'characteristically assimilated to the verisimilar and mimetic texture of the whole; it is discovered *within* the images one forms in attending to the narrative action itself'.[5] Here, Kolve's term for a symbolic form such as the tower prison is 'iconographic image' because, as he contends, Chaucer's symbolism derives from traditions of imaging which may be identified in the visual arts. Chaucer is not, however,

---

3   Ralph B. Pugh, *Imprisonment in Medieval England* (Cambridge: Cambridge University Press, 1968), 112–26 and 347–73.
4   Quotations are from The *Riverside Chaucer*, gen. ed. Larry D. Benson (Boston: Houghton Mifflin, 1987).
5   Kolve, *Chaucer and the Imagery of Narrative*, 60–1.

content with locating a single iconographic image within his mimetic image of the prison tower. He alludes to more than one, and so builds up a complexity of meaning and a depth of significance. Thus, according to Kolve in his chapter on the Knight's Tale, the prison tower is associated with the traditional images of the house of Fortune, the *prison amoureuse* and the prison of life.

To Kolve's triad of iconographic images I now wish to add a fourth. It is actually implicit in his discussion of the prison of love tradition, in the course of which he prints the following lines from Froissart's *Prison amoureuse*. They show that jealousy, as much as erotic desire, causes the lover to feel imprisoned: 'I understand by that prison in which you are placed and shut up, the languor in which you dwell when you [...] are beaten with the rods and assaults of jealousy, which are exceedingly hard and cruel to feel and know.'[6] Now the prison of jealousy, or to be more precise the castle of Jalousie, is a major locus of action within the first part of the *Roman de la rose*, which Chaucer translated and which repeatedly nourished his imagination. The castle of Jalousie, like the prison tower of Theseus, fulfils two functions: it is an important place within Guillaume de Lorris's plot, and it has a simultaneous symbolic status. Similarities of design also suggest that Chaucer modelled the castle of Theseus in part on the castle of Jalousie, which was a well-elaborated and well-known example of the custom of representing the effects of jealousy with the image of a towered, prison-like building. Kolve, commenting on the Froissart passage, asserts that 'the image of a prison could be used to render a variety of judgments upon love, and there can be no doubt that some part of that tradition is actively in service in *The Knight's Tale*'.[7] His observation is borne out by Chaucer's use of the *prison amoureuse*, but is confirmed more fully by the more direct use to which Chaucer puts the image of the castle of Jalousie.

6   Jean Froissart, *La Prison amoureuse*, ed. Anthime Fourrier (Paris: Klinksieck, 1974), 152, trans. Kolve, 96, who quotes Froissart at greater length.
7   Kolve, *Chaucer and the Imagery of Narrative*, 96.

Jalousie has decided that the rose is in danger if left in the custody of Bialacoil, for this figure, representing 'fair welcome', and aided by Venus, has allowed the lover to kiss the rose. Rather like Theseus in the harshness of his attitude, Jalousie plans that Bialacoil will be 'faste loken in a tour, | Withoute refuyt or socour' (*Romaunt*, 3839–40), and that the roses will be protected 'with siker wall' (3918). His intention is

> To make anoon a forteresse,
> T'enclose the roses of good savour.
> In myddis shall I make a tour
> To putte Bialacoil in prisoun.
> (3942–5)

The construction of the castle by Jalousie, who is, like Theseus, a builder, is described in considerable detail. First, Jalousie surrounds the area in which the roses grow with a square-shaped ditch of a hundred fathoms on each side. On this he builds a sturdy, thick wall with rock foundations. It is embattled with 'many a riche and fair touret' (4164). At each corner is a 'tour full pryncipall' (4166), complete with portcullis. In the centre of the castle is built the tower in which Bialacoil is to be imprisoned:

> And eke amydde this purprise
> Was maad a tour of gret maistrise;
> A fairer saugh no man with sight,
> Large and wid, and of gret myght.
> (4171–4)

The tower is virtually impenetrable: the mortar is specially hardened, the foundation stones are adamantine. The tower is round, 'maad in compas' (4183), and it is surrounded by a wall. Between the wall and the tower is a rose-garden 'of swete savour, | With many roses that thei bere' (4188–9), a feature similar to the garden which adjoins the tower-prison of the Knight's Tale. The castle is well-defended with weapons and archers and other embattled walls beyond the ditch. The four gates are kept by Daunger, Shame, Drede and Wikked-Tunge. Bialacoil, shut in the round tower in the middle of the garrison 'for to lyve in penaunce' (4283), is guarded by a gaoler, a hag, an 'old vekke' (4286).

The Prison of Theseus and the Castle of Jalousie 93

Figure 1 The castle of *Jalousie*, from the *Roman de la rose*, London, British Library, MS. Egerton 1069, f. 30 (15th cent.) © The British Library Board.

A knowledge of verbal and pictorial representations of the castle of Jalousie helps the reader to imagine the castle of Theseus and its prison tower (Figure 1). But how does Chaucer activate the meaning which the image of Jalousie's prison is capable of expressing? For the situation of Palamon and Arcite while they are imprisoned is the reverse of what confronts Guillaume de Lorris's lover. Chaucer's lovers cannot attain Emelye because she is outside the dungeon walls, whereas Guillaume's hero is outside the castle and cannot be received by the imprisoned Bialacoil. In a narrative characterized by reversals, Chaucer's version may be read as an ironic account of a model which he knew from the *Rose*. Perhaps detailed comparisons should not be pressed too hard between a work like the Knight's Tale, in which the anatomy of love is expressed through the complex experience of individuals, and an allegorical work like the *Rose*, in which different features of the psychology and drama of erotic love are projected into personifications. But once Arcite is released, the parallels between the two works do become more direct. Guillaume's lover is despondent because he is excluded from the castle, which contains both the prison where Bialacoil is, and the rose which is the object of his desire (*Romaunt* 4315–614). Compare the anguished envy of the banished Arcite as he longs to return to Theseus's prison tower in order to see the flower-loving Emelye in the adjacent garden:

> Thyn is the victorie of this aventure.
> Ful blisfully in prison maistow dure –
> In prison? Certes nay, but in paradys!
> Wel hath Fortune yturned thee the dys,
> That hast the sighte of hire, and I th'absence.
> For possible is, syn thou hast hire presence,
> And art a knyght, a worthy and an able,
> That by some cas, syn Fortune is chaungeable,
> Thow maist to thy desir somtyme atteyne.
> (KnT 1235–43)

Within the tower, the state of Palamon is no better. Jealousy torments him as he considers Arcite's freedom:

> 'Sith thou art at thy large, of prisoun free,
> And art a lord, greet is thyn avauntage
> Moore than is myn, that sterve here in a cage.
> For I moot wepe and wayle, whil I lyve,
> With al the wo that prison may me yive,
> And eek with peyne that love me yeveth also,
> That doubleth al my torment and my wo'
> Therwith the fyr of jalousie up sterte
> Withinne his brest, and hente him by the herte
> So woodly that he lyk was to biholde
> The boxtree or the asshen dede and colde.
> (1292–302)

Jealousy is again at issue during the confrontation between Palamon and Arcite in the grove: Emelye 'may nat now han bothe, | Al be ye never so jalouse ne so wrothe' (1839–40); and Jalousie, 'that wered of yelewe gooldes a gerland, | And a cokkow sittynge on hir hand' (1929–30), is represented in the temple of Venus. During the tournament, Arcite hunts Palamon like a tiger 'for jelous herte', and he and Palamon, who is compared to a lion, fight with 'jelous strokes' (2626–35). Afterwards, Theseus puts a stop to 'alle rancour and envye' (2732), and on his death bed Arcite states that love of Emelye and his own jealousy have been the cause of rancour and strife with Palamon (2783–5).

The two long passages just cited provide excellent examples of how mimetic and iconographic meanings combine in the Knight's Tale, along the lines described by Kolve. Arcite refers to the blissful prison of love, before blaming Fortune and her congenital instability. Palamon evokes the real misery of imprisonment – starving, weeping, wailing and woe – before alluding to the similar effects of love, which jealousy further intensifies. Each passage implies a perception of imprisonment as an existential state. The representation of jealousy as an imprisoning castle tower is an important factor in this complex process of allusion. Nor is jealousy's imprisoning power forgotten in the Miller's Tale, which in so many ways acts as a commentary on the preceding narrative. Here, an old carpenter 'ful of jalousie' (3294) acts the part of gaoler. Besotted by his young wife, he restricts her movements and activities: 'jalous he was, and heeld hir narwe in cage' (3224). Falling prey to Nicholas's plan to hoodwink him, he becomes the builder of an elaborate construction by means of which the three of them will float to safety when the floodwaters rise. On the night of the supposed catastrophe, John's house is the very image of a dark prison: 'He shette his dore withoute candel-lyght' (3634). But of course, the flood never comes, Alison and Nicholas keep their tryst, and John is deceived 'for al his kepyng and his jalousye' (3851).

Shot wyndowe (Miller's Tale, I. 3358 and 3695): An Open and Shut Case?*

What kind of a window is the 'shot wyndowe' that is such a crucial feature of the Miller's Tale? The term itself is rare: it occurs nowhere else in Chaucer's works, and is not recorded again before Gavin Douglas's translation of the *Aeneid* (1513).[1] This lack of linguistic context produced an early uncertainty about the form and meaning of *shot*. The word is found unchanged in the two earliest and best manuscripts of the *Canterbury Tales*, Ellesmere and Hengwrt, and in a majority of others, but in a significant portion of the total (some twenty of the eighty surveyed by Manly and Rickert) there is considerable variation.[2] For Miller's Tale line 3358 there are ten occurrences of *schutte*, four of *shoppe*, and two of *short*, and for line 3695 four of *shet*, eight of *shoppe*, and one of *short*. Furthermore, within the variant manuscripts there is little consistency between the two lines. For example, the same scribe will write *schutte* on the first occasion and *shoppe* on the second, or change *short* to *shoppe*, or *schutte* to *shot*.

Editors and other scholars evince a similar doubt about the precise meaning of 'shot wyndowe', and the prevailing definition is itself questionable. Thomas Wright (1847) formed the opinion that the term denotes a projecting window from which the inhabitants of the house might shoot in order to prevent forced entry.[3] This seems an unlikely use for a domestic

---

* First published in *Medium Ævum* 69 (2000), 96–103.
1 Gavin Douglas, *The Aeneid of Virgil Translated into Scottish Verse* (Edinburgh: Bannatyne Club, 1839), prologue to book VII, 380, lines 12–28.
2 John M. Manly and Edith Rickert, *The Text of the Canterbury Tales Studied on the Basis Of All Known Manuscripts*, v: *Corpus of Variants*, part I (Chicago: University of Chicago Press, 1940), 334 and 365.
3 *The Canterbury Tales of Geoffrey Chaucer*, ed. Thomas Wright, Percy Society, 24 (London, 1847), i, 134, note to line 3358.

window in late fourteenth-century Oxford, even if the periodic brawls, assaults and riots made residents feel defensive.[4] F. N. Robinson (1957) suggested that 'shot wyndowe' might designate a window equipped with a fastening bolt,[5] but there is no indication of one in the Miller's Tale. The idea was abandoned by Douglas Gray, the editor of the Miller's Tale for the *Riverside Chaucer* (1987), who gives what is now the generally accepted gloss, simply 'hinged window (one that opens and closes)'.[6] This interpretation can be traced back through Skeat (1900) – 'a hinge-shutting window'[7] – to Thomas Tyrwhitt (1775) who wrote, with more hesitancy: 'That is, I suppose, a window that was *shut*.'[8]

A wide range of other modern authorities supports the Riverside gloss,[9] and it seems churlish to quibble when there is a virtual consensus, but there are two objections. The first is this: if 'shot wyndowe' means 'hinged window' it is a redundant term, because other details in this most economic of narratives make it abundantly clear that it is a window that opens and shuts; why then would Chaucer go on to use a special term to denote its

[4] J. I. Catto, 'Citizens, Scholars and Masters', in *The Early Oxford Schools*, ed. J, I. Catto, The History of the University of Oxford (Oxford: Clarendon Press, 1984), i, 183–7.
[5] *The Works of Geoffrey Chaucer*, ed. F. N. Robinson, 2nd edn (Boston: Houghton Mifflin, 1957), 977.
[6] *The Riverside Chaucer*, 3rd edn, gen. ed. Larry D. Benson (Boston: Hiughton Mifflin, 1987), 70.
[7] *The Complete Works of Geoffrey Chaucer*, ed. Walter W. Skeat, 2nd edn (Oxford: Oxford University Press, 1900), v: *Notes to the Canterbury Tales*, 103–4. In his 'Glossarial Index', Skeat defines 'shot-windowe' as 'a window containing a square division which opens on a hinge' (vi, 232).
[8] He continues: 'It might perhaps be better to write this word (with some of the Mss.) *shet*, or *shette*.' *The Canterbury Tales of Chaucer*, ed. Thomas Tyrwhitt, 2nd edn (Oxford: Clarendon Press, 1798), ii, 428, note to line 3358.
[9] Including *A Chaucer Glossary*, comp. Norman Davis et al. (Oxford: Clarendon Press, 1979); *The Canterbury Tales by Geoffrey Chaucer: Edited from the Hengwrt Manuscript*, ed. N. F. Blake, York Medieval Texts, 2nd ser. (London: Arnold, 1980), 141; Larry D. Benson, *A Glossarial Concordance to the Riverside Chaucer*, Garland Reference Library of the Humanities 1699 (New York: Garland, 1993); and *The Complete Poetry and Prose of Geoffrey Chaucer*, ed. John H. Fisher, 2nd edn (New York: Holt, Rinehart and Winston, 1989), 61.

obvious properties? The second objection concerns the elision of *shot* and *shut*. With the exception of Wright and Robinson, commentators imply that these two words are synonymous, when in fact *shot* is not necessarily related to ME *shetten*, 'to shut', and needs to be re-examined. *OED* is of some help here, both in acknowledging that 'The precise sense of the first element [of 'shot wyndowe'] is difficult to determine', and in suggesting a connection with Middle Dutch *schotdore*, sliding door, and *schotpoorte*, portcullis. In each case, *schot* occurs in a compound noun describing an opening and shutting device that is distinctive precisely because it operates *without* a hinge. Thus, *schot* denotes not so much the action of shutting, but the nature of that action. The sliding door and portcullis 'shoot' into place, as we would say, with potential for the action of shutting being a sudden, abrupt movement.

Should we imagine the 'shot wyndowe' of the Miller's Tale as a similar kind of sliding device? To do so, it might be argued, enhances our understanding and appreciation of that joyous line in the Miller's Tale when, with a giggle and one deft action, Alisoun shuts out the astonished Absolon: '"Teehee!" quod she, and clapte the wyndow to' (3740). For Alisoun's jape to work well, she needs to remain in full control of the aperture (so to speak) and close the window quickly and decisively. A sliding window, which can be closed easily from the inside of the house, would seem to facilitate this action, whereas to reach for a wide-open window would run the risk of confrontation with an enraged suitor. Consider also the stress on speed when Alisoun first opens the window for the kneeling Absolon, 'The window she undoth, and that in haste' (3727) – surely an awkward manoeuvre if the window has to open towards him – and when Nicholas repeats her action: 'And up the wyndowe dide he hastily' (3801).[10] Yet the arrangement of these events does not *necessitate* a sliding window. Generations of readers have imagined a hinged window without registering any sense that the

---

10 'Up' as descriptive of an open window is found elsewhere in ME. Especially interesting is the expression 'Vp þou schotest a windowe', from the Auchinleck MS of *Of Arthoure and Merlin*, ed. O. D. Macrae-Gibson vol. 1, EETS, os 268 (1973), perhaps indicating a sliding device. I am grateful to David Burnley for drawing my attention to this reference.

associated dramatic business is thereby rendered clumsy. Indeed, Absolon's amazement at having kissed the wrong part of Alisoun's anatomy is such that he staggers backwards (3736), thereby enabling her to lean out, reach for, and shut a hinged window, if such it be. So we are left with a puzzling term that seems either to refer to a hinged window with a word that may or may not mean *shut*, or to a sliding window that is not strictly necessary, but which might allow certain actions to happen a little more smoothly.

The puzzle can be solved by recognizing some preconceptions that inform scholarly commentaries, and by examining the historical data. The presumption of the received gloss is that the 'hinged window' to which 'shot wyndowe' is supposed to refer is much like its modern counterpart: a glazed frame opening outwards.[11] Although it is possible that the window of a house belonging to a 'riche gnof' of Oxford, c.1380, would have had glass, it is more likely to have been unglazed: even in the fifteenth century, window glass was still regarded as a luxury item. Moreover, opening glazed windows were an even greater rarity. The usual arrangement was an unglazed opening furnished with a hinged and fastening wooden shutter on the inside of the house for warmth, privacy and security.[12] An arrangement of this sort is entirely consistent with the actions of the Miller's Tale: we may imagine Absolon knocking at the shuttered window, and the inward-opening shutter (not an outward opening glazed window) is what Alisoun and Nicholas unfasten, open and slam with such evident ease of control. In this context, a sliding window is an unnecessary complication, even if there were supporting historical examples.

[11] This is especially true of editions by north American scholars, in which 'shot wyndowe' is defined as a 'casement window', with 'casement' here indicating 'A window sash [frame] that opens outward by means of hinges' (*American Heritage Dictionary*). See for example *Chaucer's Major Poetry*, ed. Albert C. Baugh (London: Routledge and Kegan Paul, 1963), 295; and *Geoffrey Chaucer: The Tales of Canterbury Complete*, ed. Robert A. Pratt (Boston: Houghton Mifflin, 1966), 84.

[12] The surviving data for domestic windows in late medieval Oxford are scanty. See W. A. Pantin, 'The Development of Domestic Architecture in Oxford', *Antiquaries' Journal* 27 (1947), 146. However, the evidence of larger houses elsewhere is instructive: see Margaret Wood, *The English Mediaeval House* (London: Bracken Books, 1983), 351–2 and 358.

Shot wyndowe (Miller's Tale, I. 3358 and 3695) 101

So it may be appropriate to revise the gloss for 'shot wyndowe' to something like 'an unglazed window with an inward-opening shutter'.[13] But if that is the kind of window that Chaucer has in mind, and if it was the norm, and if the opening and shutting business is so well articulated regardless of the term 'shot wyndowe', why did Chaucer bother to use it? As well as having the characteristics just described, the window has certain peculiarities to which Chaucer directly and indirectly alludes, distinguishing features that may not be unconnected with our elusive term. At the first mention of 'shot wyndowe' we learn that it is conveniently located 'upon the carpenteris wal' (3358–9), and close to the bedchamber, since Absolon's crooning is audible to the slumbering John, who comments that the night visitor is 'under our boures wal' (3367). This is part of the window's attraction for the lascivious Absolon, who knows full well that it is 'upon his boures wal' (3677). Its proximity to the bed is again signalled by the ease with which Alisoun hears the parish clerk's overtures, even though they take a subdued form: 'softe he cougheth with a semy soun' (3697). Alisoun, in bed with Nicholas, is even able to conduct a conversation with Absolon, in the street outside, through the shuttered window (3708–26). As well as giving direct access to the space of the bedchamber or bower, it is also low down on the wall: Absolon plans to knock at John's window 'That stant ful lowe upon his boures wal' (3677). More, Chaucer gives us a measurement: as Absolon stands under the window it reaches (presumably its sill) to breast level, 'it was so lowe' (3696).[14] As Absolon kneels, we may imagine that the base of the window is about chin height – just the right height for his ill-fated kiss. The window-shutter is fastened, but capable of

---

13   There seems to be an inkling of this in a recent gloss, which nevertheless fails to clarify the exact nature of the window (glazed or unglazed) and shutter, and to imply a double opening 'shuttered window (hinged at the sides)'. Derek Pearsall, ed., *Chaucer to Spenser: An Anthology of Writings in English 1375–1575* (Oxford: Blackwell, 1999), 105.

14   A detail misrepresented in J. A. W. Bennett, *Chaucer at Oxford and at Cambridge* (Oxford: Clarendon Press, 1974), fig. 2b. Fig. 2a, attributed to Pantin, shows a more convincing version of Chaucer's architectonics, with the 'shot wyndowe' low down on John's chamber wall. See 35–40 on the general design of the carpenter's house.

being quickly opened, and large enough to accommodate human buttocks with enough room left to move them quickly in or out, whether Alisoun's ('at the wyndow out she putte hir hole', 3732), or Nicholas's ('Out his ers he putteth [...] | Over the buttok, to the haunche-bon', 3802–3).

Chaucer's attention to detail might be called a technique of incremental realism. As we learn more about it, an object or 'prop' with a vital function in the plot comes gradually into sharper focus, and the accumulated detail helps to make the associated actions more convincing. Seen in this light, the 'shot wyndowe' might seem to be of the size, position and kind it is merely to facilitate the hilarious ending of the story.[15] But the realism of Chaucer's fabliaux is not generally quite so mechanistic: it is driven by the need to refer to recognizable things, and to deepen the meaning of the narrative, as much as by the mechanical demands of the plot.[16] It is therefore appropriate to ask what the 'shot wyndowe' might have meant to an audience familiar with urban house design, and what (if anything) that might signify for an interpretation of the narrative.

A low, bedchamber window of a certain size giving on to the street, affording an occasional glimpse of bare buttocks – it is within the bounds of possibility that the window in question abutted a latrine. Domestic latrines within town houses of the later Middle Ages were often built against outside walls so that the effluent could be easily conveyed to the street, stream or cesspit below.[17] Ground-floor bedchambers, though by

---

15 Cf. V. A. Kolve, *Chaucer and the Imagery of Narrative: The First Five Canterbury Tales* (London: Arnold, 1984), 194.
16 Cf. Charles Muscatine, *Chaucer and the French Tradition: A Study in Style and Meaning* (Berkeley and Los Angeles: University of California Press, 1969), 59–60 and 224–6.
17 Ernest L. Sabine, 'Latrines and Cesspools of Mediaeval London', *Speculum* 9 (1934), 310, 317, 320; Sidney Oldhall Addy, *The Evolution of the English House*, rev. edn (London: George, Allen and Unwin, 1933), 113; Wood, *English Mediaeval House*, 377–88; L. F. Salzman, *Building in England down to 1540: A Documentary History* (Oxford: Clarendon Press, 1952), 280–5; Lawrence Wright, *Clean and Decent: The Fascinating History of the Bathroom and Water Closet* (London: Routledge and Kegan Paul, 1960), 47–54.

no means the rule, did occur,[18] as did ground-floor privies,[19] and the bedchamber might include a privy, as in the type of house in which Chaucer grew up in the Vintry area of London.[20] The typical domestic garderobe was some 3 feet square and consisted of a seat set on joists over a chute.[21] The chute was generally cut into a wall, and might be lined with timber, plaster, or stone.[22] It is in these terms that we might imagine a latrine within John's bower, and provided with a window for ventilation with the base of the 'shot wyndowe' on a level with the seat.[23] Such an arrangement helps to explain the ease, facility and readiness with which Alisoun and Nicholas play their pranks on Absolon, and it also gives greater credibility to a line that might otherwise seem to be inserted only to provide a rhyme: 'This Nicholas was risen for to pisse' (3798).[24] In other words, he is already heading in the direction of the 'shot wyndowe' when his rival knocks there for a second time.

Are there any grounds for linking *shot* with a privy? The most obvious explanation is the most difficult to establish, namely that *shot* is a variant of *chute*.[25] Chute in the sense of 'fall' or 'drop' was available to Chaucer in

---

18 W. A. Pantin, 'Medieval English Town-House Plans', *Medieval Archaeology* 6–7 (1962–3), 207–8. On Oxford houses see his 'Development of Domestic Architecture' and Julian Munby, '126 High Street: The Archaeology and History of an Oxford House', *Oxoniensia* 40 (1975), 280–1 and 294–5.
19 John Schofield, *Medieval London Houses* (New Haven: Yale University Press, 1994), 87.
20 Edith Rickert (comp.), *Chaucer's World*, ed. Clair C. Olson and Martin M. Crow (New York: Columbia University Press, 1948), 4 and 7, quoting from C. L. Kingsford, 'A London Merchant's House and Its Owners, 1360–1614', *Archaeologia* 74 (1923–4), 156–7. Cf. H. M. Smyser, 'The Domestic Background of *Troilus and Criseyde*', *Speculum* 31 (1956), 300.
21 Schofield, *Medieval London Houses*, 86 and 87.
22 Ibid., 87; and Sabine, 'Latrines and Cesspools', 314 and 315.
23 Cf. Wood, *English Mediaeval House*, 384–5.
24 Cf. Thomas J. Farrell, 'Privacy and the Boundaries of Fabliau in the Miller's Tale', *ELH* 56 (1989), 783–4; and D. Thomas Hanks, Jr., '"Goddes pryvetee" and Chaucer's Miller's Tale', *Christianity and Literature*, 33.2 (1984), 9.
25 I am grateful to Tim Tatton-Brown, a former director of the Canterbury Archaeological Trust, for suggesting this possibility.

Old French,[26] but it appears to have had no currency in Middle English, and the common term for a latrine chute was, simply, *pipe*.[27] *Shot-tower* is recorded as a euphemism for 'privy', but the date of its first appearance is uncertain, and its application would seem to derive from a technology that post-dates the *Canterbury Tales*.[28] More promising is the occurrence of shot as a derivative of both ME *sheten*, to eject or expel,[29] and ME *shiten*, to shit. The ambivalence of meaning enables a pun such that 'shot wyndowe' becomes associated not so much with ballistic discharges, as Wright thought, but with bodily ones.[30]

Is the existence of a garderobe within John's chamber plausible in narrative as well as linguistic terms? Within the *Canterbury Tales* there is certainly a precedent, or parallel case, of Chaucer's featuring a privy to articulate the plot of a marital deception: in the Merchant's Tale, it is a space of privacy, outside January's control, where May can momentarily escape his jealousy and read Damyan's secret love-letter, then tear it into pieces and 'in the pryvee softely it caste' (1954) – a gesture that destroys any

26 *Dictionnaire historique de la langue française*, ed. Alain Rey, 2 vols (Paris: Robert, 1993), in which see 'choir'; and cf. Anglo-Norman 'chair' in *Anglo-Norman Dictionary*, ed. Louise W. Stone and William Rothwell, Publications of the Modern Humanities Research Association, viii, fasc. I: *A-Cyvere* (London: Modern Humanities Research Association, 1977). Wood, *English Mediaeval House*, 379, 381, 385, 387, 388, uses the term 'shoot' to denote garderobe shafts, but the word appears to be a modern coinage used by archaeologists. Cf. Salzman, *Building in England*, 282, 284.
27 Schofield, *Medieval London Houses*, 86; and Sabine, 'Latrines and Cesspools', 312 and 314–15. See *MED*, s.v. 'pipe', 1b.
28 Wallace Reyburn, *Flushed with Pride: The Story of Thomas Crapper* (London: Macdonald, 1969), 73; Dulcie Lewis, *Kent Privies* (Newbury: Countryside Books, 1996), 124; and Mollie Harris, *Privies Galore* (Stroud: Sutton, 1990), 106. See *OED*, s.v. 'shot-tower', using evidence from 1835. However, the association of privies with ballistics occurs as early as the late sixteenth century: see *Sir John Harington's A New Discourse on a Stale Subject, Called the Metamorphosis of Ajax*, ed. Elizabeth Story Donno (London: Routledge and Kegan Paul, 1962), 56, and *OED*, s.v. 'shoot', *v.*, 18b.
29 *MED*, 3(a); cf. *OED*, s.v. 'shoot', *v.*, 11b, 11f, 18a.
30 Cf. Norman E. Eliason, *The Language of Chaucer's Poetry: An Appraisal of the Verse, Style, and Structure*, Anglistica 17 (Copenhagen: Rosenkilde and Bagger, 1972), 93.

illusion of romance.[31] Within the Miller's Tale, to imagine a privy helps to make some of the other details more explicable: Nicholas's rising to piss (as already noted), and perhaps also the general emphasis on countering the effects of bad odours, notably the cardamom and liquorice taken by Absolon to 'smellen sweete', and the quadrifolia placed under his tongue (3690–3), just before his first nocturnal visit. If not introduced directly to counter the offensive smells of a privy, the tale's emphasis on the fragrance of Absolon only makes the place of its denouement the more offensive, associated as it is with bad odours such as those of Nicholas's fart, itself contrasting with the sweet-smelling herbs that freshen the student's room (3205). The presence of a privy might also accentuate the wide disparity between the sublimity of Absolon's pretensions and the risible circumstances in which he enacts them: here is a would-be courtly lover, prone to wearing shoes adorned with the elaborate tracery patterns of St Paul's window,[32] conducting his amours outside a latrine window. And if we enlarge the frame of reference to the preceding tale, with which the Miller's Tale is so often compared, we can see, again, an increase in contrast to the point of grotesque travesty between the elevated tower-window of the Knight's Tale castle and the low privy window of a carpenter's house. One, with its bars, mediates privation and a desire for a distant and unwitting Emelye, seen in a memorable moment one bright morning. The other is the fulcrum of a sightless but sensory close encounter with an Alisoun who is all too responsive in returning Absolon's attentions with her 'nether-ye'.[33]

---

31 See Christine Rose, 'Woman's "Pryvetee", May, and the Privy: Fissures in the Narrative Voice in the Merchant's Tale, 1944–86', *Chaucer Yearbook* 4 (1997), 61–77. Cf. Saul N. Brody, 'Making a Play for Criseyde: The Staging of Pandarus's House in Chaucer's *Troilus and Criseyde*', *Speculum* 73 (1998), 119–28 and Smyser, 'Domestic background', 309–10.

32 Illustrated in Roger Sherman Loomis, *A Mirror of Chaucer's World* (Princeton: Princeton University Press, 1965), plate 28.

33 Cf. Michael Camille, *Image on the Edge: The Margins of Medieval Art* (London: Reaktion, 1992), 111–27; and John Leyerle. 'The Heart and the Chain', in *The Learned and the Lewed: Studies in Chaucer and Medieval Literature*, ed. Larry D. Benson, Harvard English Studies, 5 (Cambridge, Mass.: Harvard University Press, 1974), 122–3.

In another respect the tale's pattern of meaning, and particularly its play on *privy, pryvely* and *pryvetee*, is enriched if the reader is meant to envisage a privy as part of John's bedchamber. Thus Alisoun's injunction to the 'ful privee' lodger (3201) to 'wayte wel and been privee' (3295) in dealing with her husband is advice he initially follows but later ignores, with painful consequences: without waiting or considering his actions he opens the window, thrusts his buttocks out beyond the limits of the 'privy' ('out his ers he putteth pryvely, | Over the buttok, to the haunche-bon', 3802–3), and, in spite of his tremendous, blinding fart, soon feels the searing effects of the red-hot coulter wielded by Absolon. The parish clerk's enquiring after John, 'Ful prively' (3662), anticipates his own performance at the latrine window, at which he plans to knock, appropriately enough, 'Ful pryvely' (3676). The presence of a privy would also square with Chaucer's interest in small spaces – whether represented as the 'cage' of John's jealousy, his bed, Nicholas's chamber or the human body – and their violation. Indeed, Absolon's nocturnal habit of prying into a 'privy part' of the house, and the humiliation he endures, are consonant with the prologue's and tale's jocular warnings about the dangers of wanting to know too much about woman's, or God's, *pryvetee* (3454, 3558).[34] When these warnings are not heeded, Chaucer engineers a 'privy' ending that is all too public.

34 There is extensive commentary on the topic of *pryvetee* in the Miller's Tale and in Chaucer's works more generally. See especially Bernard F. Huppé, *A Reading of the Canterbury Tales* (Albany, NY: State University of New York, 1964), 75–88; Thomas W. Ross, *Chaucer's Bawdy* (New York: Dutton, 1972), s.v. 'pryvee', and his edition of *The Miller's Tale*, A Variorum Edition of the Works of Geoffrey Chaucer, ii, part 3; (Norman, Okla.: University of Oklahoma Press, 1983), note to line 3164; Paula Neuss, '*Double-entendre* in the Miller's Tale', *Essays in Criticism* 24 (1974), 330–5; E. D. Blodgett, 'Chaucerian *Pryvetee* and the Opposition to Time', *Speculum* 51 (1976), 477–85; Hanks, "Goddes pryvetee"', 7–12; Farrell, 'Privacy and the Boundaries of Fabliau', 773–95; Elaine Tuttle Hansen, *Chaucer and the Fictions of Gender* (Berkeley: University of California Press, 1992), 223–36; R. W. Hanning, 'Telling the Private Parts: "Pryvetee" and Poetry in Chaucer's *Canterbury Tales*', in *The Idea of Medieval Literature: New Essays on Chaucer and Medieval Culture in Honor of Donald R. Howard*, ed. James M. Dean and Christian K. Zacher (Newark, Del.: University of Delaware Press, 1992), 108–25; William F. Woods, 'Private and Public Space in the

Thus, the linguistic, literary and historical evidence suggests that 'hinged window', implying a glazed frame opening outwards, is an inaccurate reading of 'shot wyndowe'. In the Miller's Tale it should be imagined as an unglazed opening with a hinged internal shutter. 'Shot wyndowe', however, is a rare and striking term and may designate not this conventional arrangement for a domestic window, but a special characteristic, namely that it was a privy window, the window associated with shot in the sense of discharge, shit or chute. The existence of a privy within John's bedchamber makes some of narrative details more explicable; it enhances the scurrilous and scatological features of the tale; and it adds a further dimension to the theme of spatial transgression in which the boundaries of the private are breached and invaded.

Miller's Tale', *Chaucer Review* 29 (1994), 166–78; Frederick M. Biggs and Laura L. Howes, 'Theophany in the Miller's Tale', *Medium Ævum* 65 (1996), 269–79; and David Lorenzo Boyd, 'Seeking "Goddes pryvetee": Sodomy, Quitting and Desire in the Miller's Tale', in *Words and Works: Studies in Medieval English Language and Literature in Honour of Fred C. Robinson*, ed. Peter Baker and Nicholas Howe (Toronto: University of Toronto Press, 1998), 243–60. For further references, see T. L. Burton and Rosemary Greentree, *Chaucer's 'Miller's', 'Reeve's' and 'Cook's Tales'*, The Chaucer Bibliographies (Toronto: University of Toronto Press, 1997).

The Containment of Symkyn: The Function of Space in the Reeve's Tale*

In a previous issue of the *Chaucer Review*, Gerhard Joseph drew attention to one of Chaucer's uses of space in the *Canterbury Tales*.[1] Centring his discussion on the 'argument of herbergage' as it develops in Fragment A, he identified two opposed views of the physical world. For Palamon and Arcite the world is a spiritual prison which restricts the fulfilment of their desires, so that in the Knight's Tale, space becomes a figure of ontological problems that derive from Boethius. On the other hand the characters of the Miller's Tale, for example, take their surroundings more for granted. Domestic space is the tangible and manipulated circumstance in which Alison and Nicholas experience freedom from the carpenter's control and delight in each other. In the wider context of the pilgrimage, the Tabard also operates as a spatial image of physical enjoyment while the approach of journey's end – the final herbergage of Canterbury or, in the Parson's words, 'Jerusalem celestial' – gives a sense of curtailment and confinement to the travellers and to the tone of the narration. Joseph suggested that these antithetical apprehensions of space, one seeing it from a serious point of view as oppressive, the other from a light-hearted attitude as offering numberless possibilities for 'play', reflect the tenor and priorities of the narrative and parallel the division of the tales into those told in 'earnest' and those told in 'game'.

It is unfortunate that although space was the subject of his discussion, Joseph made no attempt to define the criteria by which the presence of this phenomenon can be determined. Nevertheless, his textual analysis was valuable in giving prominence to an important and previously neglected

---

* First published in *Chaucer Review* 14 (1980), 226–36.
1 Gerhard Joseph, 'Chaucerian "Game"–"Earnest" and the "Argument of Herbergage" in the *Canterbury Tales*', *Chaucer Review* 5 (1970), 83–96.

feature of Chaucer's poetry. But the interpretation which he offered, while he admitted it to be not the only valid one, was somewhat predictable. Given that Chaucer uses space to various effects, it might be expected that its more serious implications unfold when the general subject-matter is 'ernest' rather than when it is 'game'. Through being annexed to the 'game-ernest' polarities, space was made to seem dependent on a large and well-established issue of Chaucerian criticism. These wide terms of reference meant that while Joseph's analysis produced some impressive results with the Knight's Tale, where space is used as an image for matters of some philosophical complexity, the internal themes of the churls' tales were neglected. These tales, it was felt, make a less sophisticated use of the dimensions of the material world. In them, space is much more likely to be a functional context for the action, and that alone.

While it is true that in the churls' tales there is no equivalent of the searching philosophical speculation of the Knight's Tale, it is false to infer that a less serious tale is not capable of using space in an equally interesting way. In the Reeve's Tale, space itself becomes a talking-point; it is an important element in the articulation of the plot; the dimensions of the material world are deliberately linked to the themes of the poem; and space moves in a subtle way between the status of fact and metaphor. The present article, therefore, is an elaboration of these statements, with particular reference to the bedchamber scene where space is of special significance.

In the following discussion care has been taken to show precisely how Chaucer systematically seeks to make organic space a part of his material realism. Unless this is done, conclusions about its relation to the themes of the poems must be suspect, since they might be based on arbitrary occurrences. The question of Chaucer's deliberate use of space can be treated in two ways: the first is through comparison with any source material, when Chaucer's distinctive practices will be highlighted; the second is by examining closely the various stimuli offered by the poet which prompt the reader to infer that given passages are conceived in depth.

The closest analogue to the Reeve's Tale is found in the form of a French fabliau, probably of the thirteenth century, entitled *Le Meunier et les .II.*

clers.² Its account of the bed-swapping scene contains, in broad outline, the essential components of the 'business' which mesh with such precision in Chaucer's version. But the fabliau has very little to offer in the way of descriptive setting. In the first place, it is not clear why the two visitors should have to sleep in the same room as the miller and his family.³ The narrowness of his house is not mentioned, and indeed the opposite seems to be implied when the question of accommodation is raised 'il lo puet bien faire' (A. 153). The relative position of the beds, so important to a full appreciation of the subsequent farce, is not included in any preparatory description. Thus the presence of a cradle and its location come as a surprise (A. 237–41). For the 'huche' or tub in which the miller's daughter is locked there is some preparation, but it is an incongruous and obtrusive object, a clumsy device for demonstrating the possessiveness of the miller (A. 161–7). Similarly the means whereby the first deacon gains entrance to the tub, by presenting the girl with an andiron ring, is a contrivance blatantly introduced into the narrative (A. 176–81), depending for its success on the extreme naïveté of the girl (A. 208–20). The consequences of darkness are not much explored (A. 261–6, 301–4). The participants do not have to grope round the room, nor is there moonlight to add confusion to the closing scene. The fabliau presents only the miller and one deacon fighting, and the fight is soon over when, incredibly, the deacon wins with ease (A. 287–91). The effect which Chaucer produces of four bodies moving, banging and brawling round a confining interior, is absent.

An extension of the limits of this examination confirms that *Le Meunier et les .II. clers* has a basic disregard for those descriptive elements which, directly or indirectly, help to foster the illusion of a three-dimensional locale. One of the most marked silences of the fabliau, coming to it as we do with the Reeve's Tale in mind, is that of personal appearance. The plot demands that the miller's daughter should be attractive, 'bele et

---

2   Printed with a brief introduction by W. M. Hart, 'The Reeve's Tale', in *Sources and Analogues of Chaucer's Canterbury Tales*, ed. W. F. Bryan and G. Dempster (New York: Humanities Press, 1958), 124–47. Line references are to text A.
3   Note that the room is not in the mill but in the miller's house: A. 53–9, 136–9, 154–5.

cointe' (A. 161), but this is the nearest approach to distinguishing, either by physical features or even by name, among the five participants. Their credibility also suffers through unexplained fluctuations of what for a better word must be called character. The deacons, who at the beginning are poor, afflicted, and respectful of their Order (A. 1–18), degenerate into randy opportunists (A. 272–86); and the miller's wife, presented again with a sublime indifference to psychological probability, turns against her husband after having helped him perpetrate the fraud (A. 305–15). The place of these individuals within their society is determined by convention. The poor are the victims of a rascally entrepreneur who by virtue of his position is able to steal their corn. The situation, if not the final outcome, is general rather than unique.[4] Paralleling this indefinite social context is an imprecision about locale. The mill stands by a stream and is adjacent to a small wood, but what is important to the author is not the representing of a recognizable place but the isolation of the mill, which allows the miller to practise his tricks (A. 53–60).

Chaucer's method when working with this raw material is to particularize the typical, to make specific the general, to realize a social myth in terms of a credible fiction, in short to give substance in the fullest sense to the framework which he received. The Reeve's 'And this is verray sooth that I yow telle' (3924)[5] ought not to be underestimated, for it expresses the creative ethos of the tale: these places exist, these people lived, these events happened. The first three lines, for example, confer on the poem a three-dimensional reality of an unusual kind, for they set the tale at a place which, even at the present day, can be visited and recognized. This almost novelistic approach is maintained throughout further topographical references.[6] The

4   Some of the elements in the Reeve's Tale that tend to be praised as uniquely Chaucerian, notably social background and complex character portrayal, can be found in other fabliaux. See W. M. Hart, 'The Reeve's Tale: A Comparative Study of Chaucer's Narrative Art', *PMLA* 23 (1908), 1–44.
5   I have used *The Works of Geoffrey Chaucer*, ed. F. N. Robinson, 2nd edn (Boston: Houghton Mifflin, 1957).
6   On the topography of the tale see J. A. W. Bennett, *Chaucer at Oxford and at Cambridge* (Oxford: Clarendon Press, 1974), 105–15.

The Containment of Symkyn

individuals who inhabit this world are distinguished by their names, their different forms of speech, their appearance, their characters and separate motivations. The social standing of the miller and his family is given an intriguing local frame of reference, and Symkyn's professional relationship to the community is described. It is in reaction to his oppressive influence that Aleyn and John set out from Cambridge, to outwit him. The action therefore seems to grow organically from the opening passages. For this reason, the impression of space which the tale produces should not be considered merely as the product of objective description. The nature and complexity of the introduction create a structure for the ensuing activity in which the presence of material depth becomes not so much possible as inevitable. Such matters as Symkyn's outrageous thieving or his wife's haughtiness, although they have no direct connection with the existence of space and are not in themselves sufficient to evoke it, nevertheless imply a type of physical world in which 'behaviour' plays a crucial part. It is now time to examine an example of how, in a direct and physical sense, Chaucer deals with behaviour and in the process evokes the third dimension.

For the bedchamber scene in the Reeve's Tale there is considerable preparation. The miller himself refers to his house as confined or 'streit' (4122), and in support of this the Reeve offers an explanation of why John and Aleyn had to be lodged in the same room as Symkyn and his family: 'It myghte be no bet, and cause why? | Ther was no roumer herberwe in the place' (4144–5). The Reeve also states the distance between the miller's and clerks' beds: it is 'ten foot or twelve' (4141). Evidently it is too near for Aleyn, who complains that the cacophonous snoring of miller, wife and daughter could be heard at two furlongs (4166). The daughter's bed, says the Reeve, is 'by and by' in relation to that of her parents, but quite separate (4142–3); and he later refers to the approximate distance between the clerks' bed and that of Malyn as 'a furlong wey or two' (4199). The cradle for its part is directly at the foot of the miller's bed so that it can be rocked and the child fed (4156–7). It is amusing that the objective distance between the bed of Malyn and the miller becomes 'a twenty devel wey' (4257) after Aleyn has finished his night's mischief, unaware of more to come.

This mensuration is by and large a narrative 'plant' to give some credence to the bed-swapping episode. But it does produce an impression of the critical arrangement and space between the separate beds and cradle, spaces that are crossed several times during the night, and most dramatically by Aleyn and Symkyn in the course of their brawl. Without the necessary preparation, the farcical business and slapstick wallowing would be all the less effective. The stage has to be set.

Once the host, his family and guests are installed in their beds, the space of the room is conveyed through a series of movements which gain in tempo until the room hardly seems able to contain them. To begin with, Aleyn 'crepte' into Malyn's bed (4193), and his 'playing' with the miller's daughter contrasts with the inertia of John, who lies still like a 'draf-sak' (4199–206) until he too gets up and goes 'softely' to the cradle at the foot of the miller's bed, carrying it back 'softe unto his beddes feet' (4211–13). The movement of the miller's wife is equally expressive.[7] Unsuspecting, she walks back through the room and confidently climbs in with John 'faire and wel' (4226). Once having lured the woman to his bed, John can emulate the intimate sexual movement of his fellow. He leaps on her and allows her no respite (4228–30).

The transition from slow, stealthy, deliberate movement to fast, no-holds-barred random activity is extremely abrupt. Aleyn creeps into bed by the miller, clasps him round the neck, and tells all. Symkyn grabs the clerk by the throat and bloodies his nose. The chaos that follows soon involves his wife and John, though not Malyn. The room is bursting with strenuous activity:

> And in the floor, with nose and mouth tobroke,
> They walwe as doon two pigges in a poke;
> And up they goon, and doun agayn anon,
> Til that the millere sporned at a stoon,
> And doun he fil bakward upon his wyf.
> (4277–81)

---

7   Compare the manner in which Symkyn goes to release the clerks' horse (4057–63). He enacts a pantomine of the trickster up to no good.

The woman wakes in a state of confusion, thinking it is the clerks who are fighting (4285–91). She succeeds in finding a staff, then mistakenly strikes her husband on the head so that 'doun he gooth' again (4307) and the clerks can together deal the final blows.

Movement is conditioned in the room by darkness, and in this final scene of the Reeve's Tale it disrupts normal vision disastrously. When Symkyn's wife locates the wrong bed, she is relying on her sense of touch. Having missed the cradle at her own bed, she 'groped heer and ther' (4217) fruitlessly in empty space. Thinking she has arrived in error at the clerks' bed she sets off to find the cradle and 'gropeth alwey forther with hir hond' (4222). This transference of space perception from sight to touch is a crucial contribution to the reader's impression of the interior. It is as if forms and their relationships are made palpable. Aleyn too, having bid farewell to Malyn, gropes for a signpost and having 'fond the cradel with his hand' (4251) directs himself towards the wrong bed. And when John is rudely awakened by the ensuing fight of Aleyn and the miller, he goes feeling for a weapon: 'And graspeth by the walles to and fro, | To fynde a staf' (4293–4). The containing limits of the chamber are here literally felt. The word for 'interior' occurs at this point, and its presence further reiterates the importance placed on the presence of space in the dénouement: Symkyn's wife is more successful in finding a staff than John because she 'knew the estres bet' (4295).[8]

The accurate perception of objects in space depends on clear sight, and Chaucer takes some care to suggest that the appearance of a gloomy halflight at the end of the bedchamber scene, with the consequent improvement in visibility, is a necessary condition of the final débâcle. Although dawn is imminent,[9] it is not the light of day that brings the struggling figures into

---

8 'Interior' would seem to be the right substitute here, although *MED* (3d) defines *estres* as 'an apartment, room, hall-way, or recess in a building' while *OED* (2b) has 'inner rooms in a house'. If the miller's wife 'knew the estres bet', it seems curious that she should have mistaken her bed earlier that night; Chaucer alleviates the inconsistency by stressing the darkness surrounding that incident (4225).
9 Note the approach of dawn and Aleyn's mock aubade at 4232–39, 4249–50.

view but the silvery light of the moon, faintly but deceptively illuminating Symkyn and Aleyn. Sight is partially restored. The miller's wife

> [...] saugh a litel shymeryng of a light,
> For at an hole in shoon the moone bright;
> And by that light she saugh hem bothe two,
> But sikerly she nyste who was who,
> But as she saugh a whit thyng in hir ye.
> (4287–301)

She takes the 'whit thyng' to be Aleyn's nightcap when it is in fact her husband's 'pyled skulle', so the blow falls on the wrong head (4302–6). It is interesting that Chaucer here takes an individual's point of view and accounts for the error in subjective terms, relating it to the psychology of perception. For whether the misplaced blow is found convincing or not, Chaucer does endeavour to realize this episode, which is his invention, as convincingly as possible.

Plausibility is perhaps undermined in the closing scene by the sudden, unexpected mention of Aleyn's 'volupeer' or nightcap (4303). The clerks were not given any night attire by the miller, nor would they have brought any with them since their overnight stay was not intended. But it is the miller's wife who assumes, without thinking, that this is what she sees, and her state of confusion on waking has already been clearly indicated. When during the brawl her husband falls on her, she imagines first that 'the feend is on me falle' (4288) as she feels the weight of Symkyn on her head and John on her stomach, with whom she has been lying all night; then she imagines that the clerks are fighting each other (4291). The darkness and then shimmering light aggravate the situation so that the woman's misplaced blow is understandable, given her state of mind. And even if one might cavil at the contrived nature of the 'volupeer' there is certainly adequate preparation for the object that does receive the blow, Symkyn's head. Chaucer meticulously threads into the story a number of references, both literal and figurative, to the miller's bald, shiny, white pate, so that when it appears at the end of the poem it is accepted as a convincing target for his wife's staff. Symkyn's 'pyled skull' is a prominent aspect of his appearance from the outset.[10]

In the preceding section I hope to have demonstrated how the bedchamber scene in the Reeve's Tale is conceived in three dimensions. The question now arises as to why Chaucer should have made this particular adjustment to his source. If space, as it is analysed here, is seen merely as an aspect of narrative realism, then there is little more to be said. Space does of course serve the function of bringing to life, of giving solidity, to the individuals involved and to their actions. Since the tale takes place in a physical world recognizably like our own, the measure of appreciation is increased. And it seems appropriate that a non-intellectual tale which deals in cheating, sex and violence should be presented in this way. But the poem also indicates that space should be considered in other lights.

When Aleyn and John, weary, wet and disgruntled after chasing the warden's horse over the fens, return to the miller's house, they find Symkyn sitting smugly by the fire. The students know that the miller has triumphed: by releasing Bayard and diverting their attention, he has been able to steal some of the college's flour. The carefully phrased speech with which Symkyn greets them is clerkly, a *jeu-de-mot*, and it has space as its subject. The miller seems to have won and the clerks to have lost. Symkyn is quick to press home his advantage and stake a claim to have a wit equal to if not better than any university student. His words have a particularly pointed effect coming immediately after John's complaint that he and Aleyn have made

10   There is some debate as to what *pyled* means. W. W. Skeat in his note on the Summoner's 'piled berd' (A 627) defined 'piled' as 'deprived of hair, thin, slight' (*The Complete Works of Geoffrey Chaucer*, 2nd edn [Oxford: Clarendon Press, 1900; repr. 1963], v, 52). W. C. Curry, however, maintained that in the case of Symkyn 'piled' signifies 'probably that the hair [...] is thick (most likely bristly), and especially that it comes far down over his wide, "villainous low" forehead' (*Chaucer and the Mediaeval Sciences*, 2nd edn [New York: Barnes and Noble, 1960], 83). *OED* defines *piled* as (1) 'covered with pile, hair or fur'. But M. Copland has questioned Curry's interpretation, which, indeed, seems unlikely in the context of the Reeve's Tale, in 'The Reeve's Tale: Harlotrie or Sermonying?' *Medium Ævum* 31 (1962), 29. For other allusions in the poem to the miller's head, see 3935, 4099, 4149, 4261.

fools of themselves in the eyes of their warden and college fellows: 'Now are we dryve til hethyng and til scorn' (4110).

The subject of Symkyn's little disquisition is twofold: while dealing ostensibly with the small dimensions of the house – *this* space as opposed to the space of the fens – he also alludes to practices of learned argument and philosophical speculation. He is like the self-educated father who feels he must keep abreast of his son's university education. The tone is proud and patronizing:

> Myn hous is streit, but ye han lerned art;
> Ye konne by argumentes make a place
> A myle brood of twenty foot of space.
> Lat se now if this place may suffise,
> Or make it rowm with speche, as is youre gise.
> (4122–6)

There is a strong sense of competitiveness, of challenge, underlying these lines. 'You are students,' says Symkyn, 'you are supposed to be intelligent. Here is a problem. Now let us see if you can solve it.' His words carry the implication that clerkly wit is not much use against the native wit which he has just employed so successfully in the matter of the corn. Clerkly wit is mere words, and mere words cannot enlarge a room.

But the narrowness of which Symkyn speaks is not just related to the architectural dimensions of the house. It is the clerks' custom, he says, their 'gise', to use speech and arguments to augment and enlarge subjects of dispute. Their 'art', their university training, instructs them to do so. Now it is just this intellectual approach which has patently failed to cope with Symkyn's slyness. Aleyn and John, having conceived a plan for outwitting the miller, have put it into practice only to find that their preconceptions are no match for the wily, *ad hoc* stratagems of Symkyn. Ironically, they have succeeded in putting themselves in the wide expanse of the fens – a place a 'myle brood' – when it was their intention to remain within the narrow confines of the mill and watch the miller's every move. They expanded their 'twenty foot of space', as is the habit of students, quite irrelevantly, missed the point of their horse's disappearance, and thus allowed Symkyn to gain the upper hand.

But the students soon learn by their mistake. Abandoning pre-meditated plans and taking advantage of an unexpected state of affairs, they turn the tables on Symkyn, so that, in the event, Aleyn and John find the small space of the bedchamber quite adequate to their purposes. The cramped confines of the room and the accessibility of its occupants allow them to seduce the miller's daughter and wife without speech being necessary. Where previously the students' room for manoeuvre was under Symkyn's control, they in turn now dominate the space of the miller in his own home. In so doing, the clerks win the second trial of wit.

Symkyn, in his speech on the narrow confines of his house, draws attention to the fact that space forms the context for the contest of wit. Both parties know, though they do not admit it to each other, what the other is about. Symkyn knows that the students are aware of what he has done, and it is this awareness that helps to make his speech so rich in irony. The game of wits has been apparent from the start. It is the conscious intention of Aleyn and John ('they dorste leye hir nekke' [4009]) to beat Symkyn at his game of thieving. Symkyn immediately recognizes the lie of the land when the clerks insist on watching him at work:

> This millere smyled of hir nycetee,
> And thoghte, 'Al this nys doon but for a wyle.
> They wene that no man may hem bigyle [...]'
> (4046–8)

The repeated use of the word 'play' in a variety of contexts sustains the idea that both sides are aware of the game that is in progress. Symkyn, for his part, sees the contest very much as one between the supposedly ignorant and the supposedly learned: 'yet shal I blere hir ye, | For al the sleighte in hir philosophye' (4049–50); 'Yet kan a millere make a clerkes berd, | For al his art' (4096–7).

The miller's attitude exemplifies the driving force in his complex character: the desire to be superior, to be better than his betters, which has found expression hitherto in greed and social ambition. Now the interconnection of space and the trial of wit that forms the substance of Symkyn's speech on 'herbergage' suggest that the bedchamber episode, in which as we have seen space is constructed with such care, can be read as an image of the struggle for supremacy. The bedchamber scene epitomizes in concrete terms the involved and convoluted psychological game which the miller and the clerks have been playing. And the fight for control over the space of the bedchamber is perhaps indicative of two other themes that also give substance to Chaucer's poem.

What drove the students in the first place to go to the mill – the occasion of the contest of wit – was the increasing oppressiveness of Symkyn's dishonest practices. The space which Symkyn literally controls at the beginning of the poem is, strictly speaking, that of the mill and the house. There he has exclusive rights. But his influence is felt further afield. He has 'greet sokene', takes a great toll, of all the land about (3987–8). Because of his monopoly, he can behave dishonestly. But Symkyn oversteps the bounds of acceptable thieving, and the baneful effect of his activities becomes unbearable at Cambridge when the illness of the manciple at Soler Hall allows him extra leeway:

> For therbiforn he stal but curteisly,
> But now he was a theef outrageously,
> For which the wardeyn chidde and made fare.
> (3997–9)

The behaviour of the rascally miller impinges on his clientèle to such an extent that the students feel they must restrict such malpractices, and for this reason Aleyn and John journey to Trumpington where they 'contain' the miller by overcoming him with physical force and retrieving their lost grain, the removal of which is admitted by the miller's daughter. The clerks leave the miller as it were cut down to size, restricted to a more proper field of operation, his thieving habits curtailed. Metaphorically speaking his space, his area of influence, is reduced, and again the act of achieving this is imaged in the manoeuvres and struggles that take place within the interior of the bedchamber.

There is one further aspect of the miller's sense of his own space that is reduced: his social pretension. The opening passages of the Reeve's Tale go into great detail about the social history of the miller and his family, the

The Containment of Symkyn

overweening pride which Symkyn takes in his status, and the precariousness of his respectability. His wife is the illegitimate daughter of the town priest who learnt her haughty manners in a nunnery, and there are hopes that Symkyn will be able further to 'saven his estaat of yomanrye' (3949) by marrying his daughter well: the priest her grandfather is intending to dispose of some of 'hooly chirches good' (3983) to form her dowry. It is indicative of Symkyn's self-esteem that, on hearing that Aleyn has slept with his daughter, his first response is: 'Who dorste be so boold to disparage | My doghter, that is come of swich lynage?' (4271–2). It is the background of promiscuity, corruption and false respectability that lies exposed: Symkyn's wife and daughter have in fact behaved in accordance with their origins. Because of this, the miller's massive pretensions are deflated. The 'deynous' face he shows the world is revealed as a mask or defensive guard against revealing the flimsy basis of his self-importance. The events in the bedchamber, then, have far-reaching consequences. Symkyn's self-esteem is reduced to humiliation. The forced replacement of one by the other receives support from the vivid way in which his downfall is presented. Aleyn and John leave the miller of Trumpington sprawling helplessly in his own bedchamber. Symkyn's extensive area of influence and pretension has been brought within more realistic confines. His wit, thieving and social aspiration are all drastically reduced; he is shown contained. It is to provide a strong visual image of this his final condition that Chaucer creates a convincing three-dimensional interior. Both the presence of space and the working out of new concerns are directly attributable to Chaucer, and it seems reasonable to assume that they do form a coherent addition to the fabliau on which they are based. For the fabliau is essentially a fantasy, a wish-fulfilment, which Chaucer renders realistic and substantial by making space the vehicle of his themes.

An Optical Theme in the Merchant's Tale*

The final episode of the Merchant's Tale contains three surprising events: the restoration of January's vision, his sight of May and Damian copulating in the pear tree above his head, and the old man's eventual acceptance of May's explanation that he has been the victim of an optical illusion. Chaucer's treatment of these incidents is not adequately accounted for in the published sources and analogues. He introduced new material which derives from the medieval science of vision, or optics. Medieval optical texts furnish parallels both for Chaucer's treatment of visual deception in the ending of the Merchant's Tale and for the tale's general theme of inner blindness. These works, three of which were known to Chaucer, provide hitherto unnoticed analogues.

In her study of 1936 Germaine Dempster identified two types of deception story which share similarities with Chaucer's version.[1] The Optical Illusion type features a husband who agrees that the sight of his wife with another man was a visual deception. The Blind Husband and Fruit Tree type includes a blind husband whose sight is restored in time for him to witness the act of adultery taking place in a fruit tree. He is then persuaded by his wife that her purpose was to cure his ailment. Dempster concluded that a Novellino narrative of the Blind Husband variety is closest to Chaucer's version of the story but allowed that he could have been influenced by a

---

* First published in *Studies in the Age of Chaucer: Proceedings*, 1 (1985): *Reconstructing Chaucer*, ed. Paul Strohm and Thomas J. Heffernan, 231–43.
1 Germaine Dempster, 'On the Source of the Deception Story in the Merchant's Tale', *MP* 34 (1936–7): 133–54; and see her 'The Merchant's Tale', in *Sources and Analogues of Chaucer's Canterbury Tales*, ed. W. F. Bryan and Germaine Dempster (Chicago: University of Chicago Press, 1941), 333–56.

story of the Optical Illusion type. Additional analogues of both types have subsequently come to light, but without disturbing Dempster's findings.[2]

The ending of the Merchant's Tale is an unprecedented blend of the Optical Illusion and Blind Husband stories. The process of amalgamation may be traced from line 2354, when Pluto restores January's sight.[3] From this point onward Chaucer takes account of January's visual experience in ways which are unusual, detailed and complex. Pluto causes January to see 'as wel as evere he myghte' (2356), but, as it soon emerges, January's ability to see well is severely restricted by psychological impediments. His first reaction is to look for his wife because he dotes on her: 'was ther nevere man of thyng so fayn, | But on his wyf his thoght was everemo' (2358–9). Here Chaucer makes the first of several statements about the relations between January's state of mind and his visual experience. January is impelled as it were involuntarily to search out the object of his devotion and so catches sight of May and Damian in flagrante delicto. It is a moment of visual truth, and Chaucer indicates that, just as thought directs vision, so vision directs emotion. January cries out in anguish like a mother who fears that her child will die (2364–7).

May's explanation of what is happening is in line with the Blind Husband models: she claims that her intention was to cure January's blindness, 'to heele with youre eyen' (2372). The story would normally end here, but instead Chaucer transposes the narrative to an Optical Illusion type. The transition occurs with May's claim that she has done no more than 'strugle with a man upon a tree' (2374), so suggesting that her husband's eyes have deceived him. At this stage January is not inclined to deny the evidence of his senses. The memory image is impressed vividly on his mind:

---

[2] Charles A. Watkins, 'Modern Irish Variants of the Enchanted Pear Tree', *Southern Folklore Quarterly* 30 (1966), 202–13; Karl P. Wentersdorf, 'Chaucer's Merchant's Tale and Its Irish Analogues', *Studies in Philology* 63 (1966), 604–29; his 'A Spanish Analogue of the Pear-Tree Episode in the Merchant's Tale', *Modern Philology* 64 (1967), 320–1; and Peter G. Beidler, 'Chaucer's Merchant's Tale and the *Decameron*', *Italica* 50 (1973), 266–84.

[3] All quotations from Chaucer are F. N. Robinson, ed., *The Works of Geoffrey Chaucer*, 2dn edn (Boston: Houghton Mifflin, 1957).

> 'Strugle!' quod he, 'ye algate in it wente!
> God yeve yow bothe on shames deth to dyen!
> He swyved thee, I saugh it with myne yen,
> And elles be I hanged by the hals!'
> (2376–9)

When May retorts 'Thanne is [...] my medicyne fals' (2380), she is, of course, referring to the cure which she pretends to have effected; but there is also a sense in which she is admitting, in the form of an aside, that the explanation of her deed with Damian is inadequate as a remedy for concealing the adultery, because January refuses to believe her version of events against the visual evidence. So May switches her tactics by introducing as a supplementary explanation of what January has seen the idea that he is suffering from defective vision. This development in her strategy represents a change from what might be called a magical explanation to one which has the trappings of science. The terms in which the second explanation is presented go far beyond anything found in the Optical Illusion analogues.

The first statement in May's scientific explanation is that January has only partial sight: 'Ye han som glymsyng, and no parfit sighte' (2383). With this utterance May's account of optical phenomena becomes increasingly technical. January begins to be persuaded. Although continuing to claim that he sees 'as wel as evere I myghte' (2384), he concedes that what he saw pass between his wife and squire may have been imagined: 'me thoughte he dide thee so' (2386). The note of certainty has gone from January's recollection of his visual experience. May is quick to press home her advantage and pursues a three-pronged plan of deception. First, she appeals to science by suggesting that January's eyes are defective; second, she appeals to magic by claiming that her action in the tree has cured January's blindness; and third, she appeals to her husband's emotions by hinting that he is ungrateful:

> 'Ye maze, maze, goode sire,' quod she;
> 'This thank have I for I have maad yow see.
> Allas,' quod she, 'that evere I was so kynde!'
> (2387–9)

January capitulates and prepares to deny the existence of what has happened by suppressing the residual, still disturbing visual memory of his wife with Damian. He apologizes to May for accusing her falsely, although there still lurks the suspicion that he thought he saw the pair together, that 'Damyan hadde by thee leyn, | And that thy smok hadde leyn upon his brest' (2394–5). With astonishing speed January has moved from absolute certainty about what he saw to thinking that he saw it to banishing the image from his mind. His vision has been restored, but the effect of May's eloquence is such and his devotion to her so extreme that he might as well continue to be sightless.

To set her husband's mind completely at rest, May elaborates the scientific explanation. Just as a man waking from sleep is not always able to enjoy perfect vision until he is fully awake, so a man cured of blindness may not be able to see properly for a day or two. She suggests, menacingly, that January is likely to undergo more illusions similar to the one just experienced. He should not be too hasty in jumping to conclusions, for appearances can be deceptive (a remark which applies to May's entire argument). Finally, she warns that mental preconceptions may give rise to visual errors, an observation all too true in its application to January, whose emotions and thoughts have been so receptive to the idea that his eyes, not May, have deceived him:

> 'Ye, sire,' quod she, 'ye may wene as yow lest.
> But, sire, a man that waketh out of his sleep,
> He may nat sodeynly wel taken keep
> Upon a thyng, ne seen it parfitly,
> Til that he be adawed verraily.
> Right so a man that longe hath blynd ybe,
> Ne may nat sodeynly so wel yse,
> First whan his sighte is newe come ageyn,
> As he that hath a day or two yseyn.
> Til that youre sighte ysatled be a while,
> Ther may ful many a sighte yow bigile.
> Beth war, I prey yow; for, by hevene kyng,
> Ful many a man weneth to seen a thyng,
> And it is al another than it semeth.
> He that mysconceyveth, he mysdemeth.'
> (2396–410)

What May says has the ring of truth, considered as science, but the science is misapplied since it is used to account for an event which was not an optical illusion at all. The scientific content of her speech, therefore, has an ambivalent status. On the one hand, it impresses and persuades January more effectively than did the magical explanation May earlier espoused. This is not the only occasion on which Chaucer used scientific theory as an alternative explanation of an optical phenomenon previously accounted for in magical terms alone. When, in the Squire's Tale, a magic mirror is brought to the court of Cambyuskan, one bystander suggests that its powers may be understood 'Naturelly, by composiciouns | Of anglis and of slye reflexiouns' (SqT 229–30). On the other hand, May is patently abusing scientific knowledge for her own ends: science is shown not to have the status of objective, fixed truth, but rather to vary in its veracity according to the applications and motivations of those who employ it. One is reminded of the abuse of alchemy for personal gain as it is depicted in the Canon's Yeoman's Prologue and Tale.

The scientific element in the ending of the Merchant's Tale is not simply an isolated curiosity absent from the known analogues. It should be considered as a significant instance of the process whereby Chaucer used science imaginatively and to add stiffening to his narrative sources.[4] To inquire further into such creative practices it is necessary first to determine the intellectual context of Chaucer's references to visual theory. David C. Lindberg has described how the science of optics, or *perspectiva*, rose to preeminence among the physical sciences during the thirteenth and fourteenth centuries.[5] Influential scholars like Robert Grosseteste and Roger Bacon secured academic respectability for the discipline, drawing together optical writings by classical and Arabic authors, which they assimilated to a traditional Christian interest in the metaphysics of light

---

[4] On Chaucer's imaginative use of science see M. Manzalaoui, 'Chaucer and Science', in *Geoffrey Chaucer*, ed. Derek Brewer (London: Bell, 1974), 224–61.
[5] David C. Lindberg, *Theories of Vision from Al-Kindi to Kepler* (Chicago and London: University of Chicago Press, 1976), chs. 4–7.

and vision. The subject of *perspectiva* soon became an integral part of the arts courses at the universities. At Oxford by 1350 it was possible to study optical texts by Alhazen and Witelo as substitutes for works by Euclid.[6] Evidence of the widespread interest in optics during the fourteenth century may be found in a range of texts, from the highbrow scholastic treatise to the more popular and accessible encyclopedia, sermon exemplum and vernacular poem.

Alhazen's *De aspectibus* (written c. A.D. 1000 and translated into Latin in the early thirteenth century) was probably the most important and influential of all medieval works on *perspectiva*. The third book is devoted to the circumstances, causes, and types of visual deception. Alhazen recognizes that weak vision, such as that which supposedly afflicts January, is a significant cause of error:

> Weak sight and excess introduce error into the perception of [...] distance, for if two objects are set opposite the eye, one of which is brightly coloured and the more distant, the other weakly coloured and nearer, then (since there is no apprehension of distance without comparisons with other intervening objects) [...] the weak eye will make an uncertain comparison; and because it seems certain to the perceiver that the perception of nearer locations is more distinct than that of more distant ones, he firmly concludes that of these objects the more brightly coloured one is nearer.[7]

The Silesian scholar Witelo completed in about 1274 an authoritative compendium of optical theory, the *Perspectiva*, based on Alhazen's work and all other optical treatises extant in the West. The fourth book deals with the same topics as those found in Alhazen's book 3. Witelo points out that a weak eye takes longer than a normal, healthy eye to register visual

---

6   Pearl Kibre and Nancy G. Siraisi, 'The Institutional Setting: The Universities', in *Science in the Middle Ages*, ed. David C. Lindberg (Chicago: University of Chicago Press, 1978), 129; James A. Weisheipl, 'Curriculum of the Faculty of Arts at Oxford in the Early Fourteenth Century', *Mediaeval Studies* 26 (1964), 143–85.

7   Alhazen, *Opticae thesaurus: Alhazeni arabis libri septem [...] 1572*, 3.7.69, ed. F. Risner, Sources of Science, 94 (New York: Johnson, 1972), 101. Unless otherwise noted, the translations are mine.

events,[8] and he describes the various causes of a discrepancy which may arise between what the perceiver expects to see and what in fact he does see. It is this sort of dislocation of actual and imagined sights that May exploits so well: 'For when some object appears to visual perception as another and as if it were the real one, then the mode of apprehension makes a visual error, because the form pre-existing in the mind is applied unsuitably to another form, to which it does not correspond.'[9]

Witelo also notes how weakness of sight can increase the margin of error, giving rise to cases of mistaken identity: 'an eye affected by a bright, strongly lit colour judges all the colours it then sees to be of that same colour or of a colour mixed from it; and also through illness of the eyes a horse appears to be an ass, and Socrates is seen as Plato.'[10] We might add that a lovemaking Damian may appear to be no more than a struggling man.

There is no evidence that Chaucer was familiar with either of these works. However, he was at least aware that Alhazen and Witelo were considered to be authorities on the science of optics, for they are mentioned as such, together with Aristotle, in the Squire's Tale when the properties of the magic mirror are being debated:

> They speken of Alocen, and Vitulon,
> And Aristotle, that written in hir lyves
> Of queynte mirours and of perspectives,
> As knowen they that han hir bookes herd.
> (SqT 232–5)

Apart from the mention of Witelo, these lines derive from Jean de Meun's continuation of the *Roman de la rose*, in which there is a long speech by Nature who, in authoritative tones, explains how visual phenomena may be understood through the difficult science of optics (18013–43).[11] Here,

---

8   Witelo, *Vitellonis thuringopolini libri X [...]* (forming the second part of the *Opticae thesaurus*), ibid., 4.109, 167.
9   Ibid., 155, 187.
10 Ibid., 188.
11 Guillaume de Lorris and Jean de Meun, *Le Roman de la Rose*, ed. Daniel Poirion (Paris: Garnier-Flammarion, 1974). The relations between Nature's speech on optics

in what is demonstrably one source of Chaucer's knowledge of optical theory, we encounter a passage which almost certainly stimulated his ideas about the themes of the Merchant's Tale and about its ending. Nature and Genius agree that a mirror would have saved the lovers Venus and Mars a great deal of trouble. Venus could then have foreseen Vulcan's arrival and could have had her excuses ready to explain Mars's presence. She might also have been able to persuade Vulcan that adultery had not happened and that what he had seen was an illusion (18105–29). The similarities with the ending of Chaucer's poem do not need labouring. Mirrors, says Nature, can also cause illusions, and she associates with these the images produced in the mind's eye by mental and emotional aberrations, including those of the besotted lover (18239–46, 18357–404). The psychological state described by Nature, and its connection with mirror images, find echoes in Chaucer's description of January as he imagines the type of woman whom he would like to marry; erotic images of local beauties pass through his heart like the reflections one might receive from a mirror positioned in a marketplace (MerT 1577–87).

Jean de Meun provided Chaucer with a model for making optics the stuff of poetry; in the story of Mars, Venus and Vulcan he supplied a plot close to that followed in the ending of the Merchant's Tale, and he suggested a link, to be developed by Chaucer, between visual deception and sexual fantasy. The antecedents found in the *Roman*, and in the writings of Alhazen and Witelo, still fall short of giving a satisfactory framework within which to consider Chaucer's use of optical material in the Merchant's Tale. Further parts of that framework are to be found in encyclopedias and sermon exempla. Chaucer's use of the *Speculum maius* (*c.*1244) of Vincent of Beauvais is well known.[12] The first two books of

---

and the design of the poem as a whole have been discussed by Alan M. F. Gunn, *The Mirror of Love: A Reinterpretation of the 'Romance of the Rose'* (Lubbock: Texas Tech Press, 1951), 28–9, 49–50, 219–22, 266–73, 301; Patricia J. Eberle, 'The Lovers' Glass: Nature's Discourse on Optics and the Optical Design of the *Romance of the Rose*', *University of Toronto Quarterly* 46 (1976–7), 241–62.

12 Chaucer refers to Vincent's 'Estoryal Myrour' in *LGW* G 307. Scientific borrowings from the encyclopedia have been documented in the following articles by Pauline

the first part, the *Speculum naturale*, have much to say about vision and light. For instance, Vincent identifies three causes of defective vision like those which, according to May, afflict January. These are staring too long at an object of extreme whiteness or brightness, waking suddenly from sleep, and opening the eyes after a prolonged period in which they have been closed or in darkness, a circumstance close to January's as he stares amazed into the pear tree:

> [...] it happens that when someone for a long time has closed his eyes or has been in darkness, and afterwards has gone into the light, he does not see well until moderately changing light has entered from without, because, to reiterate the truth, vision is completed by a visual humour which runs to the eyes through the hollow optic nerves from the interior part of the brain, which said dry humour draws forth moderate colour.[13]

Chaucer's use of the *De proprietatibus rerum* of Bartholomew the Englishman (compiled 1230–40) has not been established, but it nevertheless contains material close to that which he used. One of the best-known encyclopedias of the later Middle Ages, it was translated into several vernaculars, including French (1372) and English (1398). In his seventh book Bartholomew deals at some length with the causes of defective vision and blindness, and it is possible to recognize in January a syndrome which the author describes. January is over sixty when the action of the Merchant's Tale begins, he is a bon viveur, and throughout his life he has given immoderate attention to women. On each of these three counts, according to Bartholomew, a man is likely to suffer partial or complete loss of vision.

Aiken: 'Vincent of Beauvais and Dame Pertelote's Knowledge of Medicine', *Speculum* 10 (1935), 281–7; 'Arcite's Illness and Vincent of Beauvais', *PMLA* 51 (1936), 361–9; 'The Summoner's Malady', *Studies in Philology* 33 (1936), 40–4; 'Vincent of Beauvais and Chaucer's Knowledge of Alchemy', *Studies in Philology* 41 (1944), 371–89; 'Vincent of Beauvais and the "Houres" of Chaucer's Physician', *Studies in Philology* 53 (1956), 22–4.

13 Vincent of Beauvais, *Bibliotheca mundi: Vincentii bellovacensis speculum quadruplex; naturale, doctrinale, morale, historiale [...] omnia nunc accurate recognita [...] opera et studio theologorum Benedictorum collegii Vedastini in alma academia Duacensi [...]* (Douai: B. Belleri, 1624), i, bk. 25, chap. 34, col. 1797.

A declining vitality in the humours causes gradual blindness in old age: 'ferst here yȝen wexen dymme, and þanne þey haueþ defaute of siȝt, and at þe last þe vertu of siȝt failleþ, and bey lesiþ al here siȝt'.[14] Food and drink may affect vision intermittently: 'defaute of siȝt is nout contynual but it comeþ, and gooþ, for it waxiþ, and wayneþ by diuersite of mete and of drink'.[15] Lechery also causes the eye to suffer: 'Hechinge and smertinge of yȝen comen somtyme of outward þinges, as [...] of fleischlich likinge and ofte seruyse of Venus þat corrumpiþ and dissolueþ þe spiritis and þe humour cristallyne.'[16]

January's reaction to blindness is one of possessive jealousy of May 'Lest that his wyf sholde falle in som folye' (MerT 2074). Bartholomew warns that blindness is a wretched state and causes emotional disturbance. The blind man lives in a state of anxiety and fears desertion by his friends, a fear that in January's case is fully justified: 'Selde he doþ, ouȝt sikirly; wel nyȝe alway he doutiþ and drediþ [...] þe blinde is wrecchid, for in house he dar noþing tristily doo, and in þe way he drediþ lest his felawe wole forsake him.'[17] Bartholomew ends on a moral note: 'Better is to a man to be blynde and haue his iȝen iput out þan haue iȝen and be desceyued and bigiled with fikelinge and flateringe þerof.'[18] The narrator of the Merchant's Tale makes the identical point as the plan of Damian and May to deceive the blind January gathers momentum:

> O Januarie, what myghte it thee availle,
> Thogh thou myghte se as fer as shippes saille?
> For as good is blynd deceyved be
> As to be deceyved whan a man may se.
> (2107–10)

---

14 Bartholomew, *On the Properties of Things: John Trevisa's Translation of 'Bartholomacus Anglicus de proprietatibus rerum'*, ed. M. C. Seymour et al. (Oxford: Clarendon Press, 1975), i, bk. 7, ch. 20, 364, lines 8–12.
15 Ibid., ch. 19, 363, lines 19–21.
16 Ibid., ch. 15, 359, lines 32–3; 360, lines 3–5.
17 Ibid., ch. 20, p. 365, lines 15–16, 27–9.
18 Ibid., lines 35–7.

The usefulness of optical data in pointing a moral was taken further in sermon literature. There is a remarkable and widespread collection of exempla devoted to the moralizing of information taken from the science of *perspectiva*, the *Liber de oculo morali*, compiled in the 1260s by Peter of Limoges. The work has no direct bearing on the Merchant's Tale, but it represents the tendency of preachers to make systematic use of visual phenomena as similitudes for spiritual and moral states.[19] Chaucer's probable familiarity with such exempla can be demonstrated by referring to Robert Holkot's commentary on Wisdom (written *c*.1333) which Chaucer is known to have consulted.[20] In his twenty-ninth *lectio*, Holkot relates each of the seven cardinal sins to both the spiritual and the physical blindness which they separately cause. Holkot begins with pride, which blinds by its excessive splendour. The sun is compared to the display of worldly glory, which prevents the inner eye from seeing spiritual truth by its great brightness. Showy intellectuals and fortunate and rich men are likely to be affected by this sin. The rich, powerful and ingenious ruler of Pavye comes to mind, and forcibly so as Holkot goes on to quote from a letter of Seneca to Lucilius a story similar in moral to that of the Merchant's Tale:

> [...] his [Seneca's] wife had a certain female servant, who suddenly became blind; she ceased to see. The story sounds incredible, but it is true: she did not know that she was blind, but kept asking her attendant if she might leave the house in which she lived, saying that it was too dark. Seneca adds: what makes us smile in her case happens to the rest of us; nobody understands that he is himself greedy or covetous. The blind ask for a guide while we wander without one, saying: 'I am not self-seeking, but living in my city demands great expenses. It is not my fault that I have a choleric disposition, or that I have not settled on a definite way of life; it is due to my youth.' Why do we deceive ourselves? The evil that affects us is not external, it is

---

19   For recent studies of Peter's work see David L. Clark, 'Optics for Preachers: The *De oculo morali* by Peter of Limoges', *Michigan Academician* 9 (1977), 329–43; Gudrun Schleusener-Eichholz, 'Naturwissenschaft und Allegorese: der *Tractatus de oculo morali* des Petrus von Limoges', *Frühmittelalterliche Studien* 12 (1978), 258–309.
20   Kate Oelzner Petersen, *On the Sources of the 'Nonne Prestes Tale'*, Radcliffe College Monographs, 10 (Boston: Ginn, 1898), 98–118; Robert A. Pratt, 'Some Latin Sources of the Nonnes Preest on Dreams', *Speculum* 52 (1977), 538–70.

within us, it is seated in our very vitals. For that same reason we achieve health with all the more difficulty, because we do not know that we are sick.[21]

Just as texts with a scientific bias provide a framework for May's final speech, so the moralizing of optical data gives a context for the theme of inner blindness as it occurs in the Merchant's Tale. For Seneca's moral applies to January: the true cause of his blindness is within. When January becomes physically blind, it is but the external manifestation of internal disorders. He is never more blind than when his sight is restored and May is able to persuade her husband that his eyes do not see the truth. They do, but January does not know what the truth is. Outer and inner blindness have become as one. The causes of January's lack of insight may be divided into four categories: intellectual, spiritual, erotic and emotional.[22]

January's observations on the advantages of marrying a young woman reveal a worldly wisdom which is actually a false perspicacity. Older women are too knowing, too resistant to manipulation, says January (MerT 1415–30), but, on the other hand, he is unaware of the dangers of marrying a young woman like May. He accepts the flattering words of Placebo because they are in accord with his own estimation of himself:

> And trewely, it is an heigh corage
> Of any man that stapen is in age
> To take a yong wyf [...]
> (1513–15)

Justinus's more realistic counsel – 'Ye shul nat plesen hire fully yeres thre' (1562) – is dismissed out of hand: 'Straw for thy Senek, and for thy proverbes!' (1567). January is prepared to accept only arguments which reflect his own preconceived opinions.

---

21 Robert Holkot, *M. Roberti Holkoth [...] in librum sapienttae regis Salominis praclectiones CCXIII*, [ed. J. Ryterus] ([Basel], 1586), *lectio* 29, 104. See also Seneca, *Ad Lucilium epistle morales*, epistle 50, ed. and trans. Richard M. Gummere (London: Heinemann, 1917), i, 330–3, on which my translation is based.

22 For another discussion of January's inner blindness see Robert B. Burlin, *Chaucerian Fiction* (Princeton: Princeton University Press, 1977), 207–10.

Spiritual myopia is evident when January initiates a specious discussion on paradise. He presents the dilemma as an academic one: 'Assoilleth me this question, I preye' (1654); and his manner is urbane to the point of cynicism. January understands that no man may enjoy two perfect states of bliss, that is, both on earth and in heaven. Yet his marriage to May promises to be so full of 'felicitee, [...] ese and lust, | [...] So delicat, withouten wo and stryf, | That I shal have myn hevene in erthe heere' (1642–3, 1646–7). If heaven itself is bought with tribulation and penance, how may heavenly bliss be attained by a happily married man such as himself? Although January confesses to 'drede' (1653) in thinking about this issue, it is clear that his worries about the salvation of his soul do not run very deep. Justinus points out that his master's view of the afterlife is simplistic. He offers an alternative perspective which includes a sense of the complexity and irony of human experience and of the relations between earthly and heavenly states. May, he suggests, might prove to be January's purgatory on earth, 'Goddes meene and Goddes whippe' (1671), whereby his soul will be fitted for heaven. In the event, January's inner blindness is so severe that he is impervious to the purgatory inflicted by May's actions and so also to their spiritual benefits.

January's blindness in erotic matters is clear from the passage already mentioned, in which he creates mental images of sexually attractive women before securing the real woman who will match his fantasy. January's choice of May is his own, made without consulting his advisers. The Merchant observes that this procedure is perhaps not very farsighted:

> He atte laste apoynted hym on oon,
> And leet alle othere from his herte goon,
> And chees hire of his owene auctoritee;
> For love is blynd alday, and may nat see.
> (1595–8)

The opinions of others count for nothing, such is the force of January's conviction that he is right: 'inpossible it were to repplye | Agayn his choys, this was his fantasye' (1609–10). January wanders further into the realms of erotic illusion. May, whom 'to biholde it semed fayerye' (1743), fills him with vicarious sexual pleasure and with intimations of virility (1750–64).

After a night of feverish lovemaking, and in the cold light of morning, May's perception of her husband's antics brooks no pretence: she sees him as utterly devoid of youth and sexual appeal (1851–4). January's sexual delusions help conceal from him the possibility that a younger man than he might be regarded by May as a better lover. The detection of deception in one's own home is difficult enough, suggests the Merchant, without the further impediments which January suffers. The ruler of Pavye is 'dronken in plesaunce | In mariage' (1788–9) and so has no inkling of Damian's intentions. The narrator exclaims in apparent sympathy, 'God graunte thee thyn hoomly fo t'espye!' (1792). Eventually January does espy Damian caught in the act, but it is too late because inner afflictions enable May to misdirect her husband's interpretation of what he has seen.

January's inner condition worsens with the physical blindness which suddenly affects him, for, as previously noted, it produces an emotional disturbance in the form of possessive jealousy. So extreme is January's jealousy that he restrains May's movements by always keeping a hand on her person (2087–91). Ironically, communications between May and Damian now become more visual. Owing to January's blindness, 'privee signes' (2105) can pass between them: May motions Damian into January's garden (2150–1) and then makes a further sign with her finger to tell Damian that the time has come for him to climb into the pear tree (2209–10). Blind, ignorant of the deceptions being practised, still hoping for heavenly bliss, in a state of jealousy, controlled by his dedication to the erotic image of May, and convinced that his marriage is of the best, January has given May all his worldy possessions (2160–84). His material ruination completes the process of intellectual, spiritual, erotic and emotional bankruptcy.

The theme of inner blindness in the Merchant's Tale may have been suggested to Chaucer by one of the Blind Husband stories in which the husband is presented as a jealous man, or by an Optical Illusion story in which the husband is unaware of his own shortcomings and of his wife's infidelity.[23] Such analogues provide only a hint of a theme which Chaucer was to treat in a much more complex way. Sources for the earlier phases of

---

23 Beidler, 'Chaucer's Merchant's Tale', 276–7.

the Merchant's Tale, the *Miroir de mariage* of Eustache Deschamps and the *Elegiae Maximiani*, contain passages with some reference to blindness, but Chaucer has not used them to any considerable extent.[24] It was he who enriched the idea of inner blindness and he who introduced optical material into the closing passages of the tale. The context and probably the sources of these changes are to be found in texts which deal more directly with visual phenomena, for Chaucer's innovations are rooted in the medieval tradition of *perspectiva* as it is represented in specialized scientific works, encyclopedias, vernacular poetry and sermon exempla. The analogues to be found in Alhazen, Witelo and Bartholomew should no longer be disregarded. The *Roman de la rose*, *Speculum maius* and Wisdom commentary of Holkot are known to have been used by Chaucer, and they therefore have strong claims to be considered as even closer to the origins of his inspiration.

24 Dempster, 'Merchant's Tale', 335; Albert E. Hartung, 'The Non-Comic Merchant's Tale, Maximianus and the Sources', *Mediaeval Studies* 29 (1967), 13, 18.

PART THREE

After-Images

Is the Canon's Yeoman's Tale Apocryphal?

When Chaucer died in 1400 he left behind an unfinished work, the *Canterbury Tales*, as a series of fragments. It has been the work of scribes, editors and scholars to establish the authentic components of this multi-narrative work. The first authoritative collection, as found in the Hengwrt manuscript, omits a text included in modern editions, the Canon's Yeoman's Prologue and Tale. There are strong indications that it might not be entirely Chaucer's work, but that of an imitator, thus raising questions about the received idea of Chaucer in the minds of present-day Chaucerians.

Images

The entire topic of images was an increasingly controversial one in the late fourteenth and early fifteenth centuries. John Wyclif and his Lollard followers argued that images (e.g. of saints) fostered corruption, materialism and idolatry, while their orthodox defenders maintained that images were a legitimate means of accessing religious experience. Chaucer's associate, the lawyer John Gower, adopts aspects of the reformist position in his *Vox clamantis*, only to deploy highly emotive images in condemning the rebels of 1381. Chaucer's disciple, Thomas Hoccleve, roundly condemned Wycliffite attitudes and in his *Regiment of Princes* turns Chaucer himself into a painted icon.

Journey's End: The Prologue to the *Tale of Beryn*

The unknown author who wrote the *Beryn* prologue (*c*.1420) capitalized on the reputation of the unfinished *Canterbury Tales*. He completed it by bringing the pilgrims into Canterbury and lodging them at an inn. They then visit the shrine of Thomas Becket and other local sites of interest before embarking on the return trip. The author knew the customs of pilgrims, and local topography, very well, and was also an astute reader of Chaucer's poetry. He was probably a monk of Christ Church priory and perhaps one of the keepers of Becket's shrine, writing as part of a campaign to attract visitors to the fifth jubilee of the saint's martyrdom.

Is the Canon's Yeoman's Tale Apocryphal?*

Did Chaucer write the Canon's Yeoman's Prologue and Tale or are they by an unknown imitator? The question, unthinkable to many Chaucerians, has recently been raised by N. F. Blake in his work on the Hengwrt manuscript of the *Canterbury Tales* (Aberystwyth, National Library of Wales, Peniarth 392). Hengwrt is an early copy of Chaucer's poem but it shows no trace of the link and tale associated with the Canon's Yeoman. In the introduction to his edition of the Hengwrt manuscript Blake maintains that these pieces are not authentic.[1] Before examining his case in more detail, and in order to give it some context, I shall summarize some earlier views of the Hengwrt manuscript and its notable omission. I then wish to consider some of the implications for criticism of his claims about authorship.

Manly and Rickert dated Hengwrt to between 1400 and 1410 and described it as being of 'the highest importance'.[2] In accounting for its unique order of tales, they observed that the use of a particular ink, which has now turned distinctly yellow, coincided with parts of the manuscript which could be designated on codicological grounds as insertions made later than most of the text.[3] This and other findings tended to suggest that the Hengwrt scribe worked piecemeal, without full knowledge of what the *Canterbury Tales* comprised: he did not anticipate some items

---

* First published in *English Studies* 64 (1983), 481–90.
1 N. F. Blake, ed., *The Canterbury Tales by Geoffrey Chaucer: Edited from the Hengwrt Manuscript* (London: Arnold, 1980). Professor Blake kindly allowed me to see a copy of his introduction prior to publication.
2 John M. Manly and Edith Rickert and Others, *The Text of the Canterbury Tales; Studied on the Basis of All Known Manuscripts*, 8 vols (Chicago: University of Chicago Press, 1940), i: *Descriptions of the Manuscripts*, 268 and 276. The findings and views of Manly and Rickert are conveniently collected together in their 'The "Hengwrt" Manuscript of Chaucer's *Canterbury Tales*', *National Library of Wales Journal* 1 (1939), 59–75.
3 Manly and Rickert *Text of Canterbury Tales*, i, 270–3.

which had to be included after much of the copying was done, and did anticipate some items which never materialized. Such factors implied that the Hengwrt scribe 'had not access to Chaucer's own copies or that these copies were scattered and not easy to find'. Consequently, the order of tales found in Hengwrt does not carry Chaucer's sanction. It represented for Manly and Rickert 'the earliest attempt after Chaucer's death to arrange in a single MS the tales and links left unarranged by him', many of which had circulated among friends and associates before 1400.[4] The Canon's Yeoman's Prologue and Tale are absent from Hengwrt (as is some other, less extensive material) because they did not reach the scribe in time to be included. Their authenticity need not be in doubt since they appear in each of the other four manuscripts dated to between 1400 and 1410.[5]

Doyle and Parkes have offered some modifications to the conclusions of Manly and Rickert. They allow for the possibility that the Canon's Yeoman's Prologue and Tale may have been copied into a section of the manuscript which was subsequently lost.[6] Section IV of Hengwrt (ff. 112–234), containing the Second Nun's Tale, is 'the most disturbed and fragmented in content sequence', with gaps left between tales and prologues. It shows signs of delayed copying and probably the use of a number of short exemplars which were available for a limited period of time.[7] The composition of quire

---

[4] Ibid., ii: *Classification of the Manuscripts*, 477; and see 489–90. Manly's views on the state of the *Canterbury Tales* manuscripts immediately before and after 1400 are described by Germaine Dempster, 'Manly's Conception of the Early History of the *Canterbury Tales*', *PMLA* 61 (1946), 382–90.

[5] Manly and Rickert, *Text of Canterbury Tales*, ii, 434.

[6] A. I. Doyle and M. B. Parkes, 'Palaeographical Introduction', in Geoffrey Chaucer, *The Canterbury Tales: A Facsimile and Transcription of the Hengwrt Manuscript, with Variants from the Ellesmere Manuscripts*, ed. Paul G. Ruggiers; intros. by Donald C. Baker and by Doyle and Parkes, A Variorum Edition of the Works of Geoffrey Chaucer, i (Norman, Okla.: University of Oklahoma Press, 1979), xxvi and xxviii; see also their 'The Production of Copies of the *Canterbury Tales* and the *Confessio Amantis* in the Early Fifteenth Century', in *Medieval Scribes, Manuscripts and Libraries: Essays Presented to N. R. Ker*, ed. M. B. Parkes and Andrew G. Watson (London: Scolar Press, 1978), 185–94.

[7] Ibid., xxix.

22 (ff. 161–76), containing the final 343 lines of the Franklin's Tale, the tale of 'The Nonne', and the first 238 lines of the Clerk's Prologue and Tale, exemplifies this state of affairs. It is double the normal length (16 leaves) and the Second Nun's Tale alone is written in an ink of a distinct shade, a grayer tint being used for the tales at either side. Doyle and Parkes suggest that, in the process of writing the Franklin's Tale, 'the scribe learned that he would have to place *SNPT*, the exemplar of which was not yet to hand, before *ClPT*, which he already had' and so he inserted eight extra leaves to accommodate the Second Nun's Prologue and Tale. For the copyist at this stage in his work the tale of the Nun was not one to be followed by a linked Canon's Yeoman's Tale. Doyle and Parkes attribute its absence either to the 'dislocation of exemplars of connected portions' of the *Canterbury Tales* or to the constriction of space between the Franklin's Tale and Clerk's Prologue.[8]

Blake differs from Parkes and Doyle in assuming that the scribe or editor of the Hengwrt manuscript possessed all the fragments of the *Canterbury Tales* before he started work. The assumption derives from Blake's reconstruction of the fate of the supposedly complete set of fragments possessed by Chaucer at the time of his death. He maintains that 'literary executors' engaged the Hengwrt scribe to make from these 'the first "complete" copy of the poem'. Blake accepts that changes of ink may evidence different periods of copying, but for him it does not follow that the scribe did not possess all of the fragments before undertaking his work. Blake argues that the different inks may be evidence of the scribe's or editor's developing conception of the order of the tales.[9] He also parts company with other scholars in perceiving a distinct rationale behind their arrangement. In Section IV, for example, those tales before the Second Nun's Prologue and Tale are without links while those after it are connected. 'It follows that all fragments were available to the editor before the manuscript was copied so that this order could be imposed upon them'. Coupling this conclusion,

---

8   Ibid., xxxi and xxxii.
9   N. F. Blake, 'The Relationship between the Hengwrt and the Ellesmere Manuscripts of the *Canterbury Tales*', *Essays and Studies* 32 (1979), 4–6; see also his review of the Hengwrt facsimile in 'Chaucer Manuscripts and Texts', *Review* 3 (1981), 219–32; and J. S. P. Tatlock, 'The *Canterbury Tales* in 1400', *PMLA* 50 (1935), 107.

which extends to the entire *Canterbury Tales*, with the supposition that the scribe's copytext was Chaucer's own complete set of fragments, Blake asserts that the 'corollary of this is that whatever is not in Hg may be considered spurious'.[10] The Canon's Yeoman's Prologue and Tale are therefore spurious. Blake thinks it likely that the editor of Hengwrt knew that the Canon's Yeoman's Prologue and Tale were being written to be linked to the Second Nun's Tale, so held back the tale of the Nun. But the unknown imitator's work was not ready in time and so the scribe filled in the space previously reserved with the Second Nun's Tale.

From the foregoing, incomplete account of Blake's position it can be seen that, by comparison with earlier writers on the same topic, he has adopted an unusual attitude towards the Hengwrt manuscript. It will be clear, too, that there are a number of objections to his case, as here presented. For instance, the sorting of tales in Section IV of Hengwrt into a group without links and a group with, does not necessarily mean that the editor had all of them in his possession before copying began. He may simply have divided the tales into these categories as they became available. Or, the claim that whatever is not in Hengwrt may be considered spurious is not a *corollary* since it depends in part on a proposition that is not demonstrated (that the scribe's copytext was Chaucer's own set of fragments). Or again, the notion that the editor held back the Second Nun's Prologue and Tale in the hope that the Canon's Yeoman's Prologue and Tale would be ready to be included with it does not seem to square with Blake's acceptance of a conclusion reached by Parkes and Doyle that the space reserved in the manuscript was tailor-made for 'The Nonne' alone. If the editor hoped for additional material, why did he not allow space for that too? Other points of criticism have been made by reviewers of Blake's edition of Hengwrt,

---

10   Blake, 'Relationship', 6–10. See also Walter W. Skeat, *The Evolution of the Canterbury Tales*, Chaucer Society, 2nd ser., 38 (1907; repr. New York: Haskell House, 1968), 10–11. Blake considers some literary grounds for rejecting the Canon's Yeoman's Prologue and Tale in his 'On Editing the *Canterbury Tales*', in *Medieval Studies for J. A. W. Bennett*, ed. P. L. Heyworth (Oxford: Clarendon Press, 1981) 107–9. I am grateful to Professor Blake for sending me a xeroxed typescript of his article prior to publication.

Is the Canon's Yeoman's Tale Apocryphal? 147

who tend to reinforce positions close to Manly and Rickert and Parkes and Doyle.[11] It would be risky to predict on the basis of their reception of Blake's edition whether or not his views will gain currency. Since the debate leads on all sides towards hypothesis and speculation about the early manuscript history of the *Canterbury Tales*, it is unlikely ever to be resolved on palaeographical grounds unless fresh evidence is produced.

It may therefore be helpful at this stage in the debate to give some thought to the opinions of critics on the Canon's Yeoman's Prologue and Tale. For, if nothing else, Blake's assertions have the effect of disturbing preconceptions about this part of the *Canterbury Tales*. The fountainhead of modern critical writing is Muscatine's *Chaucer and the French Tradition*.[12] For him, the tale is an example of the naturalist strain in Chaucer's work. In this mode Chaucer explores the 'world of matter', reserving a more conventional style, as in the Second Nun's Tale, for dealing with the spiritual world. The poem 'expresses [...] a distinction between false alchemy and true, between men's alchemy and God's'. Noting the lack of previous criticism, he proffers this reading as 'rather hypothetical' while admitting that few other works by Chaucer appear to give up their meaning – a warning against alchemy – quite so readily. The 'unassimilable lump' of the Canon's Yeoman's Tale can be accounted for if it is recognized that 'Chaucer's realism is ultimately symbolic'. So Muscatine draws attention to those parts of the poem which confer meaning on the practice of alchemy: it is a blind materialism, a kind of idolatry, and infernal. Here, Muscatine mentions as 'perhaps something more than coincidence' the contrast with the spiritual world of St Cecilia

---

11 The reviews known to me at the time of writing are Martin Wakelin, 'Go, Litel Book', *Times Educational Supplement*, 7 November 1980, 23; T. A. Shippey, 'Between Ellesmere and Hengwrt', *Times Literary Supplement*, 16 January 1981, 60; Barry Windeatt, 'Master Copy', *Times Higher Education Supplement*, 20 March 1981, 19; and John H. Fisher, forthcoming in *Analytical and Enumerative Bibliography*. I was able to see a typescript xerox of this review by courtesy of Mr Christopher Wheeler of Edward Arnold, London.
12 Charles Muscatine, *Chaucer and the French Tradition: A Study in Style and Meaning* (Berkeley and Los Angeles: University of California Press, 1957), 197–8 and 213–21.

in the preceding tale. She conquers fire by enduring torture whereas the alchemists' fire affects their appearance and gets out of control; and Cecilia has an inner vision but they are morally blind.

From these suggestive remarks later writers have developed an elaborate range of contrasts to show how the Canon's Yeoman's Prologue and Tale are balanced against the Second Nun's Tale. In an unpublished dissertation, J. E. Grennen demonstrated that the two tales are both parts of 'the same basic vision'. Images of unity, wisdom, faith, and good works in the Second Nun's Tale are opposed by those of multiplicity, folly, credulousness and misguided work in the Canon's Yeoman's Tale.[13] More recently, Bruce A. Rosenberg has made some observations on the crucible-like nature of Cecilia's bath, on epithets of burning in the saint's legend and on colour contrast in the two tales;[14] and K. M. Olmert, in an exploration of the moral dimensions of the Canon's Yeoman's Tale, has drawn attention to contrasting ideas of 'busyness', 'pryvetee', miracles and faith. He makes the general statement:

> The position of *The Canon's Yeoman's Tale*, following *The Second Nun's Tale*, clearly emphasizes the religious tone of *The Canon's Yeoman's Tale*, and prompts the reader to examine *The Second Nun's Tale* as a significant factor in the immediate context of *The Canon's Yeoman's Tale*, because it offers thematic opposition to it.[15]

Thus one strand of criticism of the Canon's Yeoman's Prologue and Tale derives from a consideration of their position as adjacent to the Second

---

13 Joseph Edward Grennen, 'Jargon Transmuted: Alchemy in Chaucer's Canon's Yeoman's Tale', Diss. Fordham Univ., 1960, ch. 6; for abstract see *Dissertation Abstracts International* 22 (1961–2), 859. Grennen developed his interpretations in 'The Canon's Yeoman and the Cosmic Furnace: Language and Meaning in the Canon's Yeoman's Tale', *Criticism* 4 (1962), 225–40; and 'Saint Cecilia's "Chemical Wedding": The Unity of the *Canterbury Tales*, Fragment VIII', *JEGP* 65 (1966), 466–81.
14 Bruce A. Rosenberg, 'The Contrary Tales of the Second Nun and the Canon's Yeoman', *Chaucer Review* 2 (1968), 278–91; and see his 'Reason and Revelation in the *Canterbury Tales*', Diss. Ohio State University, 1965; abstract in *Dissertation Abstracts International* 26 (1965–6), 1654.
15 K. Michael Olmert, 'The *Canon's Yeoman's Tale*: An Interpretation', *Annuale Medievale* 8 (1967), 71.

Nun's Tale. The principle of juxtaposing like with unlike in a mutually enriching way appears to be an example of the practice adopted by Chaucer with, say, the Knight's Tale and Miller's Tale. There, the fabliau with its mimicry of courtly behaviour has almost the status of a commentary on the preceding romance while offering at the same time an alternative set of values. Yet the Canon's Yeoman's Tale is unlike the Miller's Tale in the extent to which it leans on its companion tale for positive appraisal. Much can and has been said in appreciation of the Miller's Tale in its own right and it is only to perceive a further dimension of its meaning that one needs to take account of its relations with the Knight's Tale. But what critics have said in an approving way of the Canon's Yeoman's Prologue and Tale depends to a considerable and unusual extent on viewing them as the second half of a fragment which begins with the Second Nun's Tale. Now there are undoubtedly other approaches to the Canon's Yeoman's Prologue and Tale,[16] but the dominant and most influential approach adopted by present-day critics is the one that views them as complementary to the Second Nun's Tale.

Criticism of the Canon's Yeoman's Prologue and Tale is therefore in a vulnerable position when viewed in relation to Blake's view that they are spurious. If we accept, for the purpose of argument, that Blake is correct, then a major buttress supporting favourable evaluation is removed. For it is then no longer permissible to read the tale as a work designed by Chaucer to echo the themes of the Second Nun's Tale. Stripped of the advantage of its customary position in the *Canterbury Tales*, it may be that the poem will speak in a different way. I therefore wish to offer a reading of the Canon's Yeoman's Prologue and Tale as a free-standing work which is not by Chaucer and so not part of the *Canterbury Tales*. By doing this I hope to discover whether or not the poem has substantial merits independent of its generally accepted location. At the same time, this strategy will be a means of testing through criticism Blake's claim that the tale is by an unknown imitator.

---

16   e.g. Pauline Aiken, 'Vincent of Beauvais and Chaucer's Knowledge of Alchemy', *Studies in Philology* 41 (1944), 371–89; and Joseph E. Grennen, 'Chaucer and the Commonplaces of Alchemy', *Classica Mediaevalia* 26 (1965), 306–33.

For if the conclusion of the following reading is a *reductio ad absurdum*, namely that the unknown imitator is indistinguishable from Chaucer, then there will be grounds for discarding Blake's contention.

It is not an easy matter to abandon preconceptions and read the prologue and tale of the Canon's Yeoman as apocryphal. But it ought to be possible, given that readers do approach *Gamelyn* in this way even though it was once thought to be integral to the *Canterbury Tales*. The task is made more difficult because the author of the prologue has made every effort to anchor his work at a precise point in Chaucer's pilgrimage by providing indications of authenticity. The Canon and Yeoman arrive

> Whan ended was the lyf of Seinte Cecile,
> Er we hadde riden fully fyve mile,
> At Boghtoun under Blee [...]
> (554–6)

and there are later references to the pilgrimage and its organizer (620–6 and 1089).[17] There follows a description of the Canon done in the manner of a General Prologue portrait though the discerning eye of a pilgrim narrator. The Host, too, plays a familiar role. He is eager to find a teller of a 'myrie tale' (597), and adopts a commonsensical attitude towards the Canon's supposed alchemical powers, which he finds difficult to reconcile with a 'sluttissh' appearance (636). A series of probing questions then breaks down the flimsy pretences of the Yeoman and his confession is soon in full flood.[18]

If this is imitation, it is superb. The reader feels himself to be on familiar territory and, if anything, living the pilgrimage more intensely than usual. The sudden appearance of extra pilgrims is a brilliant innovation, and, as such, comparable with the Host's interruption of *Thopas*. Other literary

---

17 Line references are to F. N. Robinson, ed., *The Works of Geoffrey Chaucer*, 2nd edn (London: Oxford University Press, 1957). Lines 892–7 might also be taken as referring to the Host, who asks just such a question at 636–9.
18 See Olmert, 'Canon's Yeoman's Tale', 73–6 on the observations made by the narrator and Host; and also Lawrence V. Ryan, 'The Canon's Yeoman's Desperate Confession', *Chaucer Review* 8 (1974), 297–310.

qualities demand that the prologue be closely associated with Chaucer's work: the confessional mode is also employed in the prologues to tales by the Pardoner and Wife of Bath; and towards the end of his prologue, the Yeoman alludes to that well known topic of Chaucer's poetry and one encountered on several occasions in the links between his tales, the distinction between game and earnest (703–19).

After such a prologue the reader has high expectations of the tale, but these are not entirely fulfilled. The first section (*prima pars*) does begin by appearing to maintain some of the sophistication of what has gone before. There is an appealing irony in the notion of an alchemist's servant himself being changed from a healthy ruddiness of complexion to a leaden pallor (724–9) – the reverse of the hoped-for change from lead to gold – and in the ultimate effects of pursuing the science, which are to make men impoverished instead of wealthy (731–41). After this point, the literary effects become rather more obvious. The evaluation of alchemy as an 'elvysshe' practice which promotes hellish confusion and rancour as well as the wasting of property and wealth is made clear in so many words on a number of occasions. For example:[19]

> [...] Withouten doute,
> Though that the feend noght in oure sighte hym shewe,
> I trowe he with us be, that ilke shrewe!
> In helle, where that he is lord and sire,
> Nis ther moore wo, ne moore rancour ne ire.
> Whan that oure pot is broke, as I have sayd,
> Every man chit, and halt hym yvele apayd.
> (915–21)

The reiteration of a message and the admonitory tone in which it is delivered combine to give to the content an air of stasis, sterility and monotony after the dynamism, richness and varied voices of the prologue, as if the author is losing interest and control. This state of affairs is not helped by the sporadic listing of half-understood alchemical hardware and procedures. The Yeoman's avowal of ignorance does not exactly excite the reader's interest:

---

19   See also lines 750–3, 830–51, 884–97 and 955–71.

> Ther is also ful many another thyng
> That is unto oure craft apertenyng.
> Though I by ordre hem nat reherce kan,
> By cause that I am a lewed man,
> Yet woll I telle hem as they come to mynde,
> Thogh I ne kan nat sette hem in hir kynde [...]
> (784–9)[20]

Pars secunda differs from *prima pars* more through its degree of emphasis than through a change of theme, for as a tale it illustrates those same views on alchemy which have already been insistently made. Thus the alchemist of the tale is virtually a devil incarnate, 'a feend [...] as hymselven is' (984),[21] instead of being simply – like the alchemist described in the first part – guilty of diabolical practices. The worst fault of *pars secunda* is pointless repetition, almost as if it were written as an exercise in creating a Chaucerian tale out of the material available in the prologue and *prima pars*.[22] The narrator is right when he says 'it dulleth me to ryme' (1093). We read again of the Yeoman's loss of ruddy cheeks (1094–1100), of a conjuring trick which is repeated three times with small variations, and of a canon who is an alchemist but who is not, as is awkwardly explained, the same man as his master:[23]

> This chanon was my lord, ye wolden weene?
> Sire hoost, in feith, and by the hevenes queene,
> It was another chanoun, and nat hee,
> That kan an hundred foold moore subtiltee.
> (1088–91)

Apart from the elementary plot the major variation of *pars secunda* is in its treatment of moral blindness. The duped priest is blinded by greed:

---

20 Continued to line 829; and see 852–61.
21 See also lines 972–89 and 1065–73.
22 See A. V. C. Schmidt's remarks on the thinness of the main narrative material in his edition of *The General Prologue to The Canterbury Tales and the Canon's Yeoman's Prologue and Tale* (London: University of London Press, 1974), 44.
23 R. G. Baldwin unconvincingly argues that the Canons are, after all, identical, in his 'The Yeoman's Canons: A Conjecture', *JEGP* 61 (1962), 232–43.

> O sely preest! o sely innocent!
> With coveitise anon thou shalt be blent!
> O gracelees, ful blynd is thy conceite [...]
> (1076-8)

And he is led into believing what his eyes appear to tell him as he watches the conjuror-alchemist at work. 'Multiplying' is a cause of spiritual and intellectual myopia (1391-3 and 1413-22). A glance at the Second Nun's Tale shows that this idea is not so much new with the Canon's Yeoman's Tale as the repetition of topics already found in the life of St Cecilia. The impression of a deep-lying antithesis between the tales, as is found elsewhere in the *Canterbury Tales*, is more superficial than actual. For the lesson to which the narrator points is the same as that taught by the saint to her persecutor, Almachius: that the eye of the body is so fascinated by the material world and its precious stones (in his case an idol) that the vision of the spiritual eye is affected:

> Ther lakketh no thyng to thyne outter yën
> That thou n'art blynd; for thyng that we seen alle
> That it is stoon, – that men may wel espyen, –
> That ilke stoon a god thow wolt it calle.
> I rede thee, lat thyn hand upon it falle,
> And taste it wel, and stoon thou shalt it fynde,
> Syn that thou seest nat with thyne eyen blynde.
> (498-504)

In this fundamental respect, the Canon's Yeoman's Tale is little more than a recast version of the work which it is designed to follow.

It is then my contention that there is a gradual deterioration of literary quality from the Prologue through *prima pars* to *pars secunda* of the Canon's Yeoman's Tale. Whereas the prologue is dynamic but controlled, varied in its tone and voices and profuse in its possibilities for meaning, the tale becomes progressively more disordered, repetitive and derivative. It ends in disarray and mumbo-jumbo as the seemingly uninstructed Yeoman quotes alchemical utterances from Arnold of Villanova and Senior (1428-71). The prologue is so brilliantly conceived as part of the fabric of the *Canterbury Tales* that it is pointless to assume that it is by anyone but

Chaucer; its momentum is carried over into *prima pars* of the tale but not sustained, as if this work has been caught in the process of revision; *pars secunda* is so devoid of invention and creative energy that it may well be the work of an imitator.

Such a conclusion has separate consequences for critical writing on the Canon's Yeoman's Tale and for the assumption, borrowed from Blake, from which this argument began. The criticism inspired by Muscatine is not vitiated because much of what has been said about the relation between the Second Nun's Tale and the Canon's Yeoman's Prologue and Tale could equally well be said without the presence of *pars secunda*, and it is significant that this should be so. As for the Blake assumption we have indeed reached the absurd point of saying that the Canon's Yeoman's Prologue and Tale are not by Chaucer but two thirds is. In such circumstances the logical course of action is to reject the idea that because a part of the *Canterbury Tales* is not the Hengwrt manuscript it is not therefore genuine. Palaeography, because it deals in dates, objects and factual information, has a rhetoric of rationality which may sometimes conceal irrational thought. Criticism, allegedly subjective and impressionistic, may sometimes be a surer guide to authorship.

To say that *pars secunda* of the Canon's Yeoman's Tale may be apocryphal is actually to offer no more than a hypothetical explanation of its inadequacies since the argument is based on personal readings that have the status of unverifiable evidence. Other hypotheses are also admissible on the basis of these or similar readings. The first is more an elaboration than a contradiction. I have viewed the deterioration of literary quality in the tale from the standpoint of the prologue but it may be that the correct perspective is precisely the opposite one. It may be that *pars secunda*, though not by Chaucer, was possessed by him and provided him with the inspiration for the prologue and *prima pars*. *Pars secunda* may then have been retouched by a scribe or editor for inclusion in the *Canterbury Tales*. In that case, the Canon's Yeoman's Prologue and Tale would represent a cross-section of various stages in Chaucer's creative activity, from source material through to the conception of new pilgrims. If this were true, the

Is the Canon's Yeoman's Tale Apocryphal?

role played by *pars secunda* would be not unlike that proposed for *Gamelyn* according to Skeat, were Chaucer ever to have reworked that tale.[24]

An alternative hypothesis has recently been put forward by Hartung, who believes *pars secunda* to be authentic but not intended for inclusion in the *Canterbury Tales*. The reference to 'worshipful chanons religious' (992) which does not sit happily with a later allusion to 'Sire hoost' (1089) – if indeed Harry Bailly is being addressed – tends to support the idea that the story of a deceitful canon was meant for another audience.[25] Although Hartung's views do not square with mine, they are an attempt to account for a similar perplexity about the precise status of *pars secunda*.

The end result of my attempt to test through critical reading the authenticity of the Canon's Yeoman's Prologue and Tale is no less hedged with conditional and subjective tenses than the opinions reached through palaeography. If on both fronts the arguments are inconclusive this ought not to be taken as a sign that the debate over this work can only lead to reductive futility. On the contrary, Blake's views, controversial as they are, afford an occasion to undertake a reassessment of one of Chaucer's poems. Such an opportunity ought to be welcomed not least because, as Hartung's article shows, there lingers in the post-Muscatine world some unease about the place of a part of the Canon's Yeoman's offering within the *Canterbury Tales*. If we are not about to witness the astonishing sight of a piece of the *Tales* detaching itself from the canon of Chaucer's work, critics may nevertheless be stimulated to consider the preconceptions they take to a work because it is thought to be by Chaucer. Perhaps they will also examine afresh the Chaucerian apocrypha which, like paintings once thought to be genuine and subsequently shown to be fakes, have for too long been consigned to the limbo-land of criticism. If such issues are broached, the debate about the authenticity of the Canon's Yeoman's Prologue and Tale promises to be far-reaching in its implications.

---

24 Skeat, *Evolution*, 11.
25 Albert E. Hartung, '"Pars secunda" and the Development of the Canon's Yeoman's Tale', *Chaucer Review* 12 (1977), 111–28. See also Paull Franklin Baum, 'The Canon's Yeoman's Tale', *Modern Language Notes* 40 (1925), 153–4.

Images*

The plural in the title of this essay indicates a twofold application of the word. In the first place, 'image' denotes the familiar literary device whereby writers fashion a visual impression of a place, person or thing, whether for literal or figurative use. However, in the period covered by this book, 'image' also applied to the representation of religious objects, people and scenes (whether carved, sculpted or painted) in churches and elsewhere.[1] The use of such images was a source of much debate. My topic is the way in which the use of literary images in secular writing becomes embroiled in the controversy over religious images.

Secular and religious images, whether verbal, graphic or plastic, belong in the same frame of reference because medieval writers showed no compunction about transferring the terms of religious image-making to secular contexts, and because the interpretation of all images belongs to the same economy of mind: they function as sense signs producing mental simulacra in the imagination, which are in turn processed by the faculties of reason and understanding.[2]

The emphasis of the present essay is on two secular writers, John Gower (*c*.1340–1408) and Thomas Hoccleve (1367?–1426), who were active when

---

* First published in *A Companion to Medieval English Literature and Culture c.1350–c.1500*, ed. Peter Brown (Oxford: Blackwell, 2009), 307–21.
1 *MED* 1a, 1b, 2a.
2 James Simpson, *Reform and Cultural Revolution*, Oxford English Literary History, 2: *1350–1547* (Oxford: Oxford University Press, 2002), 389, 436–7; Douglas Kelly, *Medieval Imagination: Rhetoric and the Poetry of Courtly Love* (Madison: University of Wisconsin Press, 1978), pp. 26–9; Nicolette Zeeman, 'The Idol of the Text', in *Images, Idolatry, and Iconoclasm in Late Medieval England: Textuality and the Visual Image*, ed. Jeremy Dimmick, James Simpson and Nicolette Zeeman (Oxford: Oxford University Press, 2002), 43–4; V. A. Kolve, *Chaucer and The Imagery of Narrative: The First Five Canterbury Tales* (London: Arnold, 1984), 20–32.

the debate on images had taken a particular turn, in response to radical ideas promoted by the Lollard followers of the Oxford reformer, John Wyclif. Although both Gower and Hoccleve are clear-cut in their stated attitudes towards Lollard issues, their literary practice reveals a much more ambiguous and conflicted set of ideas.[3]

John Gower's *Vox clamantis*

For Gower in *Vox clamantis* 2.10, the word *imago* or 'image' means a religious object such as the statue of a saint.[4] He is particularly exercized by its capacity to distract believers from focusing attention on the essence of the faith, to the extent that the image, rather than what it signifies, becomes the object of veneration. Gower condemns such image-worship in forthright terms: Christians thereby become traitors to God and void of reason. For in praying to statues carved in wood and stone they are worshipping the mute products of their own creation, not their Creator. It effects an inversion, since the natural world was made to be servant, not master. Simple logic reveals the insanity of subjection to carved images, for the same tree that provides wood for a statue is also used to make a plough, or light a fire (Isaiah 44:13–20). Graven images may, however, be used in positive and constructive ways, as a means to strengthen devotion to God and the saints. But they are rendered worthless if the intention behind their manufacture is to elicit offerings from the devout, or to display the wealth of the donor. Furthermore, God explicitly prohibited to Moses any attempt

---

3   Paul Strohm, 'Hoccleve, Lydgate and the Lancastrian Court', in *The Cambridge History of Medieval English Literature*, ed. David Wallace (Cambridge: Cambridge University Press, 1999), 660.
4   Latin text in *The Complete Works of John Gower*, ed. George Campbell Macaulay (Oxford: Clarendon Press, 1899–1902), iv (1902); trans. Eric W. Stockton, *The Major Latin Works of John Gower: The Voice of One Crying and The Tripartite Chronicle* (Seattle: University of Washington Press, 1962), 109–11.

Images 159

to create a sculptured likeness (Exodus 33). The true image of God is the human body united with the faculty of reason, and it is by virtue of this creation by God that he merits worship.

The one image that should be worshipped is the sign of the Cross, in honour of the crucified Christ. It is an image accessible not only in material form as 'wood worthy of reverence' but also as an interior image (*signa*, line 553) 'stamped on our minds'.[5] The Cross is emblematic of power (the conquering of hell, overthrow of the devil, redemption of mankind), of salvation (the defeat of death) and of personal purgation (it purifies feelings, cleanses the mind, brightens the heart). The Cross therefore expresses the distilled essence of the Christian faith: all sacred things, says Gower, 'pleasantly combine [...] together in the Cross'.[6]

Gower's argument – which is part of a more general attack on clerical vices, as found in Books 3 and 4 – has a topical application. For Gower's is one among many clamorous voices, growing in number and intensity from the late 1370s, urging a reconsideration of the nature, purpose and function of representations in paint and wood of persons and scenes from biblical and devotional sources. The hostility to religious images became so intense in some quarters that they were deliberately destroyed. Henry Knighton's *Chronicle* records a case in Leicester (before 1389) involving Richard Weytestathe, a chaplain, and the vegetarian William Smith, who used a painted wooden statue of St Katherine as fuel to cook cabbage, thus inflicting a new martyrdom.[7] At roughly the same time, according to the

---

5   *Signa* is the plural of *signum*, in general 'a mark, token, sign, indication', meanings 'very frequent in all styles and periods' (Lewis and Short I); it also designates an image in the sense of a work of art (figure, statue, picture) and is synonymous with *imago* (II C).

6   See Margaret Aston, 'Lollards and the Cross', in *Lollards and their Influence in Late Medieval England*, ed. Fiona Somerset, Jill C. Havens, and Derrick G. Pitard (Woodbridge: Boydell Press, 2003), 99–113; Anne Hudson, *The Premature Reformation: Wycliffite Texts and Lollard History* (Oxford: Clarendon Press, 1988), 307.

7   *Knighton's Chronicle 1337–1396*, ed. and trans. G. H. Martin (Oxford: Clarendon Press, 1995), 292–9. See Margaret Aston, *England's Iconoclasts*, i: *Laws against Images* (Oxford: Clarendon Press, 1988), 133–4 and Hudson, *Premature Reformation*, 76. Cf.

Chronicon Anglie, Sir John Montague removed images from the chapel of the manor at Shenley and hid them but for an image of St Katherine, which he placed in a bakehouse.[8] Such episodes were not the sudden flaring of spontaneous iconoclasm in an atmosphere of revolutionary fervour, but one outcome of a controversy that had been simmering for some time. The debate pre-dates Wyclif, who – whatever the excesses of his followers – had relatively mainstream views on the uses and abuses of images.[9]

It would be a mistake to regard the debate as one that soon polarized, or remained stable. On both radical and conservative wings there were many shades of opinion and numerous intermediate positions, as the case of Walter Hilton demonstrates.[10] So, while hostility to religious imagery came to be readily associated with the Lollard position, and an occasion for persecution and death,[11] in details that position could overlap with the views of others who would not otherwise be regarded as remotely heterodox.[12] This was especially true of the debate in its formative stages, and it was towards the end of the formative stage that Gower made his

---

Sarah Stanbury, 'The Vivacity of Images: St Katharine, Knighton's Lollards and the Breaking of Idols', in *Images, Idolatry, and Iconoclasm*, ed. Dimmick et al., 131–50 and Kathleen Kamerick, *Popular Piety and Art in the Later Middle Ages: Image Worship and Idolatry in England, 1350–1500* (New York: Palgrave, 2002), 64–7.

8 Joy H. Russell-Smith, 'Walter Hilton and a Tract in Defence of the Veneration of Images', *Dominican Studies* 7 (1954), 201.

9 Aston, *Laws against Images*, 98–104; W. R. Jones, 'Lollards and Images: The Defense of Religious Art in Later Medieval England', *Journal of the History of Ideas* 34 (1973), 29–31; Anne Hudson, ed., *Selections from English Wycliffite Writings* (Cambridge: Cambridge University Press, 1978), 180.

10 Nicholas Watson, '"Et que est huius ydoli materia? Tuipse": Idols and Images in Walter Hilton', in *Images, Idolatry, and Iconoclasm*, ed. Dimmick et al., 95–111; Kamerick, *Popular Piety*, 34–7.

11 Aston, *Laws against Images*, 122. See *Two Wycliffite Texts: The Sermon of William Taylor 1406; The Testimony of William Thorpe 1407*, ed. Anne Hudson, EETS os 31 (1993), esp. 56–61.

12 Hudson, *Premature Reformation*, 301–9; Sarah Stanbury, 'Visualizing', in *A Companion to Chaucer*, ed. Peter Brown (Oxford: Blackwell, 2000), 464–5.

Images 161

intervention, subsequently endorsing it when he revised the work *c*.1386 and again *c*.1399.[13]

In order to position Gower's views in relation to the wider debate we might compare them with those expressed in a treatise setting out Lollard attitudes to images.[14] The surviving manuscript, in London, British Library MS Additional 24202, is from the early fifteenth century and occurs in a collection of religious tracts which are 'critical of the contemporary church though not all overtly heretical'.[15] Like Gower, the author of 'a tretyse of ymagis' condemns images as no more than inert objects, emphasizes the moral and spiritual waywardness of image-worship, criticizes the motives behind their making, calls on biblical authority to support his argument, reminds his readers that the living human being (especially Christ), made in God's image, is the authentic object of worship, and identifies the Cross as exempt from his strictures. At the same time, he introduces different slants, is more specific in targeting abuses and their practitioners, and extends the agenda of items linked to image-worship. All in all it is a much more pointed and polemical piece of writing than Gower's, and reads as an intervention in a continuing and fierce controversy.

For the Lollard writer, religious images entail a heresy of representation, showing Christ and the saints in a splendour far removed from the biblical record. Underneath, the images are, as for Gower, dead – no more than brightly painted stones. Their effect on the gullible and unwary is spiritually devastating. Elaborate images cause forgetfulness of their originals, contradicting what those persons stood for (simplicity, poverty, humility) and bringing their admirers into error concerning Christ, the apostles and saints, and indeed the nature of Christian belief itself. Worse, 'rude' worshippers waste their temporal goods in making offerings to images while ignoring deeds of charity to poor, needy and ill neighbours, falsely believing that the most impressive images merit the most generous gifts. But in

---

13   J. H. Fisher, *John Gower: Moral Philosopher and Friend of Chaucer* (London: Methuen, 1965), 102.
14   Jones, 'Lollards and Images', 31–7.
15   Hudson (ed), *Selections*, 179, which see for an edition of the text.

all this they are deceived, mistaking the material image for the spiritual reality it should represent, blinded to the worthlessness of the object they adore. Instead, they attribute to it semi-magical powers, even miracles, and so become little better than heathens at the mercy of the devil. Such idols are perversions of what, ideally, they might be, as Gower also recognized: the stimulus to a devout mental image, 'bokis of lewid men to sture them on the mynde of Cristis passion'.

The kind of image the Lollard writer attacks has not arisen by chance. He is as suspicious as Gower about the intentions and ulterior motives behind their manufacture. For the manipulation of images to represent more than their unadorned scriptural source is an exercise in vainglory, reflecting the sinful state of the perpetrators. They are responsible for leading the simple people into error in order to derive material gain – 'wynnyngis', or donations. They thus promote heresy by diverting to their own use the energy and money that should be targeted at charitable work. 'They' in this instance are 'rich endowid clerks' who by virtue of this practice are blatant hypocrites, preaching charity to the poor while at the same time encouraging gifts to dead images, so depriving the poor, the bedridden and the afflicted of alms, and neglecting the hungry and cold – the very people they are bound to succour as a means of attaining heavenly bliss.[16] Images are thus a means whereby proud and covetous clerks exploit and control the unwary, devices designed by the agents of Antichrist to rob the poor of faith, hope, charity and worldly goods, and to maintain themselves in pride, greed and lust. Nor is offering to images justified on biblical grounds. It is a newfangled thing with no scriptural basis. The incontrovertible anchor-point of the biblical argument is the same for the Lollard writer as it was for Gower: the first two commandments against strange gods and graven images (Exodus 20:3–4).

Again like Gower, he directs attention away from dead, false, painted representations towards true, living counterparts. Neighbours are *quick* images, so serving the poor with charity is a better way of worshipping their maker – that is, by attention to those human forms, made in the likeness of

---

16   Aston, *Laws against Images*, 124–9.

God, that replicate Christ's poverty and suffering. And since Christ took human form, the Crucifixion is for the Lollard writer, as it was for Gower, permissible as a reminder of what Christ endured – though even here the *kind* of image is important: it should be simple, uncomplicated, unadorned.

The author of 'A tretyse of ymagis', writing when the debate had become more polarized, ventures into territory that Gower does not countenance. But the underlying attitudes towards images, as expressed by Gower and the Lollard writer, are remarkably similar. And this is surprising. For if we are used to thinking of the Lollards as developing a fundamental critique of the church, one that came to be associated with political radicalism, we are no less used to regarding Gower as conservative, if not downright reactionary, with the first book of *Vox clamantis* serving as one of the chief sources of evidence.[17] The work is prefaced by a flattering dedication to Archbishop Thomas Arundel, the persecutor of the Lollards.[18] On the other hand, the later books of *Vox clamantis* mount a sustained attack on the abuses of authority, and claim to be expressing the voice of the people.[19]

Why then this sharp disparity between the sympathies implicit in Gower's attitude to images, and the vitriol he directs at the rebels of 1381? The customary explanation adduces evidence from the textual history of *Vox clamantis:* Book 2 onwards was written before the events of 1381; Book 1 was written in direct response to them, and appears to indicate a fundamental rethinking by Gower of his political stance. It may be that Gower

---

17 David Aers, 'Vox Populi and the Literature of 1381', in *Cambridge History of Medieval English Literature*, ed. Wallace (1999), 439–44.
18 Cf. *Confessio Amantis*, Prologue 346–51, 5.1803–24, in *The English Works of John Gower*, ed. G. C. Macaulay, i, EETS es 81(1900).
19 *Vox Clamantis* 3.15, lines 1267–70; 7.25, lines 1447–70. See Judith Ferster, *Fictions of Advice: The Literature and Politics of Counsel in Late Medieval England* (Philadelphia: University of Pennsylvania Press, 1996), 129–32; Paul Miller, 'John Gower, Satiric Poet', in *Gower's 'Confessio Amantis': Responses and Reassessments*, ed. A. J. Minnis (Cambridge: Brewer, 1983), 102–5; Steven Justice, *Writing and Rebellion: England in 1381*, New Historicism, 27 (Berkeley and Los Angeles: University of California Press, 1994), 207–13; Sylvia Federico, *New Troy: Fantasies of Empire in the Late Middle Ages*, Medieval Cultures, 36 (Minneapolis: University of Minnesota Press, 2003), 3–18.

was alarmed by the tendency of the rebels to target literate figures like him, a private gentleman and landowner.[20] But it is also worth considering the claims he makes for his work as a 'mirror', producing by means of memory and association what is denied to actual sight, namely a sharper and fuller perceptiveness. In this respect, Gower's choice of genre is significant because of the dream vision's particular virtues. It allows him access to truth, the significance of which 'disturbs the depths of my heart', and enables him to create a kind of distance from the turmoil of rebellion, to achieve as need demands a sense of heightened reality, to imply that what he writes is divinely inspired, and above all to represent the uprising in striking, surreal images.

There can be little doubt that Gower recognized the power of such images to alter consciousness. He claims that dream images can provide a *better* understanding of the conditions of the time than other modes of analysis by revealing deeper structures of meaning than those apparent on the surface of events. Moreover, dreams provide what he calls 'memorable tokens' of certain important occurrences. The term he uses is *signa* (line 16), the same word as the one he used in 2.10 to describe mental images formed by meditating upon the Cross as object. However, they are not a means merely of chronicling notable events in visual terms, but of rhetorical representation – that is of depicting key aspects of the revolt in ways designed to persuade the reader of their negative or positive qualities within a moral and political scheme that categorizes the uprising as deplorable.

There is no avoiding the striking contradiction between Gower's attitude to images in 2.10, where he counsels restraint, and in Book 1, where images of his own sprout and flourish in abundance as if from some *Vox clematis*. But the contradiction may be more apparent than real. It could be that he, 'moral' Gower, was acutely aware that, as a writer, he was himself by analogy a creator, manipulator and controller of images and hence responsible for ensuring that the effects they achieved were consonant with the intentions behind them. For both sections are about the tendency of the ignorant to go astray and lose reason when confronted by a powerful,

---

20 Andrew Galloway, 'Gower in his Most Learned Role and the Peasants' Revolt of 1381', *Mediaevalia* 16 (1993), 329–47.

influential and attractive force – be it that of a visually impressive religious icon, or of Fortune, herself a kind of political idol,[21] or that of a demagogue offering the enticing prospect of redress for wrongs suffered to 'stupid minds' prone to imagine more than they should (2). Second, *Vox* 2.10 is concerned with images that are books for the unlettered and which must therefore be tightly controlled, whereas the book as a whole is written in Latin for the intelligentsia, whom Gower presumably trusts to take from images the meanings they are intended to convey.[22] Finally, as order is re-established in the aftermath of revolt, man resumes his proper place, made in the image of God, and with reason his paramount faculty once the delusory images produced in the ferment of revolt have evaporated (1.18). Man as the image of God and Reason, we know from 2.10, is worthy of worship. The correct hierarchy is restored, subservience and subjection reinstated (1.21) after being turned upside-down by wild, animalesque forces. It is the surrendering of reason to religious enthusiasm, of the 'rational' to the 'brutish', and the subservience of the worshipper-cum-idolator before a thing that should be servant, not master, that the abuse of religious images entails. It is perhaps no coincidence that at this particular place in Book I of *Vox clamantis* Gower should address the Cross as a token of salvation – that one image exempted from his strictures and which acts here as a constant reminder of integrity, stability and dependable truth.

For the most part the images Gower creates in Book 1, his 'memorable tokens', are the very antithesis of what he associates with the Cross, for they express again and again the inversion of hierarchical order, and contempt for its gradations. The longest lasting inversion is that of the dream itself, not merely as a mirror image of the peasants' uprising, but in enabling Gower to show how the revolt gave reality itself a different hue, a dreamlike quality, it having been for him a living nightmare of transgression, of space invaded, of boundaries broken and privacy violated. Even the sanctioned, festive, socially rehabilitating inversions associated with the June feast of

---

21   Kurt Olsson, 'John Gower's *Vox clamantis* and the Medieval Idea of Place', *Studies in Philology* 84 (1987), 147.
22   Fisher, *John Gower*, 105–6.

Corpus Christi – the day on which the rebels entered London – suddenly become serious and menacing, the invasion a parodic Corpus Christi procession bent on desecration.[23]

Among the topsy-turvy images Gower describes paradise becomes hell, reasonable people become madmen, peasants become animals, domestic beasts revert to a wild state, arable land lies fallow, country invades city, citizens are rusticated, the subservient become masters, freemen become constrained, the weak defeat the strong, the sheep assault their shepherd, new Troy (London), undergoing its own fall, becomes an anti-Troy with no heroes (though plenty of traitors). Gower himself feels dehumanized, dislocated, bewildered.[24] The outcome of this relentless dynamic is the production of images memorable precisely because they capture the process of inversion, the metamorphosis of one thing into another to produce hybrids, grotesques; pigs that are wolves, asses that become lions, farmhands who are frogs. In all this, Gower draws on a library of imagined forms familiar to his readers from the Bible and Ovid and elsewhere.[25]

If it is difficult to detect in the proliferation of images in Book 1 of *Vox clamantis* any of the reticence and resistance to images Gower evinced in 2.10, it is the case that in Book 1 he deploys images in response to a particular occasion and need, in order to achieve certain effects and purposes, not in order to have them admired for their own sake. Again, there is a sense of relief when the chimeras of the revolt fade, the invented images become redundant, and he turns to the one true image of the Cross. And we should also note the relative lack of rhetorical colour in the following books. If Gower was not a crypto-Lollard he certainly shared some of the Wycliffites' misgivings about images. At the same time he abrogated to himself the creation and control of elaborate awe-inspiring, vivid representations of a

---

23 Paul Strohm, *Hochon's Arrow: The Social Imagination of Fourteenth-Century Texts* (Princeton: Princeton University Press, 1992), 45–56.
24 Olsson, 'Gower's *Vox clamantis*', 145.
25 Bruce Harbert, 'Lessons from the Great Clerk: Ovid and John Gower', in *Ovid Renewed: Ovidian Influences on Literature and Art from the Middle Ages to the Twentieth Century*, ed. Charles Martindale (Cambridge: Cambridge University Press, 1988), 83–7.

Images 167

world turned upside-down. While he remained true to his Lollard-leaning views on the function of images, that did not prevent him from dedicating his work to a persecutor of heretics, or from condemning popular demand for the kinds of social and religious reform for which he had earlier seen a need.[26] Hoccleve, the subject of the next section, is no less contradictory in his attitude to images, but his starting-point is very different.

Hoccleve's *Regiment of Princes*

It is not unusual to find in the margin of a late medieval manuscript a drawing of a hand with an extended index finger. A two-dimensional outline in ink, often hastily sketched, and inserted by a scribe or reader, it indicates a noteworthy section of the text.[27] However, on folio 88 of London, British Library, MS Harley 4866 (after 1411) the convention is transformed almost beyond recognition.[28] The pointed hand depicted there is not schematic, but lifelike, executed in skin-coloured tints, and shaded to suggest depth and modelling (Figure 2). It is a right hand, attached to an arm, and the arm to the body of a man who is familiar from the polychrome covers of modern books: Geoffrey Chaucer.[29] It accompanies the text of the *Regiment of Princes* by Hoccleve, a work that is part autobiography, part mirror for

26 Siân Echard, 'Gower's "bokes of Latin": Language, Politics and Poetry', *Studies in the Age of Chauce* 25 (2003), 123–56.
27 For examples, see the index entry for '*Note bene*/index signs […] hands' in Ann Eljenholm Nichols, Michael T. Orr, Kathleen L. Scott and Lynda Denison, *An Index of Images in English Manuscripts from the Time of Chaucer to Henry VIII. c.1380–c.1509: The Bodleian Library, Oxford*, i: *MSS Additional–Digby* (Turnhout: Harvey Miller, 2000).
28 Kathleen L. Scott, *Later Gothic Manuscripts, 1390–1490*, 2 vols, A Survey of Manuscripts Illuminated in the British Isles, 6 (London: Harvey Miller, 1996), ii, 160–2.
29 Nicholas Perkins, *Hoccleve's 'Regiment of Princes': Counsel and Constraint* (Cambridge: Brewer, 2001), 119–21.

Figure 2 Portrait of Geoffrey Chaucer, from the *Regement of Princes* by Thomas Hoccleve (London, British Library, MS Harley 4866, f. 88) © The British Library Board.

princes, part petition,[30] and addressed to Henry of Monmouth, Prince of Wales (the future Henry V).

The familiarity of the portrait should not obscure its extraordinary impact within its original context. Here is Thomas Hoccleve's Chaucer in a manuscript which may have been executed under the author's direct supervision[31] – Chaucer as Hoccleve remembered him and wished him to be remembered in a portrait dating from the time of the poem's completion in 1411.[32] According to his own testimony, among the qualities valued by

30 Larry Scanlon, 'The King's Two Voices: Narrative and Power in Hoccleve's *Regement of Princes*', in *Literary Practice and Social Change in Britain 1380–1530*, ed. Lee Patterson (Berkeley and Los Angeles: University of California Press, 1990), 216–47; Anna Torti, *The Glass of Form: Mirroring Structures from Chaucer to Skelton* (Cambridge: Brewer, 1991), 87–106.
31 Thomas Hoccleve, *The Regiment of Princes*, ed. Charles R. Blyth (Kalamazoo, Mich.: Medieval Institute Publications for TEAMS, 1999), 16–17. All quotations are from this edition.
32 For Hoccleve's life see John Burrow, *Thomas Hoccleve*, Authors of the Middle Ages, 4 (Aldershot: Variorum, 1994).

Images 169

this clerk of the privy seal were Chaucer's skills as a writer, his piety and his dependability as a source of wisdom and authority. So the picture shows him holding a rosary in his other hand, wearing a *penner* or inkhorn around his neck, dressed in gown and headgear of a sober grey colour and with a carefully composed facial expression, created in three-quarter profile, suggesting that its owner is serious, of an age that commands respect and focused (he looks and points steadily in one and the same direction). Furthermore, the image 'leaps out of the page': it is the only image embedded in the text of the *Regiment of Princes*; it appears, unexpectedly, towards the end of the poem; its lush colours contrast with the monochrome of the script; its size (approximately 7 cm × 4 cm) is relatively large in relation to the whole page; and by being placed against a flat, lozenge-pattern background, and overlapping the frame with his hand, Chaucer seems – in contrast to the linearity of the text – three-dimensional, as if leaning out of a window in a wall to call attention to some significant event.

The significant event is the production of this extraordinary image. Chaucer points to lines in the text where their author explains:

> [...] I have heere his liknesse
> Do make, to this ende, in sothfastnesse,
> That they that han of him lost thoght and mynde
> By this peynture may ageyn him fynde.
> (4995–8)

Viewed as an event in the history of art, the image is indeed significant,[33] but its more immediate function is different: while the portrait draws attention to the text, the text also directs attention to the portrait, informing the reader's response to it. For Hoccleve, the image of Chaucer is intended not

---

33   James H. McGregor, 'The Iconography of Chaucer in Hoccleve's *De Regimine Principum* and in the *Troilus* Frontispiece', *Chaucer Review* 11 (1977), 338–50; Jeanne E. Krochalis, 'Hoccleve's Chaucer Portrait', *Chaucer Review* 21 (1986), 234–45; David R. Carlson, 'Thomas Hoccleve and the Chaucer Portrait', *Huntington Library Quarterly* 54 (1991), 283–300; Alan T. Gaylord, 'Portrait of a Poet', in *The Ellesmere Chaucer: Essays in Interpretation*, ed. Martin Stevens and Daniel Woodward (San Marino, Calif.: Huntington Library, 1995), 121–42.

merely as an icon of literary greatness, but also as a means to an end – as a way in which those who have forgotten Chaucer's significance ('lost thoght and mynde') can recapture it. That process might well be stimulated through Chaucer's outward appearance, as shown in the portrait, but the true ends in view are the inner qualities of Chaucer's writing – qualities that might then be further internalized in the life or poetry of the admiring reader. It is an image designed to stir reading (or listening) memories, to encourage a return to Chaucer's writings, to aid thoughtfulness, to incorporate Chaucer posthumously, as an icon of national identity, in Prince Henry's political agenda,[34] and to reinforce the authority of Hoccleve's role as an adviser to princes by linking his poem vividly with a revered writer who wrote poems of advice to the Prince's father, Henry IV.[35]

The lines quoted above are embedded in two stanzas, headed by the image, which describe in greater detail the process Hoccleve has in mind, which is analogous to the use of images in religious meditation:

> Althogh his lyf be qweynt, the resemblance
> Of him hath in me so fressh lyflynesse
> That to putte othir men in remembrance
> Of his persone, I have heere his liknesse
> Do make [...]
>
> The ymages that in the chirches been
> Maken folk thynke on God and on his seintes
> Whan the ymages they beholde and seen,
> Where ofte unsighte of hem causith restreyntes
> Of thoghtes goode. Whan a thyng depeynt is
> Or entaillid, if men take of it heede,
> Thoght of the liknesse it wole in hem breede.
> (4992–5005)

---

34 Derek Pearsall, 'Hoccleve's *Regiment of Princes:* The Poetics of Royal Self-Representation', *Speculum* 69 (1994), 398.
35 Perkins, *Hoccleve's 'Regiment of Princes'*, 118–19; Scanlon, 'King's Two Voices', 240–2.

Not to have imaginative access to Chaucer is a grievous error, comparable to the neglect of religious images.[36] If the images found in churches are left unseen the result is moral torpor and the inhibition of virtue: 'restreyntes | Of thoghtes goode'. Actually looking at them, on the other hand, makes people think about god and the saints. But they are a stimulus to devotion, not objects of worship or admiration in themselves. Hoccleve's interest is not in the sign, useful and functional though it may be, but in what it signifies. Furthermore, paintings and carvings, once viewed with attention, or 'heede', are possessed internally, imaginatively, and can be summoned up as it were by remote access. That in turn provokes meditation: 'Thoght of the liknesse it wole in hem breede'. Thus the production of an image (Chaucer) commissioned by Hoccleve enables others to possess him in their internal lives, much as Hoccleve does.

At least, that is his pious wish, founded upon what might be seen as a naive understanding of the identity between outer show and inner nature. Such naivety might well be strategic in a poem designed to promote the integrity of a prince whose father usurped the legitimacy of Richard II's reign.[37] Other problems hedge his endeavours. The *Regiment*, of which there are forty-three complete or substantial copies, is 'far and away Hoccleve's most successful poem in its day'.[38] The manuscripts of the poem circulated nor only in court circles, but also among religious, gentry and professional owners; its readers included priests, physicians, lawyers, administrators and writers.[39] But the portrait survives only in two manuscripts: Harley 4866 and British Library MS Royal 17.D.vi (an inferior version). It has been

---

36   Ethan Knapp, *The Bureaucratic Muse: Thomas Hoccleve and the Literature of Late Medieval England* (University Park: Pennsylvania State University Press, 2001), 119–24.
37   Paul Strohm, *England's Empty Throne: Usurpation and the Language of Legitimation 1399–1422* (New Haven: Yale University Press, 1998), 180–6.
38   J. A. Burrow, 'Hoccleve and Chaucer', in *Chaucer Traditions*, ed. Morse and Windeatt (1990), 56. See also Perkins, *Hoccleve's 'Regiment of Princes'*, 151–4 and Simpson, *Reform and Cultural Revolution*, 204.
39   Perkins, *Hoccleve's 'Regiment of Princes'*, 171–7. See also M. C. Seymour, 'The Manuscripts of Hoccleve's *Regiment of Princes*', *Transactions of the Edinburgh Bibliographical Society* 4 (1974), 255–8.

removed from a third (British Library MS Arundel 38), while a seventeenth-century copy has been inserted in a fourth (Philadelphia, Rosenbach Museum and Library, MS 1083/10).[40] Was the cult of Chaucer too esoteric to have produced the kind of general and widespread effect Hoccleve wanted? Worse, the very basis on which the mechanism of devotion rests is itself contested. Hoccleve acknowledges as much only to dismiss it, as if a more elaborate rehearsal of the counter-arguments to his project might result in its being fatally undermined. In the third stanza on folio 88 he writes:

> Yit sum men holde oppinioun and seye
> That noon ymages sholde ymakid be.
> They erren foule and goon out of the wey;
> Of trouthe have they scant sensibilitee.
> Passe over that! Now, blessed Trinitee,
> Upon my maistres soule mercy have;
> For him, Lady, thy mercy eek I crave.
> (5006–12)

The allusion is to the contemporary attacks on religious images such as had surfaced in Lollard circles. As we have seen, such attacks argued that, far from providing a means to spiritual improvement, religious images are an impediment and a distraction – objects of admiration in their own right, and thus the focus of idolatry.[41] That Hoccleve was ideologically opposed to reformist thought we know from an earlier section of the poem (211–399) in which John Badby, burnt for heresy at Smithfield in 1410, is given short shrift for denying transubstantiation (another Lollard issue).[42] But

---

40 Derek Pearsall, *The Life of Geoffrey Chaucer: A Critical Biography*, Blackwell Critical Biographies, 1 (Oxford: Blackwell, 1992), 285–91; Pearsall, 'Hoccleve's *Regement of Princes*', 395–6; Perkins, *Hoccleve's 'Regiment of Princes'*, 155–9.
41 Pearsall, 'Hoccleve's *Regement of Princes*', 405–6.
42 Peter McNiven, *Heresy and Politics in the Reign of Henry IV: The Burning of John Badby* (Woodbridge: Boydell Press, 1987), 199–219; and cf. Hoccleve's diatribe against the Lollard rebel Oldcastle in *Hoccleve's Works: The Minor Poems*, ed. Frederick J. Furnivall and I. Gollancz, EETS es 61 (1892) and 73 (1897), rev. edn Jerome Mitchell and A. I. Doyle repr. in one vol. (1970), 8–24, esp. lines 409–24.

the very act of appropriating religious ideology to serve secular ends itself undermines the orthodox position that Hoccleve ostensibly adopts. The controversy over the right use of religious images is sidestepped and put to questionable use as a means of giving iconic status to a literary saint – itself a manoeuvre designed to curry favour with the regime-in-waiting. What also undermines Hoccleve's stated political position on images is his literary practice. The internalizing of Chaucer's image, far from leading to some higher, unassailable truth, as was the intention of such practice in a pious context, instead drives the poet ever more inward, to an examination of his own subjectivity. It is, indeed, a process that validates inwardness as an end in itself, rather than as a means to transcendence of self.

I will take as my example the topic of old age. In his portrait, Chaucer is relatively venerable, depicted as he might have looked towards the end of his life, with grey hair and beard. (He died at the age of sixty, or thereabouts.) Now the key authority figure in the *Regiment of Princes* is 'A poore old hoore [grey-haired] man' who happens to walk by when Hoccleve's persona is in a state of abject anxiety, aggravated by insomnia (120–6). The old man greets him courteously, but Hoccleve is too immersed in his 'seekly distresse' to reply. Yet the old man is concerned about Hoccleve's melancholic state of 'drery cheere, | And [...] deedly colour pale and wan' (127–8) in which, as he later says, his wits have become 'disparpled' [scattered] (209). Having recognized that his true nature has become distorted ('Al wrong is wrestid'), the old man attempts to shock him out of introversion and into normality by asking 'Sleepstow, man? | Awake!' and shaking him 'wondir faste'. Hoccleve answers at last with a sigh and a 'who is there?' and 'this olde greye' replies 'I [...] | Am here' (130–4).

Who this 'I' is becomes an intriguing question as the rest of the prologue develops. At first Hoccleve is rude and arrogant and tries to send him away, saying that the old man's words are annoying and only make a bad situation worse. But the old man, now calling Hoccleve 'My sone' (143) in a paternal or pastoral, and certainly a caring, mode, won't go. Instead he offers relief from sorrow through conversation, therapy through dialogue or confession: 'If that thee lyke to ben esid wel, | As suffre me with thee to talke a whyle' (148–9). He identifies Hoccleve's problem as stemming in part from his relative youthfulness and lack of experience but, discovering that Hoccleve is literate, the old man looks forward to a complete cure, for 'Lettred folk han gretter discrecion' (155). Still Hoccleve rejects his overtures, scorning the old man's self-appointed role as a doctor, and disparaging his appearance outright: 'Cure thyself that tremblest as thow goost, | [...] thou art as seek almooste | As I' (163–7). In spite of his advice on the use of images, Hoccleve has not, at this stage of his story, learnt how to penetrate outward appearances. Nor does he believe that the old man can possibly understand his condition: 'thou woost but litil what thow meenest' (173).

But the old man persists, gradually teasing a confession out of his new-found son, and pointing out that to be isolated and alienated may lead to madness, 'a dotid heede' (200). So he offers his services as a guide, and the conversation now turns to a wide range of topics, including poverty, extravagance, the temptations of youth, money, reputation, marriage, sexuality and patronage. Hoccleve is much encouraged by his exchanges with the old man, who swears loyalty, old and poor as he may be: 'swich as that I am, sone, I am thyn' (1992). Hoccleve, for his part, has formed an equally close bond and does not wish to be parted:

> 'What, fadir, wolden yee thus sodeynly
> Departe fro me? Petir, Cryst forbeede!
> Yee shall go dyne with me, treewely.'
> 'Sone, at o word, I moot go fro thee neede.'
> 'Nay, fadir, nay!' 'Yis, sone, as God me spede.'
> 'Now, fadir, syn it may noon othir tyde,
> Almighty God yow save and be youre gyde.'
> (1996–2002)

Hoccleve is sufficiently recovered and energized to begin the *Regiment* proper, in which he offers counsel to the Prince of Wales on the management of 'images' more generally, while at the same time petitioning him for the payment of his overdue annuity. Before he begins, he invokes Chaucer, calling him 'maister deere and fadir reverent' (1961).

The old man has been variously identified as almsman, go-between, surrogate for Hoccleve, alter ego, truth-teller, Carmelite friar, and academic doctor. But such is the consanguinity of the Chaucer in Hoccleve's portrait and the old man in the prologue to the *Regiment of Princes* that

Images

the latter might be thought of, if not as an animated version of the former, at least as a figure with strong affinities. Here is the elderly guide taking an active role in the life and imagination of Hoccleve, much as Chaucer's works did.[43] As the old man says to the narrator of the *Regiment*: 'swich as that I am, sone, I am thyn' (1992). However, the Chaucerian ambience is not focused only on the old man. For the debate on youth and age, and the contempt of the young for the old and its dire consequences, see the Pardoner's Tale. For the comic exchange between the old man and Hoccleve ('Awake!' 'It's me!') see Mercury's exchange with Morpheus in the *Book of the Duchess* (178–86). See the same poem for an account of melancholy and the effects of insomnia, and for a therapeutic dialogue between a reluctant, introverted, sorrowing man and a persistent interlocutor – a dialogue that includes the repeated line borrowed by Hoccleve: 'Thow wot full litel wot thou wenest' (*BD* 743, 1137, 1305).

While it is important to be aware of allusions, and to recognize the affinities between Chaucer and the old man, there is nothing resolved or mechanistic about the processes at work here. On the contrary, the image and influence of Chaucer in Hoccleve's prologue are dynamic, shifting, heartfelt, subject to constant renegotiation. For Hoccleve, 'Chaucer' (the man and his works as indivisible entity) is not a mine to be quarried but a father-figure with whom to engage in an act of filial piety designed at once to understand and possess for himself the source of his own existence as a writer.[44] Thus 'Chaucer' – the man and his narratives – becomes a structure of thought and feeling, a way of thinking through independently, and articulating, Hoccleve's own preoccupations, and of writing about them in ways that are at once original and recognizable by a particular reading community.

---

43   Lee Patterson, "What is me?": Self and Society in the Poetry of Thomas Hoccleve', *Studies in the Age of Chaucer* 23 (2001), 465–6.
44   A. C. Spearing, *Medieval to Renaissance in English Poetry* (Cambridge: Cambridge University Press, 1985), 103–10; Ethan Knapp, 'Eulogies and Usurpations: Hoccleve and Chaucer Revisited', *Studies in the Age of Chaucer* 21 (1999), 247–73; Ruth Nissé, '"Oure Fadres Olde and Modres": Gender, Heresy, and Hoccleve's Literary Politics', *Studies in the Age of Chaucer* 21 (1999), 278–91; Patterson, '"What is me?"', 461–3.

What all of this points to is something of the complexity of the relationship between text and image. In decrying the Lollard position on religious images, as it applies by extrapolation to his own case, Hoccleve was right but for the wrong reasons.[45] Certainly the image of Chaucer works by association, and the topic of age is one which becomes a source of meditation and debate with the prologue to the *Regiment*. But in so doing the image changes its nature, moving from a visual to an imaginative status, and undergoing refraction through the regular literary devices of characterization, dialogue and dramatic situation. It might be that the literary image is so complex and different that the Lollard case ceases to apply. All of which opens up a discursive space quite at odds with the poem's larger project, which is to reinforce political and religious orthodoxy as a way of enhancing what might be called the image of Prince Henry. Insofar as legitimacy and succession were issues that needed to be addressed under the general rubric of the Prince's image, the integrity of Hoccleve's literary descent from Chaucer might be seen as a way of expressing a literary analogy that reinforces the legitimacy of the future Henry V – except that, as we have seen, the literary expression of a father and son relationship is full of fissures, discontinuities, ruptures and anxiety.[46]

The late medieval debate on images, whether one examines it within contexts that are religious or secular, material or literary, is one that admits of no easy resolution. For it is founded upon a series of linguistic and religious paradoxes that cannot be neatly divided into discrete positions. Two of the basic tenets of the Christian faith – that Christ was God made flesh, and that each person was an image of God – conferred on human existence and the material world an inherent sanctity, however much they were despoiled by sin. Furthermore, the narratives of Christ's life, and the legends of the saints who modelled themselves on his example, were constructed in terms of episodes that led naturally to the repetition and memorializing of key persons and events, and so to the veneration of symbolic

---

45 Knapp, *Bureaucratic Muse*, 129–34; Sarah Tolmie, 'The *Prive Scilence* of Thomas Hoccleve', *Studies in the Age of Chaucer* 22 (2000), 285.
46 Strohm, 'Hoccleve, Lydgate', 645.

representations. Those representations had their ultimate sanction in the canonical texts of a Bible brim-full of images subtly deployed across the whole gamut of literary artifice – texts that were themselves subject to a huge accretion of commentaries that expounded the hidden significance, the underlying patterns, of holy writ.

Once the whole notion of image-making – whether verbal or material – became politicized, as it did in the 1380s, then it became incumbent upon individuals to take positions on a divisive issue could not be easily resolved. It is not surprising, therefore, that practitioners of literary images, such as writers of the calibre of Gower and Hoccleve, find themselves impaled on the horns of a dilemma. While they ostensibly adopt and articulate one position (different in each case), their literary practice points in another direction. To this extent their work witnesses to their struggle to reconcile the imperatives of their social existence (as producers of literature within a network of patron, audience, and political faction) with the often contradictory and uncomfortable priorities that develop as a consequence of reflective writing.

Journey's End: The Prologue to the *Tale of Beryn**

Manuscript 455 (formerly 55) at Alnwick Castle, Northumberland, contains an imperfect version of the *Canterbury Tales*. The order of the tales is eccentric, though perhaps deliberate, and after the Canon's Yeoman's Tale there occurs, on fols 180–235, a unique copy of an apocryphal work generally known as the *Tale of Beryn*.[1] It is followed by the end of the Summoner's Tale (2159–294).

The entire manuscript is written in the same hand, dated between 1450 and 1470. Dialectal and textual evidence suggest that the scribe or his copy-text came from the south-east Midlands. Marks of subsequent ownership locate the manuscript in Devon: it was in the possession of various families at Pilton, Barnstable and Tavistock during the sixteenth century, and by the end of the following century it had travelled to Exeter, where it was owned by a prebendary, Thomas Long. The latter moved to Norwich, and the manuscript was there purchased (evidently then in an unbound state) by the 'Honourable Mrs. Thynn' of Cawston, near Norwich. A member of the Thynn family married a Lord Percy, and the manuscript probably travelled by this route to the Duke of Northumberland's library, where it has been since the early nineteenth century.[2]

---

*   First published in *Chaucer and Fifteenth-Century Poetry*, ed. Julia Boffey and Janet Cowen, King's College London Medieval Studies, 5 (London: King's College Centre for Late Antique and Medieval Studies, 1991), 143–74.
1   J. Zupitza, ed., *Specimens of All the Accessible Unprinted Manuscripts of the Canterbury Tales: The Doctor-Pardoner Link, and Pardoner's Prologue and Tale*, Chaucer Society, first ser., 81 (1892; repr. New York: Johnson, 1967), xvi; Bowers, John M., 'The *Tale of Beryn* and the *Siege of Thebes*: Alternative Ideas of the *Canterbury Tales*', *Studies in the Age of Chaucer* 7 (1985), 33–8.
2   *The Works of Geoffrey Chaucer*, ed. J. Urry (London: Lintot, 1721), k³; Royal Commission on Historical Manuscripts, *Third Report* (London: HMSO, 1872), 112b; Caroline F. E. Spurgeon, *Five Hundred Years of Chaucer Criticism and Allusion*

According to some authorities, the first printed version of *Beryn* appeared in John Stow's 1561 edition of Chaucer's works,[3] but it is nowhere to be found in that volume, or in other early editions of Chaucer.[4] In fact the prologue and tale of *Beryn* did not appear in print until 1721, when they were included in John Urry's posthumous *The Works of Geoffrey Chaucer*. Urry's editor, Timothy Thomas, records that the text of *Beryn* is a transcript made by Urry's amanuensis, a Mr Thomas Ainsworth. Elsewhere he apologizes that, owing to the lack of other copies, *Beryn*'s verse was never 'compleated', as was that of the other contents of the book.[5] *Beryn* therefore escaped the worst excesses of Urry's editorial practices, dedicated to metrical corrections designed 'to restore [... Chaucer] to his feet again'[6] – practices vilified by many subsequent writers.[7]

1357–1900, 3 vols (1925; rpt. New York: Russell and Russell, 1960), i, 325; John M. Manly and Edith Rickert, *The Text of the Canterbury Tales Studied on the Basis Of All Known Manuscripts*, 8 vols (Chicago: University of Chicago Press, 1940), i, 387–95; The *Tale of Beryn*, ed. M. E. M. Tamanini, Diss. New York University, 1969, 1–5, 52.

3 *IMEV*, item 3926; H. S. Bennett, *Chaucer and the Fifteenth Century* [corrected edn], Oxford History of English Literature, 2, pt 1 (Oxford: Clarendon Press, 1948), 317.

4 Geoffrey Chaucer, *The Works 1532, with Supplementary Material from the Editions of 1542, 1561, 1598 and 1602*, ed. W. Thynne, intro. D. S. Brewer (Menston: Scolar, 1969).

5 *Works*, ed. Urry, i³–k¹, k⁴, 7M².

6 Spurgeon, *Five Hundred Years*, i, 325.

7 *The Canterbury Tales of Chaucer*, ed. Thomas Tyrwhitt, 2nd edn, 2 vols (Oxford: Clarendon Press, 1798), i, pp. x, xiii; J. Ritson, *Bibliographia Poetica: A Catalogue of English Poets, of the Twelfth, Thirteenth, Fourteenth, and Sixteenth, Centurys, with a Short Account of Their Works* (London: Nicol, 1802), 20; *The Works of Geoffrey Chaucer*, in *The Works of the English Poets, from Chaucer to Cowper*, [ed. A. Chalmers,] (London: Johnson, 1810), i, p. xiv; Walter W. Skeat, *The Chaucer Canon, with a Discussion of the Works Associated with the Name of Geoffrey Chaucer* (Oxford: Clarendon Press, 1900), 143.

Bell reprinted Urry's text of Beryn in the sixth volume of his *Poets of Great Britain*,[8] as did Anderson for his *Poets of Great Britain* in 1793,[9] and Chalmers in 1810 for his *Works of the English Poets*.[10] Rather more interest was taken by Thomas Wright for his edition of 1851.[11] He tried to trace the manuscript used by Urry, but was unsuccessful, and had to content himself with altering 'the more apparent errors', using 'only the corrections that are self-evident'. In the absence of the manuscript it is not entirely clear on what basis Wright made his emendations, but he nevertheless declares cheerfully that 'Urry's faithlessness to his manuscript is quite extraordinary', and 'he not only often misread his original, but he introduced foolish alterations of his own'.[12] Wright's edition does, however, include some useful annotations.

Beryn has not been happy in its editors. The first edition of *Beryn* as a text independent of the *Canterbury Tales*, one based on a re-examination of the Northumberland manuscript, was that by F. J. Furnivall and W. G. Stone, published for the Chaucer Society in 1876, with ancillary material appearing in 1887. Reissued for the Early English Text Society in 1909, it remains the only generally available complete edition. Unfortunately, the text is marred by extensive editorial intervention, Furnivall having been (in his own words) 'affected for a time with the itch of padding out lines by needless little words in square brackets', on the grounds that 'the MS. is often faulty in metre, and not a correct copy of the original poem'.[13] Darton published an abbreviated and sanitized translation of *Beryn* in 1904, interpolated with some material from Lydgate's *Siege of Thebes*.[14] In 1930,

---

8   *The Poetical Works of Geoffrey Chaucer*, ed. J. Bell, 14 vols (Edinburgh: Apollo Press, 1782–3), vi (1782), 120–74.
9   *The Poetical Works of Geoffrey Chaucer*, in *A Complete Edition of the Poets of Great Britain*, ed. R. Anderson, 14 vols (Edinburgh: Mundell, 1792–1807), i (1793), 239–73.
10 *Works*, [ed. Chalmers], i, 634–69.
11 *The Canterbury Tales of Geoffrey Chaucer*, ed. Thomas Wright, 3 vols, Percy Society, 24–6 (London: 1847–51), 191–318.
12 Ibid., xxiii, 191n.
13 *The Tale of Beryn, with a Prologue of the Merry Adventure of the Pardoner with a Tapster at Canterbury*, ed. F. J. Furnivall and W. G. Stone, EETS es 105 (1909), xi.
14 *Tales of the Canterbury Pilgrims Retold from Chaucer and Others*, trans. F. J. H. Darton, 2nd edn (London: Wells Gardner, Darton, 1904), 278–365.

French and Hale included in their anthology the trial scene from the tale, taken from the Furnivall and Stone edition, lines 2910–3894.[15] Loomis and Willard in 1948 printed lines 1–308 of the prologue in a modernized version, at the same time baptizing the Pardoner with the name 'Hugh' (actually a misreading of ME 'huch' = 'which', at line 176).[16] In 1958 Kaiser included in his revised version of *Medieval English* lines 130–204, 231–50 and 267–99 of the Furnivall and Stone prologue.[17] It was not until 1969 that a full modern edition appeared, based on a rereading of the manuscript (in photographic reproduction) and taking due account of the variants proposed by previous editors. Regrettably Tamanini's work is relatively inaccessible because it exists only in the form of a doctoral thesis. A modern, readily available, edition of *Beryn* is long overdue, as is a detailed literary analysis of its content. Recently one scholar appeared to believe that after Urry's edition of *Beryn* the manuscript disappeared from view. 'It has not since been located' (Blake 1985, 8).[18]

Since Furnivall and Stone's edition the entire composition has been known as the *Tale of Beryn*. It is a misleading title in that it does not indicate the existence of two connected narratives (in one of which Beryn does not feature), and because it does not follow the usual convention of the *Canterbury Tales* in giving the title to the teller. It is the tale of Beryn insofar as the second half is about Beryn, not by him as narrator. For reasons which will become evident, it is the first part of the composition which is of more interest at present. That is not to say that the story about Beryn, comprising 4024 lines in couplets, does not merit a detailed examination. On the contrary, a lively narrative with considerable emotional appeal, which has

15 W. H. French and C. B. Hale, eds, *Middle English Metrical Romances* (1930; repr. New York: Russell and Russell, 1964), 899–930.
16 Roger Sherman Loomis and Rudolph Willard, eds, *Medieval English Verse and Prose in Modernized Versions* (New York: Appleton-Century-Crofts, 1948), 373–8.
17 R. Kaiser, ed., *Medieval English: An Old English and Middle English Anthology*, 3rd edn, rev. (Berlin: Kaiser, 1958), 494–6.
18 N. F. Blake, *The Textual Tradition of the Canterbury Tales* (London: Arnold, 1985), 8.

been summarized elsewhere, threads through a fascinating range of themes, such as the nurturing of children, the consequences of familial and social misgovernment, gambling and its effects, the different and opposing characteristics of youth and old age, the problems of inheritance after remarriage, the uses and abuses of trade, true and false hospitality, the relative justice of different legal systems and the deceptiveness of story-telling.[19] Unfortunately, Beryn's tale has suffered neglect because of its association with Chaucer – not merely because the writing is inferior to his, but also because nothing within the tale appears to reflect or shed light on the *Canterbury Tales*. The 731 lines which precede it, however, seem to have been composed out of an infectious enthusiasm for what Chaucer had accomplished, and to provide a commentary on it. They describe the arrival of the pilgrims in Canterbury, their accommodation at a pilgrim inn, their visit to the shrine of St Thomas and events at the inn on the night before their departure, when the Pardoner's tryst with Kitt the tapster is thwarted.[20]

The critical reception of *Beryn*, most of which has concentrated on the prologue, falls into two main categories. Some writers, and chiefly those of an earlier period, stress the overpowering influence of Chaucer. More recently, the author has been credited with considerable independence in the exercise of his literary skills. Not unusually, critics maintain an ambivalent attitude, gauging the poet's achievement as at once derivative and innovative. In 1774, Thomas Warton wrote that the prologue to Beryn had 'some humour and contrivance'.[21] At the turn of the century, Ritson recognized 'a writer of uncommon merit'.[22] Furnivall also responded positively: 'worse than Chaucer's though the hand of the *Beryn*-writer is, a bit, and a good bit, of the Master's humour and life-likeness, the latter verser

---

19   *Tale of Beryn*, ed. Furnivall and Stone, viii–x; French and Hale, eds, *Middle English Metrical Romances*, 899–900; Karen A. Winstead, 'The *Beryn*-Writer as a Reader of Chaucer', *Chaucer Review* 22 (1988), 226–7.
20   Bowers, '*Tale of Beryn*', 28–33.
21   Thomas Warton, *The History of English Poetry, from the Close of the Eleventh Century to the Commencement of the Eighteenth Century*, 2 vols (London: 1774–8), i, 455.
22   Ritson, *Bibliographia Poetica*, 20.

has in his Prologue. Chaucer's characters are well kept up.'[23] In the early part of this century, George Saintsbury condemned the *Beryn* author's handling of metre, but found that he is 'not by any means so un-Chaucerian in matter and temper'. As for the prologue, 'the narrative power is by no means inconsiderable'.[24]

Double negatives were not for Kittredge, who responded warmly to 'that highly interesting document, the Tale of Beryn', noting that the prologue 'is worth a moment's notice'. He praised the cathedral scene as 'more edifying, and equally vivid' by comparison with events in the hostelry: 'Particularly diverting is the behavior of the Miller and others of his sort'. Kittredge also recognized that, imitator though the *Beryn* author might be, he was also an astute reader of the *Canterbury Tales* who interpreted them remarkably like Kittredge himself:

> All this is a poor substitute for what Chaucer would have given us, if he had lived to finish his work. But there is some merit in the performance, and it certainly evinces a lively sense of the actuality of Chaucer's Pilgrims. The author of *Beryn* did not mistake the Canterbury Tales for a volume of disconnected stories. He recognized the work for what it really is – a micro-cosmography, a little image of the great world.[25]

Subsequent writers before mid-century might admire the way in which the *Beryn* writer by and large maintained the consistency of Chaucer's characters,[26] but might also be less forthcoming, one finding in 1948 that 'The Prologue has some of Chaucer's realistic vigor but none at all of his sly humor or happy turn of phrase', a remark reiterated in 1967.[27]

---

23 *Tale of Beryn*, ed. Furnivall and Stone, vii.
24 George Saintsbury, 'The English Chaucerians', in *Cambridge History of English Literature*, ed. A. W. Ward and A. R. Waller, 15 vols (Cambridge: Cambridge University Press, 1867–1922), ii (1908), 216.
25 G. L. Kittredge, *Chaucer and His Poetry* (Cambridge, Mass.: Harvard University Press, 1915), 157–8.
26 E. J. Bashe, 'The Prologue of *The Tale of Beryn*', *Philological Quarterly* 12 (1933), 1–16.
27 A. C. Baugh, 'The Middle English Period (1100–1500)', in *A Literary History of England*, ed. Baugh, 2nd edn, 4 vols (London: Routledge and Kegan Paul, 1967), i, 292.

Tamanini, whose work heralded a reappraisal of the *Beryn* author, nevertheless adopted a familiar position in applauding the way in which he followed the *Canterbury Tales*: 'He hardly achieved a true imitation of Chaucer's work, but [...] he followed more than just the characters and the pilgrimage setting of Chaucer. In the prologue he imitated character and situation with some of the realistic gusto and narrative art of Chaucer'.[28] A year later it was clear that the negative estimate still had a following when one critic wrote that the achievement of Lydgate's *Siege of Thebes* and of *Beryn* 'rests so heavily on a knowledge of the original that they could never stand alone'.[29] As late as 1985 another critic was content to maintain the position of a Saintsbury in stating that, although the *Beryn* poet lacks 'his master's gifts as a versifier, he had a fine ear for colloquial dialogue, as well as real talents for inventing and staging comic action'. The writer goes on to praise ingenuity in the narrative structure, an eventfulness superior to that of the General Prologue, and dramatic vitality.[30]

Thus the received critical image of the *Beryn* author is that of a slavish imitator who enjoyed occasional bursts of confidence. Generally speaking, commentators have been mesmerized by the prologue's associations with the *Canterbury Tales* and unable or unwilling to evaluate it on its own terms. During the past decade, however, *Beryn* has been subjected to some thoughtful rereadings informed by modern critical theory, by an interest in genre and by an appreciation of Chaucerian aesthetics. As a result, the *Beryn* author has grown in stature to emerge as a writer interesting both in his own right and as a perceptive early reader of the *Canterbury Tales*. In 1983, Kohl read the prologue to *Beryn* (and that to Lydgate's *Siege of Thebes*) as a 'metafiction' which comments on Chaucer's General Prologue to the end of 'pouring ridicule on his moral view of the world'. Kohl's argument might carry more force if he had paid closer attention to the text. He says without irony that 'the Pardoner makes his arrangements in a kind

---

28 *Tale of Beryn*, ed. Tamanini, 39.
29 R. H. Robbins, 'The English Fabliau: Before and After Chaucer', *Moderna Språk* 64 (1970), 234.
30 Bowers, '*Tale of Beryn*', 27–8, 50.

of brothel' (actually a pilgrim inn), that the Wife of Bath and Prioress 'while the afternoon away sitting in the back garden of their inn' (actually the parlour), and he bases a part of his argument on a line composed by Furnivall (line 683) as one of that editor's 'improvements' to the text.[31] Two years later, in an article again spoilt by erroneous or misleading references to the narrative of the *Beryn* prologue, Darjes and Rendall focused on the author's manipulation of the fabliau which occupies the major part of the story. They found that his use of detail is even more sparing than that of traditional fabliau authors, that he does not take advantage of the opportunity to include sexual 'spice', but that in representing everyday speech and character he is considerably more successful.[32] In the most sophisticated critical study of prologue and tale yet to appear, Winstead argues that the *Beryn* author's work is finely tuned to Chaucer's modulations of style and technique:

> It conveys an understanding of Chaucer's irony, his playful manipulation of generic conventions, his methods of linking components in a work through parallelism and variation, and his juxtaposition of styles, tones, genres and subject matter in order to create meaning. Although none of these devices is unique to Chaucer, Chaucer developed and polished these techniques, and they are today considered hallmarks of his style. Evidently the *Beryn*-writer, already in the fifteenth century, perceived these same features as distinctly Chaucerian.[33]

***

A fully informed critical debate on the merits of the prologue to *Beryn* cannot avoid the issue of its relationship with the *Canterbury Tales*. Too often, though, that relationship has been seen as derivative when a more constructive approach might have placed the prologue in much the same comparative position as one of Chaucer's tales is often placed in relation to its source material. By this means the distinctive and positive qualities

---

31   S. Kohl, 'Chaucer's Pilgrims in Fifteenth-Century Literature', *Fifteenth-Century Studies* 7 (1983), 226, 229, 234.
32   Bradley Darjes and Thomas Rendall, 'A Fabliau in the Prologue to the *Tale of Beryn*', *Mediaeval Studies* 47 (1985), 418–19.
33   Winstead, '*Beryn*-Writer', 231–2.

Journey's End: The Prologue to the Tale of Beryn 187

of the poem under discussion become clear. Certainly the critical debate on the *Beryn* author has recently been furthered, and become more interesting, thanks to the efforts of the writers just named. What now follows is an attempt again to enlarge that discussion, but by returning in the first place to questions of authorship, date of composition and audience. A consideration of such factors affects our understanding of the function of the prologue and that in turn has implications for its critical interpretation.

Although Urry may have believed that *Beryn* was a lost work by Chaucer,[34] Thomas, Urry's editor, was not persuaded of its authenticity:

> It may (perhaps with some shew of reason) be suspected that Chaucer was not the Author of them, but a later Writer, who may have taken the hint from what is suggested in V. 796 of the Prologues, that the Pilgrims were to tell Tales in their Return homewards; but as to that the Reader must be left to his own Judgement.[35]

In Urry's edition, the idea that *Beryn* is of different, or at least doubtful, authorship is sustained by keeping prologue and tale quite separate from the *Canterbury Tales*, towards the end of the volume and in a sequence of miscellaneous works most of which are not by Chaucer.

Warton tested the stylistic evidence for himself and concluded: 'I cannot allow that this Prologue and Tale were written by Chaucer. Yet I believe them to be nearly coeval.'[36] When *Beryn* and other apocryphal works were subsequently republished, as by Anderson, they appeared with a disclaimer: 'all evidence, internal and external, is against the supposition of their being the production of Chaucer.'[37] Skeat dealt the death blow, at once appearing to resent Urry's discovery of *Beryn* and acknowledge its usefulness:

> it is necessary to say that he added two new pieces to the pile; both of them undoubtedly spurious, though the first is of some importance, and both have a certain interest of their own.[38]

---

34 Spurgeon, *Five Hundred Years*, i, 325.
35 *Works*, ed. Urry, k³.
36 Warton, *History of English Poetry*, i, 456.
37 *Poetical Works*, ed. Anderson, i, p. vi.
38 Skeat, *Chaucer Canon*, 143.

It was hardly necessary of Saintsbury to reiterate: 'Chaucer's own it cannot possibly be'.[39]

The key to the authorship of *Beryn* lies in the colophon (fol. 235):

> Nomen Autoris presentis Cronica Rome
> Et translatoris Filius ecclesie Thome.

(The name of the author presenting the chronicle of Rome, and the translator, is 'son of the church of Thomas'.)

According to one scholar, 'author' and 'translator' are both applicable to the person who fashioned *Beryn* as a chronicle of Rome (where *Beryn* was born), for he brought to the French tale of Bérinus precision in rendering it into English and a flair for extensive modification.[40] But what does 'son of the church of Thomas' mean? For Furnivall it meant 'a Canterbury man – monk, I suppose', and he glossed the colophon: 'A Canterbury monk wrote this Tale'.[41] McIntosh was more circumspect: 'The identity of the author is as yet unknown. The colophon of the manuscript suggests a man in holy orders [...] but there is no proof that he was a monk of Canterbury, although his familiarity with that city is clearly shown in the prologue'.[42] Manly and Rickert, however, were relatively confident: 'The most natural interpretation of "Filius ecclesie Thome" makes him a monk of Canterbury, and this is confirmed [...] by his intimate knowledge of the town and the doings of the pilgrims'.[43]

If 'son of the church' is indeed fairly clear evidence that the author was in holy orders, there is certainly a difficulty in presuming too hastily that he was a monk of Canterbury. If he had been, then he might have indicated a more obvious connection with one or the other of the two great monastic institutions which the city sustained: Christ Church and St Augustine's

---

39 Saintsbury, 'English Chaucerians', 216.
40 H. M. McIntosh, 'The Literary Background of the *Tale of Beryn*', Diss. University of Chicago, 1931, 45–117.
41 *Tale of Beryn*, ed. Furnivall and Stone, vii, 120.
42 McIntosh, 'Literary Background', 1.
43 Manly and Rickert, *Text of the Canterbury Tales*, i, 392.

abbey. There is, however, another possibility which may be entertained. It is that 'church of Thomas' refers specifically to the place where the shrine of St Thomas Becket, and associated cults, were accommodated within the cathedral. For the location of the shrine, Trinity Chapel, was 'called almost universally [...] "St Thomas' Chapel"'.[44] The author of *Beryn* might then be one of the monks charged with custodial duties associated with the shrine and its devotions, such as the articulate John Vyel (*fl.* 1399–1444) or Edmund Kyngyston (*fl.* 1401–1428), who were serving as guardians of the shrine in 1428.[45]

Internal evidence tends to support the hypothesis that the author was a monk with detailed knowledge of pilgrim practices. Attitudes towards representatives of the church within the prologue suggest his own status. Although the main functions are to indicate the courtesy of the Knight, and to reflect actual practice, the 'prelatis' (presumably the Monk, Friar, and Prioress) are twice treated with due deference. At the church door they, together with the Parson and his companions, are allowed to enter first (137),[46] and they are again given special attention before the evening meal (386–8). More revealing, however, is the indulgent representation of monks with minor roles within the prologue, and of the pilgrim Monk himself. The monk who has the task of sprinkling pilgrim visitors with holy water does so (with the author glancing at the General Prologue, line 167) 'with a manly chere' (138). The individual who, at the shrine, names and talks about the holy relics, offering them to be kissed, is a 'goodly monke' (167). Most interesting of all, an episode is devised for the pilgrim Monk which enables references both to a literate member of the Canterbury monastery (such as the author may have been), and to the legendary hospitality to

---

44 Daniel Knapp, 'The Relyk of a Seint: A Gloss on Chaucer's Pilgrimage', *ELH* 39 (1972), 3.
45 D. H. Turner, 'The Customary of the Shrine of St Thomas Becket', *Canterbury Cathedral Chronicle*, No. 70 (1976), 16–22.
46 References are to *Tale of Beryn*, ed. Furnivall and Stone. I have emended lines from that edition on the basis of photographs of the text of MS Alnwick 455 taken by me in September 1985. For permission to reproduce the MS for the purposes of research I am grateful to Mr Colin Shrimpton of the Northumberland Estates Office.

be found there. He invites the Parson and Friar to join him in visiting an acquaintance, 'my brothir in habit and in possessioune' (271) who has been pressing him by letter for three years to make a visit. They are received with memorable generosity:

> For of the best that myght be found, and therwith mery chere
> They had, it is no doubt, for spycys and eke wyne
> Went rounde aboute, the gascoyn and eke the ruyne.
> (278–80)

On this occasion there is no hint of animosity between Monk and Friar, but elsewhere friars receive short shrift. There is an element of conventional satire, but nevertheless the author is not likely to have belonged to one of their orders.[47] One incident uses Chaucer's idea of the Friar as a ladies' man sharply to disparage this pilgrim and to illustrate why friars have lost esteem and respect. At the entrance to the church he attempts winsomely ('fetously'), but without success, to gain control of the holy water sprinkler. His motive is not a pious one, it is in order to see the Nun's face. His spirituality, like hers (GP 142, 150) has become misdirected: 'So longid his holy conscience to se the Nonnys fase' (140–4). Other opportunities are taken to associate friars with vicious living. For example, Kitt provokes the sexual affections of the Pardoner 'As thoughe she had lernyd cury fauel of som old frer' (362).

The detail with which he describes pilgrim practices and behaviour supports the idea that the *Beryn* author was a member of the Christ Church community with particular responsibilities at the shrine of Becket. He is familiar, in the first place, with customary matters: the Knight allows the prelates to enter the church door first because he 'knewe righte wele the guyse' (136); the monk with his sprinkler 'did as the manere is' (139); and after the shrine has been visited the pilgrims purchase badges 'as manere and custom is' (171). The stress here and elsewhere on income generated by the shrine is consonant with the responsibilities of the temporal guardian in keeping account of the offerings, undertaking audits, paying the assistant

---

47 Bashe, 'Prologue', 5–6.

clerks and making payments of other kinds.[48] Other procedures followed by the *Beryn* pilgrims are equally authentic. The offerings to be made at the shrine are 'sylvir broch and ryngis' (134), kinds of gift often connected with that place;[49] the pilgrims kneel at the shrine, tell their beads, praying to St Thomas, and kiss the relics as they are displayed and named by an attendant monk; they then visit 'other placis of holynes' within the church (163–70), presumably other sites associated with Becket, like the Martyrdom, at which the guardians of the shrine and their clerks also performed duties; and buy pilgrim badges.[50] Nor does the author ignore the effect of the cathedral on those seeing it for the first time. The stained glass, in particular, still one of the glories of the building, distracts the Pardoner and Miller and others until they are 'half amasid' (158) and have to be ushered forward by the Host, still 'goglyng with hire hedis' (163).[51] That the glass should receive special attention is a further indication of the

[48] Turner, 'Customary of the Shrine', 17.
[49] W. A. Scott Robertson, 'The Crypt of Canterbury Cathedral', Part 2, *Archaeologia Cantiana* 13 (1880), 510–11; C. Eveleigh Woodruff, 'The Financial Aspect of the Cult of St Thomas of Canterbury as Revealed by a Study of the Monastic Records', *Archaeologia Cantiana* 44 (1932), 29.
[50] Cecil Brent, 'Pilgrims' Signs', *Archaeologia Cantiana* 13 (1880), 111–15; Robertson, 'Crypt of Canterbury Cathedral', 516–22; A. P. Stanley, *Historical Memorials of Canterbury*, 11th edn (London: Murray, 1912), 217; Raymonde Foreville, *Le Jubilé de saint Thomas Becket du XIIIe au XVe siècle (1220–1470): étude et documents* (Paris: S.E.V.P.E.N., 1958), 12–13; Knapp, 'Relyk of a Seint', 3–5; Turner, 'Customary of the Shrine', 19; John V. Fleming, 'Chaucer and Erasmus on the Pilgrimage to Canterbury: An Iconographical Speculation', in *The Popular Literature of Medieval England*, ed. Thomas J. Heffernan, Tennessee Studies in Literature, 28 (Knoxville: University of Tennessee Press, 1985), 155–6; M. Mitchiner, *Medieval Pilgrim and Secular Badges* (London: Hawkins, 1986), 64–144.
[51] Bashe, 'Prologue', 8; Madeline Harrison Caviness, *The Early Stained Glass of Canterbury Cathedral: Circa 1175–1220* (Princeton: Princeton University Press, 1977); and her *The Windows of Christ Church Cathedral, Canterbury*, Corpus vitrearum Medii Aevi, 2 (Oxford: Oxford University Press for the British Academy, 1981).

author's preoccupations: income at the shrine was used for the upkeep of the windows in the shrine precincts.[52]

Manly and Rickert dated MS Alnwick 455, on palaeographic grounds, to between 1450 and 1470.[53] Doyle agrees in general, but accepts the possibility of an earlier date: 'it is probably of the third quarter of the 15th century, certainly not earlier than the second'.[54] Given that *Beryn* is copied from an unknown exemplar, perhaps from the author's own copy of the work, the date of composition can be set some years earlier than the date of the surviving manuscript. Thus the palaeographic data indicate that the poem must have been composed at the latest by the mid 1460s, and at the earliest by about 1420.

Bennett, on unspecified grounds, dated the composition of *Beryn* to 'after 1400'.[55] It is certainly clear that the author of *Beryn* had access to a reasonably complete version of the *Canterbury Tales*. He was familiar with the General Prologue and the fabliau tales of Fragment I, with the Friar's Tale and Summoner's Tale. He also knew the Canon's Yeoman's Prologue, Pardoner's Tale and Merchant's Tale. Now the earliest surviving collection of the *Canterbury Tales*, that represented by the Hengwrt manuscript (which itself omits the Canon's Yeoman Prologue and Tale), dates from the first years after 1400,[56] so it is reasonable to assume on this evidence that *Beryn* is unlikely to have been composed before about 1410. Pearsall dates *Beryn* to the beginning of the fifteenth century, while Tamanini,

---

52 Turner, 'Customary of the Shrine', 21.
53 Manly and Rickert, *Text of the Canterbury Tales*, 388.
54 Tamanini, ed., *Tale of Beryn*, 1, n. 2.
55 Bennett, *Chaucer and the Fifteenth Century*, 317.
56 A. I. Doyle and M. B. Parkes, 'Palaeographical Introduction', in *The Canterbury Tales: A Facsimile and Transcription of the Hengwrt Manuscript, with Variants from the Ellesmere Manuscript*, ed. Paul G. Ruggiers, Variorum Edition of the Works of Geoffrey Chaucer, 1 (Norman: University of Oklahoma Press, 1979), xx–xxi.

Journey's End: The Prologue to the Tale of Beryn

after a careful consideration of the evidence, similarly opts for 'early in the fifteenth century'.[57]

As with the question of authorship, some internal evidence needs to be weighed. The Canterbury inn at which the pilgrims stay, the 'Cheker of the hope' (14), was built by Prior Chillenden, specifically for the pilgrim trade, between 1392 and 1395.[58] (Its title refers to the inn sign, presumably a square checkerboard enclosed within a hoop of wood or metal.) It remained the most prominent purpose-built accommodation for pilgrims until 1437–8, when The Sun was erected by Christ Church priory, even closer to the cathedral, adjacent to one of the main gates of approach.[59] If the *Beryn* author had been writing after 1438 it is likely that he would have sited the action of the prologue at The Sun by virtue of its closeness to the cathedral and its novelty as a building. That he chose the Cheker of the hope indicates that it was at the time of writing the most suitable setting. The eastern section of the building still stands in Canterbury, at the west corner of Mercery Lane and the High Street. The stone arcades of the ground floor are now occupied by shops.

Again, when the Knight and his companions find time on their hands they go to inspect the defences of the city: the wall and the 'wardes' or defensible gates of Canterbury. The Knight proceeds to deliver an authoritative talk to his son (237–44). There is a degree of topicality in the episode, since the city's defences were extensively rebuilt (under the supervision of Henry Yevele) in the later fourteenth and early fifteenth centuries, in response to the threat of French invasion. Work was under way by 1378

---

57 Derek Pearsall, *Old English and Middle English Poetry*, Routledge History of English Poetry, 1 (London: Routledge and Kegan Paul, 1977), 298; Tamanini, ed., *Tale of Beryn*, 76.
58 Stanley, *Historical Memorials*, 213–14; C. Eveleigh Woodruff, 'A Monastic Chronicle Lately Discovered at Christ Church, Canterbury: With Introduction and Notes', *Archaeologia Cantiana* 29 (1911), 65, 69.
59 T. Tatton-Brown, *Medieval Inns in Canterbury* (Canterbury: Canterbury Archaeological Trust, 1987).

and had been completed by 1409.[60] It is particularly interesting that the Knight should mention attack by gun – 'the perell and the doubt | For shot of arblast' (241) – and the appropriate form of defence, since provision was made at West Gate, reconstructed by about 1380 at the expense of archbishop Simon Sudbury, for the firing of guns, the gunports for which are still visible.[61] Its novelty as a fortification, and indeed the novelty of using guns in siege warfare in the late fourteenth and early fifteenth centuries, provide a plausible context for the Knight's activities and remarks. West Gate is 'the earliest known fortress in this country designed specifically for defence with guns'.[62]

The evidence so far presented tends to suggest that the prologue to *Beryn* was composed at the earlier end of the possible period between 1420 and 1460. But what could have prompted a monk of Christ Church, of all people, to compose a bawdy farce about one of Chaucer's pilgrims two decades after Chaucer's death? That it was not unknown for Benedictine monks to compose continuations of the *Canterbury Tales* in the early fifteenth century is clear from the case of John Lydgate, who was familiar with a similar range of Canterbury tales, and whose prologue to the *Siege of Thebes* describes the author, in the course of a pilgrimage to Canterbury after a recovery from illness, meeting Chaucer's company at the city inn where they had chosen to stay.[63] The following morning the entire company sets off on the return journey, intending to dine at Ospringe. Before

60   John H. Harvey, *Henry Yevele c.1320 to 1400: The Life of an English Architect* (London: Batsford, 1944), 61; Hilary L. Turner, *Town Defences in England and Wales: An Architectural and Documentary Study AD 900–1500* (London: Baker, 1971), 148–54; S. S. Frere, S. Stow and P. Bennett, *Excavations on the Roman and Medieval Defences of Canterbury*, The Archaeology of Canterbury, 2 (Maidstone: Kent Archaeological Society, 1982), 21–4; John H. Harvey, 'Henry Yeveley and the Nave of Canterbury Cathedral', *Canterbury Cathedral Chronicle* No. 79 (1985), 8.
61   Frere, Stow and Bennett, *Excavations*, 107–19.
62   A. R. Dufty, 'Review of *Castles and Cannon: A Study in Early Fortification in England*, by B. H. St J. O'Neil', *Archaeological Journal* 119 (1962), 369.
63   A. C. Spearing, 'Lydgate's Canterbury Tale: The *Siege of Thebes* and Fifteenth-Century Chaucerianism', in *Fifteenth-Century Studies: Recent Essays*, ed. Robert F. Yeager (Hamden, Conn.: Archon Books, 1984), 337; Rosamund S. Allen, 'The *Siege of Thebes*:

they are a bow shot from Canterbury the Host asks the new arrival to tell a tale, and he obliges, passing on the way the village of Boughton (lines 1–176, 1047–60).

Lydgate's composition is generally dated to 1420 or soon after,[64] and in the same year one finds another monk, this time of Christ Church itself, composing a poem in Latin extolling the virtues of a pilgrimage to the shrine of St Thomas. Copies were affixed, much like modern advertisements, at various prominent positions within Canterbury cathedral, and also on the door of St Paul's cathedral in London.[65] The reason for this literary activity by a Canterbury monk, and perhaps the occasion for Lydgate's prologue, was that 1420 was one of the years of jubilee. Jubilees occurred every fifty years to mark the anniversary of the martyrdom of St Thomas. For this, the fifth jubilee year, more than a normal effort was necessary on the part of the prior and convent. The prior's accounts show a steady decline in takings at the shrine and at other locations during the preceding years. In 1396 the total was £503. 0s. 10d., but by 1410 it had fallen to £265. 18s. 4d.[66] The jubilee year a decade later was promoted and prepared for with unusual care. Financial considerations were one factor. The jubilee also provided an occasion to assert orthodoxy and demonstrate the effectiveness of indulgences against the invective of the Lollards, who had singled out devotion to St Thomas as an example of the false piety of pilgrimage and of idolatry sustained by shrines, images and relics.[67]

Efforts were made well in advance of 1420 to secure from Pope Martin V a plenary indulgence, traditionally all but synonymous with the word

---

Lydgate's Canterbury Tale', *Chaucer and Fifteenth-Century Poetry*, ed. Boffey and Cowen (1991), 122–42.
64   Johnstone Parr, 'Astronomical Daring for Some of Lydgate's Poems', *PMLA* 67 (1952), 253–6.
65   Foreville, *Jubilé de saint Thomas*, 134–5.
66   Woodruff, 'Financial Aspect', 22.
67   J. F. Davis, 'Lollards, Reformers and St Thomas of Canterbury', *University of Birmingham Historical Journal* 9 (1963), 1–15; Anne Hudson, ed., *Selections from English Wycliffite Writings* (Cambridge: Cambridge University Press, 1978), 153–4; Fleming, 'Chaucer and Ersamus', 152–4.

'jubilee'.[68] Martin, whose policy was hostile to the incipient autonomy of the English church, withheld his approval. When it was not forthcoming, four doctors in theology examined at Canterbury the indulgence granted by Honorius VI for the first jubilee in 1220, and declared that it was still effective.[69] Such independence of action was accompanied by a propaganda campaign designed to demonstrate the legitimacy of the plenary indulgence to be enjoyed by those attending the celebrations. In addition to the composition of a Latin poem, notices were drafted and affixed to prominent places at St Paul's in London, Christ Church and Ospringe and, at the turn of the year, a monk – probably Richard Godmersham – composed in the form of a letter a treatise on the fifth jubilee, in effect a chronicle-cum-apologia and anti-Lollard polemic.[70]

In the event the jubilee, which took place in early July, was a great success. Occurring in an atmosphere of international peace and reconciliation (it was the year of the Treaty of Troyes), the fifth jubilee has been called the apogée of Canterbury pilgrimage.[71] Such was the crowd of people who packed into the cathedral for Mass on 7 July that the preacher, the Augustinian Thomas Tynwith, had to repeat his homily three times. Significantly, the chosen text, *Annus jubileus est* (Leviticus 25:10), allowed for a further iteration of how the jubilee enabled remission of the punishment and guilt occasioned by sin. The city bailiffs claimed that 100,000 people came to the city, and were satisfactorily fed and housed, thanks to the co-operation of the local citizens.[72] The jubilee celebrations lasted for fifteen days and, as far as the prior was concerned they were financially satisfactory: his accounts for 1420 show a steep climb in offerings at the shrine and elsewhere, to £644.[73]

68 Foreville, *Jubilé de saint Thomas*, 21–8, 34.
69 Ibid., 37–45, 61–6, 115–18; E. F. Jacob, *Archbishop Henry Chichele* (London: Nelson, 1967), 43–6.
70 Foreville, *Jubilé de saint Thomas*, 52–6, 101–13, 129.
71 Ibid., 17.
72 Ibid., 18, 142–3, 180–1.
73 Woodruff, 'Financial Aspect', 22.

It is not unreasonable to assume that the prologue of *Beryn* was composed as part of the process of promoting the jubilee of 1420, written by a monk of Christ Church, who was probably a guardian of the shrine, to encourage visitors and gifts. Suitably published by being read aloud to appropriate audiences, it would have been capable not only of entertaining, but of creating the pleasing impression among listeners that by visiting Canterbury they would become nothing less than Chaucer's pilgrims incarnate, enacting his fiction, enjoying the jokes and bonhomie, and playing out the appropriate roles. In the course of so doing they would bring the *Canterbury Tales* to fruition by arriving in the city and visiting the shrine where, in the normal course of events, they would make offerings, such as the rings and brooches described by the *Beryn* author, and buy pilgrim badges: 'Ech man set his sylvir in such thing as they likid' (173).

The way in which the prologue is structured provides some sense of the circumstances of its 'publication'. The author adopts a Chaucerian persona, which he uses, as in the opening lines, to establish his values, set the tone of the narrative, thicken the meaning of the story with some sententious statement, or emphasize a particular theme. Subsequently appearing at regular intervals, his interjections of a dozen lines or so would also have indicated to an audience the stage which the narrative had reached and what was to be expected in the way of content. As structural members of the composition they divide the action into segments roughly equivalent to the span of a listener's attention and provide both a breathing space and an opportunity to re-engage interest. Such functions are especially clear in the remarks which conclude the Pardoner's first visit to Kitt, in which the audience is thrice told what it is about to *hear* (119–29).

The nature of the intended audience is indicated by the content of the prologue. It is written on the assumption that its auditors are intelligent, literate, and in particular that they are familiar with the *Canterbury Tales*. The author has studded his composition with references to Chaucer's poetry which operate at various levels of subtlety but which do not work at all if the recipients are ignorant of what Chaucer wrote. The appeal of the prologue is in this respect to a group of initiates, of educated people in the know, who carry an awareness of or an affection for the *Canterbury Tales* as part of their cultural outlook. That the author of *Beryn* has chosen a fabliau as the genre on which to base his prologue is a further indication that it is targeted at a bourgeois or would-be aristocratic audience, and one which would not have omitted the likes of the Merchant, who is treated with a certain amount of preference: it has been argued that fabliaux were customarily intended for a mixed audience on the cusp between bourgeois and seigneurial affiliations.[74]

The repeated emphasis on 'curtesy' and 'gentilnes' in a variety of favourable contexts, however much these may be Chaucerian themes, indicates more sharply the outlook of those for whom the prologue was originally intended.[75] An appeal to such values would have been particularly effective and appropriate, given the extent to which the pilgrimage to Canterbury continued to enjoy royal attention and patronage throughout this period.[76] The prologue is appealing to and reinforcing the values and ideals of behaviour of those who, if not born to courtly ways, regard themselves as at least capable of adopting and emulating them with reasonable accuracy. There are two approaches to 'curtesy' and 'gentil' behaviour within the prologue. They are taken for granted as desirable qualities, assumed standards which operate among people of certain aspirations; and they are represented as unattainable by others, who become the target of comedy.

Thus, Kitt acts with mock deference to the Pardoner, flattering him by presuming that he is 'gentil' (as in the General Prologue, line 669) and 'nobill' (56–7). Later, she lavishes praise on his generosity in paying a groat – an excessive amount – for the hot pie that she has brought him. Again he is a 'gentill sire' and, in order not to offend his 'curtesy' rather than accept the proper payment she puts the entire amount in her purse (88–93). However, when the Pardoner, that evening, stalks into Kitt's bedroom, she reproaches

---

74   Charles Muscatine, *The Old French Fabliaux* (New Haven: Yale University Press, 1986), 46.
75   Derek Brewer, 'Class Distinction in Chaucer', *Speculum* 43 (1968), 298–300.
76   Stanley, *Historical Memorials*, 229–30; James Hamilton Wylie and William Templeton Waugh, *The Reign of Henry the Fifth* (Cambridge: Cambridge University Press, 1929), iii, 10, 18–19, 21; Foreville, *Jubilé de saint Thomas*, 15–16; D. Seward, *Henry as Warlord* (London: Sidgwick and Jackson, 1987), 84–5, 89; W. M. Ormrod, 'The Personal Religion of Edward III', *Speculum* 64 (1989), 858.

Journey's End: The Prologue to the Tale of Beryn

him: 'Yee shuld have coughid when ye com – wher lern ye curtesy?' (323). Here, appeals to 'curtesy' and 'gentilnes' are being used by Kitt as crude instruments of control, as a means of exploiting the Pardoner's vanity so that he becomes vulnerable to her manipulations. The values of behaviour are themselves not denigrated: the satire focuses on the Pardoner, who would imagine that what Kitt implies about his ideals is true. Similarly it is the people, not the ideal, who are the target when the Pardoner and Miller fancy that they can interpret heraldic images in the stained glass of the cathedral, 'Countirfeting gentilmen the armys for to blase' (150).

Meanwhile, other members of the company subscribe to the qualities of 'curtesy' and 'gentilnes' in the knowledge that it is appropriate for them to do so, and as a modus vivendi whereby social relations can be conducted with a minimum of difficulty. The Knight, motivated by 'gentilnes' in the manner of his prototype, acts authoritatively in insisting that 'the prelatis' enter the church before 'the curtesy' (135–7). Subsequently, a word from the Knight is sufficient to smooth over the beginnings of an argument between Friar and Host, one in which the 'curtesy' and 'gentilnes' of each begins to be brought into question: the Friar grants that the Host was courteous in agreeing to feed the company in return for stories, but wonders if he has in practice honoured his commitment, and appeals to the Knight as a witness. For his part, the Host says that the Friar's 'gentilnes' in remembering the agreement ought to be enough (suggesting thereby that it is deficient) and that there is therefore no need to call witnesses. The Knight, as arbiter, sides with the Host and the matter is closed (214–26).

The practice of 'curtesy' and 'gentilnes' by others is widespread and goes beyond similar behaviour in the *Canterbury Tales*. The Monk asks the Parson and Friar 'for curteysy' to join him for his visit to a fellow monk (268); the Prioress assents to the Wife of Bath's invitation to drink wine in the garden of the inn 'as vomman taught of gentil blood and hend' (287); the pilgrims of higher social status, given priority treatment on arrival at the inn (19) and better food 'as curtesy axith', return the compliment by paying for everyone to drink wine – 'Wherfor they did hir gentilness ageyn to al the rout' (403–5); and the Host and Merchant, 'wexen somwhat wroth' at the noise caused by the revellers as they try to compute the accounts, 'preyd him curteysly to rest for to wend' (420–1). For the Host in particular there is a practical use for 'curtesy' in that he may appeal to it for help in running the day-to-day arrangements of the pilgrimage.

The range of social groups among the author's listeners is suggested by some of the interjections by means of which a working relationship with the audience is sustained and developed. He declares that those who value their reputation ('worship') and well-being should avoid the likes of Kitt, her lover and the hosteller: 'no man that lovith his worshipp and hele' (466) should have dealings with them. When it comes to the names which the Pardoner calls Kitt once he has discovered her duplicity the writer stops short for fear of causing offence: such names would not occur to those who (like his audience) are respectable people – either merchants ('men of good'), or men of good reputation ('worship') or high social standing: 'Huch to rech hir wer noon honeste | Among men of good, of worship and degre' (517–18). (This tactic is, of course, only a stimulus for the imaginations of such worthy people to be set racing.)

Women, as forming a distinct group, also feature in the author's understanding of the kind of audience that he is addressing. Once again, a direct reference to the recipients of the narrative is linked with a nice sense of their feelings and general outlook. Commenting on Kitt's success in duping the Pardoner, he uses it as evidence of the success of women in general at deceiving men. But at this he begins to retrace his ground, so leaving the nature of women a matter for debate in case he should offend 'ladies [...] | Or els gentil vomen', who legitimately employ 'daliaunce [...] sportis and [...] goodly chere'. Members of such 'estatis' are not his target but others, lower down the social scale, like Kitt. This is an engaging and adroit passage, designed to tease the audience. It introduces a controversial topic, only to leave it as it were in his listeners' laps while the author decorously disengages himself from any suggestion that he would want to utter words of criticism against any women who might be present (436–46).

If there is some justice in the preceding remarks about the authorship, date and audience of the prologue to *Beryn*, it follows that there are certain consequences for its interpretation as a work of literature. For its main purpose ceases to be that of imitation. Instead, its function becomes that of an occasional piece for which the existence of the *Canterbury Tales*, as a recently composed and well known collection of narratives, was a convenient, but by no means necessary, stimulus. The author's representation of the Pardoner, for example, owes as much to the preoccupations of a Canterbury monk in 1420 as it does to its Chaucerian model.

Superficially, the *Beryn* Pardoner is recognizably the same figure as the one created by Chaucer. The anger which he manifests in response to the Host's attack (PardT 956–7) surfaces again on his being rebuffed by Kitt. On that occasion there is also an example of his vindictiveness, such as he sometimes manifests in the pulpit (PardP 421–2), when he calls his would-be mistress 'namys many mo then oon, | Huch to rech hir wer noon honeste' (516–17). The Pardoner's legendary avarice is kept in play in his plan to seal back the money he gives to Kitt (373–6). And his abuse of the authority vested in him as a representative of the church is instanced in his interpretation of Kitt's supposed dream to his own advantage (106–15).

At the same time, the *Beryn* author subjects the Pardoner to a much lengthier and more detailed treatment than any other of Chaucer's characters. He singles out the Pardoner for humiliation, especially by dwelling on his hypocrisy, blasphemy and lechery. That process is best demonstrated by means of an example, one which simultaneously reveals the subtlety of the writer's techniques: the Pardoner's first encounter with Kitt. From the outset, the Pardoner is – unusually for him – unwittingly on the receiving end of a deception (what he would call a 'jape'), while all the time believing that Kitt is his prey and that he is in control of the situation. After the Pardoner has absented himself from the rest of the company, Kitt greets him affectionately, with a 'Welcom, myne owne brother' and 'frendly look, al redy for to kys' (22–3). The Pardoner responds in kind, and is here described with a wry cadence worthy of Chaucer: he is 'ilernyd of such kyndnes' (24), embraces her about the waist, and 'made hir gladly chere' as though he had known her for a year (25–6). The Pardoner has fallen for the bait and is now led into a trap. Kitt calls the Pardoner into that part of her tapstry where, affecting an erotically inviting pathos, she says that she lies 'my selff al nyght al nakid | Without mannys company syn my love was ded' (28–9). There follows a virtuoso display of histrionics to demonstrate the depth of her feeling for the 'dead' Jenkyn Harpour (32–9). The Pardoner comes in on cue, proceeding to exploit Kitt's grieving by again laying an affectionate hand around her waist, so offering the sympathy and consolation which might be expected by virtue of his profession, but which he now deploys for his own ulterior motives.

Kitt sneezes, and the Pardoner suggests that this is an indication that her grieving or 'penaunce' (43) is coming to an end. Kitt appears to be keen to accept the Pardoner's suggestions, sprinkling her own response with pious-sounding remarks: 'God forbede it els!' (44). False piety has here become a language for expressing erotic attachment, itself false in the case of Kitt and doomed to failure in the case of the Pardoner. Under its cover, the Pardoner gradually transfers attention from Kitt's 'grief' to his own desire. Blessing the God 'of mendement of hele, and eke of cure' he chucks her erotically under the chin and exclaims 'Allas! that love ys syn!' (46–8), words serving at once to confuse divine and sexual love, and to associate the Pardoner with the libidinous attitudes of the Wife of Bath. If there is a Wife of Bath in this episode it is not the Pardoner but Kitt who, like Dame Alys, has mastered one who would master her. The Pardoner continues: 'For be my trewe conscience yit for yewe I smert, | And shal this month hereaftir, for yeur soden disese' (50–1) – an ambiguous statement, describing at once the Pardoner's professed sympathy for Kitt's bereavement while also conveying quite other emotions. He proceeds to flatter Kitt, putting himself forward as a candidate for her new lover, by taking her grieving as evidence that she is 'trewe' in love, and that therefore the man who might win her love would be fortunate indeed (52–4). Thus the 'death' of Jenkyn Harpour, and her 'soden disese', which is 'green in yeur mynde' (54) become the cause of the Pardoner's own sorrow, ostensibly through legitimate compassion but implicitly because of his unfulfilled desire for her. By the time that the Pardoner concludes 'Ye made me a sory man – I dred ye wold have stervid' (55) the emphasis is predominantly sexual. Thus the lechery of the Pardoner, under cover of priestly authority, is laid bare.

The courting of Kitt is an episode which also demonstrates the extent to which the *Beryn* author's Pardoner is a fundamentally different creature from Chaucer's Pardoner, whose most immediate sexual attachment is to a member of his own sex.[77] Elsewhere, too, the *Beryn* author shifts emphasis: he is at pains to stress the isolation of the Pardoner from the rest of the company, and his unattractiveness, in a way that Chaucer never did.[78] He is shown as self-seeking, unsharing, separate from the companionship of others, anti-social, gloating inwardly, scheming to himself to another's disadvantage, secretive – and all this to no avail. Thus the first description of him, at the Cheker of the hope, shows him realizing (perhaps resentfully) that the 'statis' are being ordered food first, and that the Host is too busy to pay any attention to him. This he discerns 'al pryvely and asyde swervid' (19–20) to try his luck with the tapster. His devious characteristics are again represented when he remains at the inn while the other pilgrims pursue diversions elsewhere. Then he 'pryvelich when al they were goon | Stalkid into the tapstry' (298–9) and 'stappid into the tapstry wonder pryvely' (309). Having made arrangements with Kitt he keeps his success slyly to himself while others near him are, as they eat, full of 'sportis and of cher' (390): 'But the Pardonere kept hym close and told nothing of | The myrth and hope that he had, but kept it for himselff' (394–5). Retentive and furtive, a creature of darkness, the Pardoner waits until the merriment has subsided. Each pilgrim goes to rest, 'Save the Pardonere, that drewe apart and wayted hym at rest | For to hyde hymselff till the candill wer out' (424–5).

Such behaviour may lie in the logic of Chaucer's portrait, and be not inconsistent with it, but if so his shaming by the Host has had a devastating effect. He is now a man diminished in confidence, in rhetorical skill, in the success with which he dupes others. He has become a notable failure, rather than the admirable blackguard of the General Prologue (GP 707–14), someone who is pathetic, ineffectual, reduced to a dog-like existence. At Kitt's door he tries to attract her attention, 'And scrapid the dorr welplich and wynyd with his mowith, | Aftir a doggis lyden as ner as he couth' (481–2), at which Kitt's lover shouts 'Away, dogg, with evil deth!' (483). Undeterred, but livid with anger, 'The Pardonere scrapid efft agayne'

77 Darjes and Rendall, 'Fabliau in the Prologue', 427–30.
78 Frederick Tupper, 'The Pardoner's Tavern', *JEGP* 13 (1914), 563–5.

(507), only to be beaten like a dog when Kitt's lover opens her door. It is altogether fitting, then, that someone behaving 'spitouslich' (520) should spend the night in the litter of a 'spetouse' dog (635–48).

Why should the Pardoner be systematically pilloried and vilified by the *Beryn* author? Certainly the process was initiated by Harry Bailly, but it is continued with inordinate relish and gusto. Chaucer's Host, having been addressed as a man 'envoluped in synne' is invited to 'kisse the relikes everychon, | Ye, for a grote! Unbokele anon thy purs' (PardT 942–5). The Pardoner himself receives short shrift, and it is particularly on account of the signs of his false authenticity, his bogus relics – actually animal bones and rags – that the Host launches a virulent attack.[79] In rejecting the Pardoner's proposal the Host claims that the Pardoner would make his soiled 'olde breech' into a relic if he could, perhaps implicitly making a contrast with a true relic, the breeches of St Thomas, kept at Canterbury;[80] and, swearing by another true relic, 'the croys which that Seint Eleyne fond', he threatens to cut off the Pardoner's testicles so that 'They shul be shryned in an hogges toord!' (PardT 948–55).

In such graphic distinctions between true and false relics, and true and false shrines, lies the clue to the reason for the *Beryn* writer's subsequent attack. For it is the Pardoner's role, both historically and as established in the *Canterbury Tales*, to offer for cash payment access to an indulgence.[81] But this is exactly what a pilgrimage to Canterbury did (if in a less obvious way), the relics of St Thomas providing the conduit through which God's grace was effective – 'pilgrimage' and 'indulgence' being, by this time,

---

79 Lawrence Besserman and Melvin Storm, 'Forum: Chaucer's Pardoner', *PMLA* 98 (1983), 405–6.
80 Knapp, 'Relyk of a Saint', 5–14; Melvin Storm, 'The Pardoners Invitation: Quaestor's Bag or Becket's Shrine?', *PMLA* 97 (1982), 815.
81 J. J. Jusserand, *English Wayfaring Life in the Middle Ages (XIVth Century)*, trans. Lucy Toulmin Smith, 3rd edn (London: Unwin, 1925), 312–37; A. Williams, 'Some Documents on English Pardoners, 1350–1400', in *Mediaeval Studies in Honor of Urban Tigner Holmes, Jr.*, ed. J. Mahoney and J. E. Keller, University of North Carolina Studies in the Romance Languages and Literatures, 56 (Chapel Hill, NC: University of North Carolina Press, 1965), 197–207.

virtually interchangeable terms.[82] The Pardoner and his kind represented, to those responsible for propagating and sustaining the cult of St Thomas, serious competition.[83] That a figure such as the Pardoner would have seemed a *bête noire* from a Canterbury viewpoint is clear from Archbishop Chichele's preoccupation with regulating indulgences by restricting their use and the activities of their purveyors. The subject featured in the English Concordat with the papacy in 1418, the first clause of which criticizes those who diverted money from the parochial clergy 'by reasons of divers indulgences and letters of faculties granted by the apostolic see'. Again, in 1424–25, Chichele's constitution concerned unlicensed pardoners and the collection of money for indulgences.[84] Hence the Pardoner is a legitimate target for a monastic author charged with the care of an important shrine. The Pardoner as a travelling shrine, a purveyor of false relics and cash absolutions, is a threat to those who might consider themselves to be the guardians of true relics and the means of obtaining legitimate forgiveness for sin, however much the use of similar money-raising agents was at other times condoned by the Canterbury chapter.[85] Even the gifts which Chaucer's Pardoner solicits – 'silver broches, spoones, rynges' (PardT 908) – bear a striking resemblance to those which the *Beryn* author anticipates for the shrine of St Thomas.

Another kind of reform which the archbishop and chapter promoted was directed at heretics. In a series of trials after the Lollard uprising of 1414

---

82 Christian K. Zacher, *Curiosity and Pilgrimage: The Literature of Discovery in Fourteenth-Century England* (Baltimore: Johns Hopkins, 1976), 45–6; Melvin Storm, '"A Culpa et a Poena": Christ's Pardon and the Pardoner's', *Neuplologische Mitteilungen* 83 (1982), 440–2.
83 Woodruff, 'Financial Aspect', 26–9.
84 *The Register of Henry Chichele Archbishop of Canterbury 1414–1443*, ed. E. F. Jacob et al., 4 vols (Oxford: Oxford University Press, 1937–47), iii (1945), 88–98 and iv (1947), 194–6; Jacob, *Chichele*, 36–7, 41.
85 *Register of Chichele*, ed. Jacob, iv, 260–2; Alfred L. Kellogg and Louis A. Haselmayer, 'Chaucer's Satire of the Pardoner', *PMLA* 66 (1951), 265; Fleming, 'Chaucer and Erasmus', 160–4. My thanks are due to Pamela King for pointing out the relevance of Chichele's policies.

they heard evidence, recorded recantations, and inflicted punishments.[86] To a member of the Christ Church convent sensitized by Lollard trials to the heretics' satire on indulgences and their purveyors, on relics, images and pilgrimage (particularly to Canterbury), the activities of Chaucer's Pardoner could have read as a similar travesty of the activities in which he and his convent were engaged, especially at the time of jubilee.[87] The *Beryn* prologue, insofar as it denigrates the Pardoner and promotes pilgrimage to St Thomas's relics, might have served as a salvo in the pamphleteering war, consistent with the active suppression of Lollard heresy in which the author and his archbishop and convent were then engaged.[88] For Harry Bailly's attack would have warmed the heart of any Canterbury monk hoping to sustain the pilgrim trade. The Host (treated with admiration in the *Beryn* prologue) shames the Pardoner into an angry silence and so saves the day for the shrine of St Thomas. The humiliation and exposure of the Pardoner are, then, processes begun in the *Canterbury Tales* and continued, for his own reasons, by the *Beryn* author, to a point at which the Pardoner and his role became markedly different.

One further factor helps to explain the extremity of the *Beryn* author's attack. The documents concerning the arrangements for the fifth jubilee indicate that Pope Martin V was not entirely pleased with decisions taken by the archbishop and prior without his consent, particularly in the granting of a plenary indulgence, an act which the pope claimed as his prerogative. Likening Archbishop Chichele and Prior Wodenesburgh to 'damned angels' who were guilty of 'unheard-of presumption and reckless sacrilege', he sent two emissaries to Canterbury in 1423 for a post-mortem.[89] It may be that

---

86 Jacob, *Chichele*, 69–72.
87 Knapp, 'Relyk of a Saint', 18–21; Jones, 'Lollards and Images'; Storm, 'Pardoner's Invitation', 810–13; Charles A. Owen, 'Forum: Chaucer's Pardoner', *PMLA* 98 (1983), 254; Besserman and Storm, 'Forum'.
88 *Register of Chichele*, ed. Jacob, iii, pt 1 and iv, pt 1; Anne Hudson, *The Premature Reformation: Wycliffite Texts and Lollard History* (Oxford: Clarendon Press, 1988), 124–5, 164.
89 Woodruff, 'Financial Aspect', 23; Foreville, *Jubilé de saint Thomas*, 181–2; Jacob, *Chichele*, 47–8.

in attacking Chaucer's Pardoner, who 'streight was comen fro the court of Rome' with his wallet 'Bretful of pardoun comen from Rome al hoot' (GP 671, 687) a monk of Christ Church was also expressing the antagonism felt by him, his brothers and his superiors towards papal authority, and their sense of grievance at Pope Martin's reluctance to grant their request.

To credit the *Beryn* author with some independence of motive has the effect of allowing a revaluation of his achievement. That the prologue is derivative goes without saying, but it is far from being slavish imitation. The imaginative life of Chaucer's composition has been internalized to the point where the *Beryn* author can confidently enjoy creative integrity, if not absolute autonomy. His liberties with the Wife of Bath's character, components of which are attributed to the Pardoner, and especially to Kitt, have already been noted in passing, but deserve closer attention because they provide support for the contention that the *Beryn* author is not so much a plagiarizing hack as a sophisticated writer who 'possessed' the *Canterbury Tales* to the point where he could reconstruct its features in his own idiom, according to his own priorities and with a clear understanding of genre.

Hailed by many a modern reader as one of the most memorable and successful of the personalities whom Chaucer creates, the Wife of Bath is given little prominence by the *Beryn* author. Her one appearance occurs after supper when, 'so wery she had no will to walk', she takes the Prioress by the hand and invites her 'Pryvely' into the garden of the inn to inspect the plants and then share some wine with the innkeeper's wife in her parlour (281–3). The Prioress accepts, and so they enter, 'Passyng forth sofftly into the herbery' (289). This muted representation of Dame Alys is consistent with her practice of spending much time with a female 'gossib' (WBP 243, 529, 544, 548), and her enjoyment of walking from house to house to hear 'sondry talys' (WBP 547), but mention of her other quirks and enthusiasms is omitted. That is because, as suggested earlier, the *Beryn* author has another use for them, for in Kitt the characteristics of the Wife of Bath find a new form.[90] Here is a woman who behaves as Alys did in her youth: she is sexually experienced; anticipates and betters the wiles of an (admittedly

---

90 Darjes and Rendall, 'Fabliau in the Prologue', 423–7.

bogus) clerk; reaps financial reward from her stratagems; and is master not only of the Pardoner but also of her regular lover, for whom she devises a role in the humiliation of the Pardoner. She even copies one of the Wife of Bath's most successful ploys (WBP 575–84) in telling the Pardoner of a presumably invented dream, a ploy that flatters the Pardoner by allowing him to display his 'authority' as an interpreter, and which encourages him to think that she is ripe for sexual approach (99–116).

The 'recycling' of Chaucerian characters occurs also in the case of the Pardoner, whose disappointment in love recalls that of Absolon in the Miller's Tale.[91] Thus the sudden dousing of the Pardoner's expectations at Kitt's door as he demands the return of his pilgrim's staff, traditionally associated with tumescent male desire,[92] is not unlike the deflation of self-image which Absolon undergoes at Alison's shot-window:

> For who hath love longing, and is of corage hote,
> He hath ful many a myry thought tofore his delyte,
> And right so had the Pardonere, and was in evil plighte;
> For fayling of his purpose he was nothing in ese.
> (494–7)

Through anger and jealousy he becomes 'almost wood' (501), and when he considers that another man has enjoyed Kitt's company at his expense his thoughts turn to 'vengaunce' (503), before he asks for the return of his staff 'spitouslich' (520). Failing in his bid for retribution, he can only 'curs his angir to aswage, | And was distract of his wit and in grete dispeyr' (628–9). Absolon, similarly affected by 'love-longynge' (MilT 3679), suffers the indignity of kissing Alison's backside and experiences the same emotions as the Pardoner on realizing that Nicholas has supplanted him: 'on his lippe he gan for anger byte, | And to hymself he seyde, "I shall thee quyte"' (MilT 3745–6). In a frenzied state he rubs his mouth with the detritus of the ground outside the carpenter's shop, suddenly cured of his erotomania, 'heeled of his maladie' (MilT 3757). Absolon, of course, takes

---

91 Ibid., 421–3.
92 Zacher, *Curiosity and Pilgrimage*, 109.

quite effective revenge in assaulting Nicholas with a hot coulter, and to this may be compared the success of the Pardoner in hitting Kitt's lover on the nose with a ladle.

The migration of detail from its 'original' source in the *Canterbury Tales* to new locations in the prologue to *Beryn*, the borrowing of descriptions and turns of phrase originally associated with one character for use with another, may be taken as evidence of artistic failure on the author's part. Alternatively, it may indicate that literary 'character', as it is generally understood today, was not, to a medieval writer, inviolate, but more a loose amalgam of ingredients from various sources, any one of which could be borrowed and recombined elsewhere. Such a technique of personal delineation is, after all, one that Chaucer himself used, as Jill Mann has shown.[93] It is a principle of composition which extends beyond character to the architecture of the narrative itself. Two tales in particular, those of the Miller and Reeve, are quarries for the *Beryn* author's building materials, as the reappearance of 'Absolon' in the guise of the Pardoner already suggests.

The sparring of Kitt and Pardoner, using wit and words, is in the same vein as the contest between native wit (or low cunning) and educated intelligence which informs both the Miller's Tale and the Reeve's Tale. There, clerks are set against ignorant people and (eventually) win. In the *Beryn* version of this scenario the tables are turned and a supposedly clever clerk is discredited by the more subtle manoeuvres of his adversary which, ironically, include his being blinded by flattery along the lines of 'you clerks are so much cleverer than the like of us' (a strategy earlier used, but with less success, by the Miller of the Reeve's Tale, 4122–6). Turns of phrase echo the source of the *Beryn* author's inspiration. He asks his audience 'who is that a vomain coud nat make his berd'? (436) and the Pardoner later grieves at the 'makeing of his berd' (622) at the hands of a woman. The proverbial expression is amusing applied to the Pardoner, who is notoriously clean-shaven (GP 689–91), but it also recalls Symkyn's comment as

---

[93] Jill Mann, *Chaucer and Medieval Estates Satire: The Literature of Social Classes and the General Prologue to the 'Canterbury Tales'* (Cambridge: Cambridge University Press, 1973).

he sees through the attempts of John and Aleyn to outwit him: 'Yet kan a millere make a clerkes berd' (RvT 4096).

Again, the prologue to *Beryn* is an 'argument of herbergage', to use the Cook's phrase (CkP 4329), along the lines of that adumbrated in his own fragmentary tale, and explored at length in the preceding two. In this species of tale crucial concerns are who lodges with whom, in which bed, and with which other person. The 'herbergage' topic and its likely outcome are announced at the moment when the Pardoner seeks out Kitt for the second time. 'He wold be loggid with hir, that was his hole entencioun' (301), although in the event 'hym had bette be iloggit al nyght in a myere | Then he was the same nyght' (304–5). The accommodation which the pilgrims find at the Cheker of the hope, termed 'hire herbegage' (379), is satisfactory enough, and the Pardoner, who expects that he will be sharing Kitt's bed, congratulates himself on being 'iloggit [...] best' and at no cost, for he intends to pick her purse (374–6). He is, of course, disappointed in Kitt on both counts, and so prays to St Julian, the patron saint of hospitality, that her own travels be damned, 'That the devill hire shuld spede on watir and on londe, | So to disseyve a traveling man of his herbegage' (626–7). The Pardoner suffers his final ignominy when he is forced to seek his 'logging' in a dog's litter. Even then 'The warrok' will not let him rest (632–48).

Once the nocturnal fracas gets under way the main source of influence shifts to the Reeve's Tale.[94] As in The Reeve's Tale, a dark interior, sleeping figures, and an individual intent on erotic adventure are the prelude to farcical happenings (473–7 and RvT 4153–98). In pursuit of the Pardoner, Kitt's lover is described as 'Graspyng aftir with the staff' (528) to hit the Pardoner, whom he 'fond' (529), recalling indirectly the way in which John the clerk 'graspeth by the walles to and fro, | To fynde a staf' (RvT 4293–4). Later, in a more cautious frame of mind, Kitt's lover encourages Jak the innkeeper to go and fetch light because 'thow knowest bette then I | Al the estris of this house' (555–6), a familiarity with an interior shared by the miller's wife in the Reeve's Tale, who is more successful than John in finding a staff because she 'knew the estres bet' (RvT 4295). Deceptive appearances,

---

94 Darjes and Rendall, 'Fabliau in the Prologue', 430–1.

caused by the glimmering of the moon as it reflects on Symkyn's bald head, cause the final uproar of the Reeve's Tale (RvT 4297–301). As if Jak remembers the fate of the Trumpington miller he declines to fetch light 'For by the blysyng of the cole he myght se myne hede' (561). So the action continues in absolute darkness, with the Pardoner finding a ladle when 'he graspid ferthermore to have somwhat in honde' (573) and with the Host, hurting his shin, obliged 'to grope where to sete' (591) much as, in the pantomime of the Reeve's Tale, Symkyn's wife 'groped heer and ther' and 'gropeth alwey forther with hir hond' (RvT 4217, 4222) in order to find the cradle which signals (or so she thinks) that she has found her own, adjacent, bed. Fortunately for the Pardoner, and necessarily if the pilgrim company is to return to London intact, he endures no physical and public defeat – not least because, by contrast with the moonlit scene at Trumpington, Jak and Kitt's lover cannot find their quarry (605) and so they take the latter's advice, 'Sith the moon is down, for to go to rest' (610). When the pilgrims do set out the next morning the Reeve and his tale are not entirely forgotten: in order to avoid detection the Pardoner hides among his companions 'And evirmore he held hym amydward the route' (670). The Reeve, for other reasons, rode at the rear, 'And evere he rood the hyndreste of oure route' (GP 622).

The prologue to *Beryn* is a tale based in contemporary city life in the manner of the fabliaux of Fragment I of the *Canterbury Tales*. It reveals as much about medieval Canterbury as the Miller's Tale does about Oxford, the Reeve's Tale does about Cambridge and its environs, and the Cook's Tale begins to do about London.[95] Mention has already been made of the authentic descriptions of Christ Church, its architecture, pilgrim trade and monastery; of the city and its defences; and of the functioning of a major pilgrim inn, the Checker of the hope. Typical of the verisimilitude

---

95 Beryl Rowland, 'What Chaucer Did to the Fabliau', *Studia Neophilologica* 51 (1979), 207–8.

with which such places are treated is the author's description of the inn garden or 'herbery'[96] in which the Wife of Bath and Prioress walk: there

> [...] many a herbe grewe for sew and surgery,
> And al the aleyis feir and parid and raylid and imakid,
> The sauge and the isope ifrettid and istakid,
> And othir beddis by an by fressh idight,
> For comers to the hoost righte a sportful sight.
> (290–4)

Such topographical detail is entirely in keeping with, say, Chaucer's account of John's house and its neighbourhood in Oxford, or Symkyn's fenland mill at Trumpington.[97]

In the process of his creative engagement with Chaucer's narratives, the *Beryn* author maintains a keen sense of what is appropriate to the genre, thereby producing one of the rare examples of an English fabliau.[98] The descriptive realism usually associated with this species of narrative has already been amply demonstrated. But once the climactic action of the night gets under way the realism slips into another gear. There are then numerous references to the furnishings, fittings, and internal design of the Cheker of the hope as the three men blunder about in the dark: the candles (425, 473), the opening and locking mechanism on Kitt's door (477–9), the hosteller's bed (531), the key to the kitchen (544), the bedchamber of Jak's wife, which is above Kitt's (545), the hall where guests take supper, also on an upper floor, where there is a fireplace (550–2), the pans, watercans and ladle (565–6, 574, 587), the dog's litter under the stairs (632–3). Now this amount of detail has the effect of making the interior of the inn seem credible and tangible, but in a sense that is a side-effect. The primary purpose is functional: everything mentioned has a use in the unfolding of

---

96 Frank Crisp, *Mediaeval Gardens, 'Flowery Medes' and Other Arrangements of Herbs, Flowers and Shrubs Grown in the Middle Ages*, ed. Catherine Childs Paterson, 2 vols (London: Bodley Head, 1924), i, 20–3.

97 J. A. W. Bennett, *Chaucer at Oxford and at Cambridge* (Oxford: Clarendon Press, 1974), 34–40, 111–12.

98 Winstead, '*Beryn*-Writer', 226; Robbins, 'English Fabliau', 1970.

the action, and is introduced, like a stage property, because it is necessary. Once the usefulness of the object or place has passed, it is forgotten. Such 'disposable realism', if that is an appropriate term, is a familiar feature of the genre.[99]

Also characteristic of the fabliau is a strong dramatic element. It finds expression chiefly through dialogue and through episodes of fast action. In addition, the *Beryn* author attends to the expressiveness of movement, posture, gesture and facial expression. This makes the dramatic content of his composition considerably more interesting than it might be in a run-of-the-mill fabliau, and suggests on his part a keen appreciation of the language of the human body. He deploys body language sparingly, using it in the main as a means of communication between the Pardoner and Kitt. As with other forms of language, she is considerably more successful than he is in using it as an instrument of power and control. Thus he signals to her his attitude and intentions in conventional straightforward terms: an embrace (25, 40), a tweak of the chin (47), an amorous look: he 'unlasid his both eyen liddes, | And lokid hire in the visage paramour amyddis' (67–8), a hand on her breast (313). Kitt reads the signs and turns them to her own advantage. But the Pardoner is completely taken in by Kitt's own performance, not least because she is a much better amateur actress. Thus to engage his sympathy for the invented death of Jenkyn Harpour she enacts an impressive range of emotionally charged actions. She weeps, wiping her eyes gently 'with hire napron feir and white iwassh' (33), the very picture of female distress. The tears are superlatively pitiful, and ludicrous to the audience, if not to the Pardoner: 'As grete as eny mylstone upward gon they stert' (35). Weeping and wailing, she wrings her hands 'For love of hir swetyng that sat so nyghe hire hen' (36) and concludes her no doubt well rehearsed business with a display of misery that invites an affectionate gesture: 'She snyffith, sighith and shooke hire hede and made rouful chere' (39).

---

99 Charles Muscatine, *Chaucer and the French Tradition: A Study in Style and Meaning* (Berkeley and Los Angeles: University of California Press, 1957), 59–67.

Beneath the gaiety or 'chaff' of the narrative lies, in Chaucerian manner, a rather more serious content or 'fruit' or, to use the *Beryn* author's own variant of the familiar metaphors, 'yolke' within the 'white' (732). Its notable manifestation concerns the question of fellowship, adopted from the *Canterbury Tales* as an ideal with an alarming propensity to disintegration.[100] However, the location of the main threat to fellowship is moved away from the quarrelsome relations of the pilgrims themselves and towards an external situation, that of the scheming of Kitt and her accomplices.

At the outset, 'feleshipp' refers to the company of pilgrims (118, 370, 675). It has positive connotations and is actively supported as an improving species of social organization by the Host, who reminds the Miller and Pardoner that they are 'in company of honest men and good' (159). Falling in with the will of the majority and imitating their actions – in this case worshipping at the shrine of St Thomas – will, he suggests, have a beneficial effect, 'For who doith aftir company may lyve the bet in rest' (162). But in spite of the Host's best efforts, rival fellowships, complete with a rival 'covenaunte' (300) of an unsavoury or subversive kind, exist and flourish. If they do not directly threaten the dominant fellowship of pilgrims and their values of honesty, courtesy and good reputation, they at least indicate the potential for social and moral division. Thus Kitt encourages the Pardoner to 'Ete and be mery' and break his fast rather than wait for the 'feleshipp' of the other pilgrims (71–2). False fellowship is particularly associated with the alliance formed by Kitt, her lover and Jak the hosteller, one which prompts even the *Beryn* author to comment sympathetically on what is in store for the Pardoner:

> It was a shrewid company – they had served so many oon
> With such manere of feleshipp, ne kepe I nevir to dele,
> Ne no man that lovith his worshipp and his hele.
> (464–6)

Later they are called 'the felisshipp that should nevir thryve' (534), and it is with certain relief that the Pardoner escapes a second drubbing by hiding

---

100 Zacher, *Curiosity and Pilgrimage*, 87–101.

among the pilgrims, the 'feleshippe' proper (657, 675) or the 'company', as it is here repeatedly described (656, 661, 666). The Pardoner feigns merriment in order to merge better into his surroundings: he 'made lightsome cher' (663) and sings (671). It is as if he has learnt the value (or at least the usefulness) of the true fellowship which this pilgrimage represents and perhaps even of being 'gentil' (658).

The *Beryn* author was one of the earliest poets working in the English tradition to register the 'anxiety of influence', that sense of being indebted to, yet needing to escape from, the work of an earlier English writer. Much of what Spearing says of Lydgate's attempts, in the *Siege of Thebes*, to come to terms with Chaucer's legacy, is also true of the author of the prologue: his perception of a *tessera*, or loose end which forms a link, in the form of the incompleteness of Chaucer's work; his deliberate use of allusions to Chaucer's poetry; his ability to free himself from dependence upon his master; his reliance on an audience well versed in Chaucer's poetry; and his periodic success in achieving irony and an eloquence perfectly appropriate to sense.[101] The major difference lies in what the two poets respond to, which in turn has consequences for the kind of writing each produces. Thus Lydgate's *Siege* 'completes' the Knight's Tale with another romance, and in so doing its author affects a high style of latinate language full of formal rhetorical devices. The *Beryn* author, for his part, 'completes' the sequence begun by the fabliau tales which follow the Knight's Tale, choosing for that purpose a demotic style. It is almost as if Lydgate and the *Beryn* author, writing at the same time and both Benedictine monks, were collaborators in a project designed to continue and complete the *Canterbury Tales*.

Whatever the truth of the matter, the *Beryn* prologue deserves to be considered more carefully for the evidence it provides about the reception of the *Canterbury Tales* in the fifteenth century. It has become generally accepted that, following the dispersal, retirement, or death of Chaucer's immediate public, the wide range of his writing fell on deaf ears. Early fifteenth-century readers, it is said, set more store by his love lyrics and

---

101 Spearing, 'Lydgate's Canterbury Tale'.

dream visions than by *Troilus* and the *Canterbury Tales*. That secondary audience, as recently described by Strohm,[102] is said to have existed in the later years of Chaucer's life, then to have enlarged rapidly after his death. Socially, it extended wider and deeper than the knights and esquires of the king's households, lawyers, chancery figures and other civil servants who have been identified as members of the Chaucer circle. Instead, its base was in a literate middle estate of landed gentry and prosperous merchants with a fascination for aristocratic mores, a social order relatively unaffected by the rhythms of professional careers and the vagaries of court patronage. In terms of literary taste, at least on the evidence of anthologies, it was narrowly predisposed towards compositions self-evidently courtly.[103]

Embedded in the prologue to *Beryn*, as we have seen, are courtly aspirations, and so it would appear to appeal to much the same kind of audience. Beneath the surface excitement there is a deep-rooted conservative, orthodox element. Hierarchies are not challenged, genres are not violated. On the other hand, the poetry of the prologue is of a radically different kind from that of other Chaucerian compositions of the early fifteenth century designed for the emergent élite. Unlike those works, it is prepared to embrace, and to respond to, some of Chaucer's most innovative writing, writing which was otherwise unpopular in the fifteenth century.[104] It may be, then, that the *Beryn* author's audience is in two senses transitional: it spans the period between Chaucer's last years and the 1420s, showing that the *Canterbury Tales* in all their variety enjoyed continuing appeal beyond Chaucer's immediate circle; and it simultaneously accepts the imaginative stimulation of Chaucer's work while wanting to reassert unquestioned, traditional values in a way that was to become more and more the norm.[105]

102 Paul Strohm, 'Chaucer's Fifteenth-Century Audience and the Narrowing of the "Chaucer Tradition"', *Studies in the Age of Chaucer* 4 (1982), 3–32.
103 Pearsall, *Old English and Middle English Poetry*, 212–14; Richard Firth Green, *Poets and Princepleasers: Literature and the English Court in the Late Middle Ages* (Toronto: University of Toronto Press, 1980), 9–10; Strohm, 'Chaucer's Fifteenth-Century Audience', 18.
104 Ibid., 24–5.
105 Ibid., 27.

The continuity of appeal from the *Canterbury Tales* through to the prologue to *Beryn* indicates that there was in his larger, secondary audience an element which possessed a keen appreciation of a wide range of his techniques.[106] If, on Chaucer's death, there was a 'dispersion' of his literary public, the narrowing of literary taste did not occur until later, in the 1420s rather than the 1400s.[107] It is difficult therefore to accept Strohm's conclusion:

> Available evidence suggests that Chaucer's public did indeed fail to renew itself, and that by the early years of the fifteenth century it had ceased to exist as a public likely or able to provide a setting encouraging to the creation of literary works.[108]

The evidence available from the prologue to *Beryn* suggests otherwise. Granted that the author was in all probability, like other imitators, on the fringes of court culture, he was nevertheless central in articulating for another, as yet unidentified, section of Chaucer's audience the manifold attractions of the *Canterbury Tales*.

---

106   Winstead, '*Beryn*-Writer', 232.
107   Strohm, 'Chaucer's Fifteenth-Century Audience', 8.
108   Ibid., 15.

Bibliography

Primary and Reference Sources

Alhazen, *De aspectibus*, ed. Risner in *Opticae thesaurus ... 1572* (1972).
Alighieri, Dante, *The Divine Comedy*, ed. and trans. John D. Sinclair, rev. edn (London: Oxford University Press, 1971).
Bartholomaeus Anglicus, *On the Properties of Things: John Trevisa's Translation of 'Bartholomaeus Anglicus De proprietatibus rerum'*, ed. M. C. Seymour et al., 3 vols (Oxford: Clarendon Press, 1975–88).
Benson, Larry D., *A Glossarial Concordance to the Riverside Chaucer*, Garland Reference Library of the Humanities, 1699 (New York: Garland, 1993).
Bible: *Biblia sacra iuxta vulgatam Clementinam*, ed. Alberto Colunga and Laurentio Turnado, 4th edn, Biblioteca de Autores Cristianos 14. 1 (Madrid: Editorial Catolica, 1965).
——: *The Holy Bible: Douay Version Translated from the Latin Vulgate (Douay A.D. 1609: Rheims, A.D. 1582)* (London: Catholic Truth Society, 1956).
Browne, Sir Thomas, 'On Dreams', in *The Works of Sir Thomas Browne*, ed. Keynes, vol. 3 (1964), 230–3.
——, *The Works of Sir Thomas Browne*, ed. G. Keynes, new edn, 4 vols (London: Faber, 1964).
The Brut, or the Chronicles of England, ed. Friedrich W. D. Brie, 2 vols, EETS os 131 (1906) and 136 (1908).
Bryan, W. F. and Dempster, Germaine, eds, *Sources and Analogues of Chaucer's Canterbury Tales* (New York: Humanities Press, 1958).
Burton, T. L. and Greentree, Rosemary, *Chaucer's 'Miller's', 'Reeve's' and 'Cook's Tales'*, The Chaucer Bibliographies (Toronto: University of Toronto Press, 1997).
Chaucer, Geoffrey, *The Canterbury Tales: A Facsimile and Transcription of the Hengwrt Manuscript, with Variants from the Ellesmere Manuscripts*, ed. Paul G. Ruggiers; intros. by Donald C. Baker, A. I. Doyle and M. B. Parkes, A Variorum Edition of the Works of Geoffrey Chaucer, 1 (Norman: University of Oklahoma Press, 1979).

——, *The Canterbury Tales by Geoffrey Chaucer: Edited from the Hengwrt Manuscript*, ed. N. F. Blake (London: Arnold, 1980).

——, *The Canterbury Tales of Geoffrey Chaucer: A New Text, with Illustrative Notes*, ed. T. Wright, in *Early English Poetry, Ballads, and Popular Literature of the Middle Ages*, vols 24 and 26, Percy Society 68 (1847) and 91 (1851).

——, *The Canterbury Tales of Chaucer*, ed. Thomas Tyrwhitt, 2nd edn, 2 vols (Oxford: Clarendon Press, 1798).

——, *The Canterbury Tales of Geoffrey Chaucer*, ed. Thomas Wright, 3 vols, Percy Society, 24–6 (London: 1847–51).

——, *Chaucer's Dream Poetry*, ed. Helen Phillips and Nick Havely (London: Longman, 1997).

——, *Chaucer's Major Poetry*, ed. Albert C. Baugh (London: Routledge and Kegan Paul, 1963).

——, *The Complete Poetry and Prose of Geoffrey Chaucer*, ed. John H. Fisher, 2nd edn (New York: Holt, Rinehart and Winston, 1989).

——, *The Complete Works of Geoffrey Chaucer*, ed. W. W. Skeat, 2nd edn, 7 vols (London: Oxford University Press, 1899).

——, *The General Prologue to The Canterbury Tales and the Canon's Yeoman's Prologue and Tale*, ed. A. V. C. Schmidt (London: University of London Press, 1974).

——, *The Miller's Tale*, ed. Thomas W. Ross, A Variorum Edition of the Works of Geoffrey Chaucer, vol. 2, part 3 (Norman, Okla.: University of Oklahoma Press, 1983).

——, *The Poetical Works of Geoffrey Chaucer*, ed. J. Bell, 14 vols (Edinburgh: Apollo Press, 1782–3).

——, *The Poetical Works of Geoffrey Chaucer*, in *A Complete Edition of the Poets of Great Britain*, ed. R. Anderson, 14 vols (Edinburgh: Mundell, 1792–1807), vol. 1 (1793).

——, *The Riverside Chaucer*, 3rd edn, ed. Larry D. Benson et al. (Boston: Houghton Mifflin, 1987).

——, *The Tales of Canterbury Complete*, ed. Robert A. Pratt (Boston: Houghton Mifflin, 1966).

——, *Tales of the Canterbury Pilgrims Retold from Chaucer and Others*, trans. F. J. H. Darton, 2nd edn (London: Wells Gardner, Darton, 1904).

——, *The Works 1532, with Supplementary Material from the Editions of 1542, 1561, 1598 and 1602*, ed. W. Thynne, intro. D. S. Brewer (Menston: Scolar Press, 1969).

——, *The Works of Geoffrey Chaucer*, in *The Works of the English Poets, from Chaucer to Cowper*, [ed. A. Chalmers,], vol. 1 (London: Johnson, 1810).

——, *The Works of Geoffrey Chaucer*, ed. F. N. Robinson, 2nd edn (Boston: Houghton Mifflin, 1957).

——, *The Works of Geoffrey Chaucer*, ed. J. Urry (London: Lintot, 1721).

Chichele, Henry, *The Register of Henry Chichele Archbishop of Canterbury 1414–1443*, ed. E. F. Jacob et al., 4 vols (Oxford: Oxford University Press, 1937–47).

Cicero, *De re publica; De legibus*, ed. and trans. Clinton Walker Keyes (London: Heinemann, 1928).

——, *Somnium Scipionis*, in Macrobius, *Ambrosii Theodosii Macrobii Commentarii in Somnium Scipionis*, ed. Jacob Willis, 2 vols (Leipzig: Teubner, 1963).

Clanvowe, Sir John, *The Works of Sir John Clanvowe*, ed. V. J. Scattergood (Cambridge: Brewer, 1965).

Davis, Norman; Gray, Douglas; Ingham, Patricia; and J. M. Wallace-Hadrill, comps, *A Chaucer Glossary* (Oxford: Clarendon Press, 1979).

Les Débats du clerc et du chevalier dans la littéraire poétique du moyen-âge, ed. Charles Oulmont (Paris: Champion, 1911).

de Condé, Jean, '*La Messe des oiseaux*' et' '*Le Dit des Jacobins et des Fremeneurs*', ed. Jacques Ribard (Geneva: Droz, 1970).

de Deguileville, Guillaume, *The Pilgrimage of the Lyfe of the Manhode: Translated Anonymously into Prose from the First Recension of Guillaume de Deguileville's Poem 'Le Pèlerinage de la vie humaine'*, ed. Avril Henry, 2 vols EETS os 288 (1985) and os 292 (1988).

——, *The Pilgrimage of the Soul: A Critical Edition of the Middle English Dream Vision*, ed. Rosemarie Potz McGerr, Garland Medieval Texts, 16 (New York: Garland, 1990).

de Lorris, Guillaume and de Meun, Jean, *Le Roman de la Rose*, ed. Daniel Poirion (Paris: Garnier-Flammarion, 1974).

de Margival, Nicole, *Le Dit de la panthère d'Amours*, ed. Henry A. Todd, SATF (1883).

Dempster, Germaine, 'The Merchant's Tale', in *Sources and Analogues*, ed. Bryan and Dempster (1958), 333–56.

Deschamps, Eustache, *Le Lay de franchise*, ed. Saint-Hilaire, in *Œuvres complètes* vol. 2 (1880), 203–14.

——, *Œuvres complètes de Eustache Deschamps*, ed. le marquis de Queux de Saint-Hilaire and G. Raynaud, 11 vols, SATF (1878–1903).

Dives and Pauper, ed. Priscilla Heath Barnum, 2 vols, EETS os 275 (1976) and os 280 (1980).

Douglas, Gavin, *The Aeneid of Virgil Translated into Scottish Verse* (Edinburgh: Bannatyne Club, 1839).

Li Fablel dou Dieu d'amors, in *Les Débats du clerc et du chevalier*, ed. Oulmont (1911), 197–216.

French, W. H. and Hale, C. B., eds, *Middle English Metrical Romances* (1930; repr. New York: Russell and Russell, 1964).

Frere, S. S.; Stow, S.; and Bennett, P., *Excavations on the Roman and Medieval Defences of Canterbury*, The Archaeology of Canterbury, 2 (Maidstone: Kent Archaeological Society, 1982).

Froissart, Jean, *Chronicles*, ed. and trans. Geoffrey Brereton, rev. edn (Harmondsworth: Penguin, 1978).

——, *Le Paradis d'Amour; L'Orloge amoureus*, ed. P. Dembowski (Geneva: Droz, 1986).

——, *La Prison amoureuse*, ed. Anthime Fourrier (Paris: Klincksieck, 1974).

Gordon, R. K., trans., *The Story of Troilus as Told by Benoît de Saint-Maure, Giovanni Boccaccio, Geoffrey Chaucer, Robert Henryson* (New York: Dutton, 1964).

Gower, John, *The Complete Works of John Gower*, ed. G. C. Macaulay, 4 vols (Oxford: Clarendon Press, 1899–1902).

——, *Confessio Amantis*, ed. J. A. W. Bennett, in his *Selections from John Gower* (Oxford, 1968).

——, in *The English Works of John Gower*, ed. G. C. Macaulay, vol. 1, EETS es 81(1900).

——, *The Major Latin Works of John Gower: The Voice of One Crying and The Tripartite Chronicles*, trans. Eric W. Stockton (Seattle: University of Washington Press, 1962).

——, *Selections from John Gower*, ed. J. A. W. Bennett (Oxford: Clarendon Press, 1968).

——, *Vox Clamantis*, ed. Macaulay, in *Complete Works*, iv: *The Latin Works* (1902), 1–313.

Grandson, Oton de, *Le Songe Saint Valentin*, ed. Piaget in his *Oton de Grandson* (1941), 309–23.

Harington, Sir John, *Sir John Harington's A New Discourse on a Stale Subject, Called the Metamorphosis of Ajax*, ed. Elizabeth Story Donno (London: Routledge and Kegan Paul, 1962).

Hart, W. M., 'The Reeve's Tale', in *Sources and Analogues*, ed. Bryan and Dempster (1958), 124–47.

——, 'The Reeve's Tale: A Comparative Study of Chaucer's Narrative Art', *PMLA* 23 (1908), 1–44.

Havely, N. R., ed. and trans., *Chaucer's Boccaccio: Sources of 'Troilus' and the 'Knight's' and 'Franklin's Tales'*, Chaucer Studies, 3 (Cambridge: Brewer, 1980).

Higden, Ranulph, *Polychronicon*: C. Babington and J. R. Lumby, eds, *Polychronicon Ranulphi Higden Monachi Cestrensis; together with the English Translations of John Trevisa and of an Unknown Writer of the Fifteenth Century*, 9 vols, Rolls series 41 (1865–86), i (1865).

Historia vitae et regni Ricardi secundi, ed. George B. Stow, Haney Foundation series, 21 (Philadelphia: University of Pennsylvania Press, 1977).

Hoccleve, Thomas, *Hoccleve's Works: The Minor Poems*, ed. Frederick J. Furnivall and I. Gollancz, EETS es 61 (1892) and 73 (1897), rev. edn Jerome Mitchell and A. I. Doyle repr. in one vol. (1970).

———, *The Regiment of Princes*, ed. Charles R. Blyth (Kalamazoo: Medieval Institute for TEAMS, 1999).

———, *The Regiment of Princes*, ed. M. C. Seymour, in his *Selections from Hoccleve* (1981).

———, *Selections from Hoccleve*, ed. M. C. Seymour (Oxford: Clarendon Press, 1981).

Holkot, Robert, *M. Roberti Holkoth ... in librum sapientiae regis Salominis praelectiones CCXIII ...* [ed. J. Ryterus] ([Basel], 1586).

Hudson, Anne, ed., *Selections from English Wycliffite Writings* (Cambridge: Cambridge University Press, 1978).

John of Salisbury, *Policraticus*: as *Frivolities of Courtiers and Footprints of Philosophers*, trans. Joseph B. Pike (Minneapolis: University of Minnesota Press, 1938).

Kaiser, R., ed., *Medieval English: An Old English and Middle English Anthology*, 3rd edn, rev. (Berlin: Kaiser, 1958).

Knighton, Henry, *Knighton's Chronicle 1337–1396*, ed. and trans. G. H. Martin (Oxford: Clarendon Press, 1995).

Langland, William, *Piers Plowman: An Edition of the C-Text*, ed. Derek Pearsall (London: Arnold, 1978).

———, *The Vision of Piers Plowman: A Critical Edition of the B-Text*, ed. A. V. C. Schmidt (London: Dent, 1978).

Loomis, Roger Sherman, *A Mirror of Chaucer's World* (Princeton: Princeton University Press, 1965).

——— and Willard, Rudolph, eds, *Medieval English Verse and Prose in Modernized Versions* (New York: Appleton-Century-Crofts, 1948).

Machaut, Guillaume de, *Le Dit dou lyon*, ed. Hoepffner, in *Œuvres de Guillaume de Machaut*, vol. 2 (1911), 159–237.

———, *The Fountain of Love (La Fonteinne amoureuse) and Two Other Love Vision Poems*, ed. and trans. R. Barton Palmer, Garland Library of Medieval Literature, series A, vol. 54 (New York: Garland, 1993).

———, *The Judgment of the King of Navarre*, ed. and trans. R. Barton Palmer, Garland Library of Medieval Literature series A, vol. 45 (New York: Garland, 1988).

———, *Œuvres de Guillaume de Machaut*, ed. Ernest Hoepffner, 3 vols, SATF (Paris, 1908–21).

Macrobius, *Commentary on the Dream of Scipio*, trans. William Harris Stahl, Records of Civilization, Sources and Studies, 48 (New York: Columbia University Press, 1952).

Maidstone, Richard of, *Concordia: The Reconciliation of Richard II with London*, trans. A. G. Rigg, ed. David R. Carlson (Kalamazoo: Medieval Institute for TEAMS, 2003).
Manly, John M. and Rickert, Edith, *The Text of the Canterbury Tales Studied on the Basis Of All Known Manuscripts*, 8 vols (Chicago: University of Chicago Press, 1940).
Mum and the Sothsegger, ed. Mabel Day and Robert Steele, EETS os 199 (1936).
Nichols, Ann Eljenholm; Orr, Michael T.; Scott, Kathleen L.; and Denison, Lynda, *An Index of Images in English Manuscripts from the Time of Chaucer to Henry VIII. c.1380–c.1509: The Bodleian Library, Oxford, Vol. 1: MSS Additional–Digby* (Turnhout: Harvey Miller, 2000).
Of Arthoure and Merlin, ed. O. D. Macrae-Gibson, 2 vols, EETS, os 268 (1973) and os 279 (1979).
The Parlement of the Thre Ages, ed. M. Y. Offord, EETS os 246 (1959).
Pearsall, Derek, ed., *Chaucer to Spenser: An Anthology of Writings in English 1375–1575* (Oxford: Blackwell, 1999).
Piaget, Arthur, *Oton de Grandson: sa vie et ses poésies*, Mémoires et Documents Publiés par la Société d'Histoire de la Suisse Romande, série 3, tom. 1 (Lausanne: Payot, 1941).
The Poems of the Pearl Manuscript: Pearl, Cleanness, Patience, Sir Gawain and the Green Knight, ed. Malcolm Andrew and Ronald Waldron (London: Arnold, 1978).
Rey, Alain, ed., *Dictionnaire historique de la langue française*, 2 vols (Paris: Robert, 1993).
Rickert, Edith, comp., *Chaucer's World*, ed. Clair C. Olson and Martin M. Crow (New York: Columbia University Press, 1948).
Risner, F., *Opticae thesaurus: Alhazeni arabis libri septem ... Vitellonis thuringopolini libri X ... 1572*, Sources of Science, 94 (New York: Johnson, 1972).
Ross, Thomas W., *Chaucer's Bawdy* (New York: Dutton, 1972).
Ritson, J., *Bibliographia Poetica: A Catalogue of English Poets, of the Twelfth, Thirteenth, Fourteenth, and Sixteenth, Centurys, with a Short Account of Their Works* (London: Nicol, 1802).
Rolle, Richard, *English Writings of Richard Rolle, Hermit of Hampole*, ed. Hope Emily Allen (Oxford: Clarendon Press, 1931).
——, *The Fire of Love*, trans. Clifton Walters (Harmondsworth: Penguin, 1972).
Royal Commission on Historical Manuscripts, *Third Report* (London: HMSO, 1872).
Scott, Kathleen L., *Later Gothic Manuscripts, 1390–1490*, 2 vols, A Survey of Manuscripts Illuminated in the British Isles, 6 (London: Harvey Miller, 1996).
Seneca, *Ad Lucilium epistolae morales*, ed. and trans. Richard M. Gummere (London: Heinemann, 1917).
Sir Orfeo, ed. A. J. Bliss, 2nd edn (Oxford: Clarendon Press, 1966).

Somnia Danielis: Steven R. Fischer, *The Complete Medieval Dreambook: A Multilingual, Alphabetical 'Somnia Danielis' Collation* (Bern: Lang 1982).
Spurgeon, Caroline F. E., *Five Hundred Years of Chaucer Criticism and Allusion 1357–1900*, 3 vols (1925; repr. New York: Russell and Russell, 1960).
Stone, Louise W. and William Rothwell, eds, *Anglo-Norman Dictionary* (London: Modern Humanities Research Association, 1977).
Strayer, Joseph R., ed., *Dictionary of the Middle Ages*, 12 vols (New York: Scribner's, 1982–9).
The Tale of Beryn, ed. M. E. M. Tamanini, Diss. New York University, 1969.
The Tale of Beryn, with a Prologue of the Merry Adventure of the Pardoner with a Tapster at Canterbury, ed. F. J. Furnivall and W. G. Stone, Part 1, Chaucer Society, 2nd series, 17: Supplementary Canterbury Tales, 1 (London: 1876).
——, Part 2, Chaucer Society, 2nd series, 24: Supplementary Canterbury Tales, 2 (London: 1887).
——, EETS es 105 (1909).
Two Wycliffite Texts: The Sermon of William Taylor 1406; The Testimony of William Thorpe 1407, ed. Anne Hudson, EETS os 31 (1993).
Usk, Adam, *The Chronicle of Adam Usk 1377–1421*, ed. and trans. C. Given-Wilson (Oxford: Clarendon Press, 1987).
Usk, Thomas, *The Testament of Love*, ed. Skeat in *Complete Works of Geoffrey Chaucer*, 2nd edn, vol. 7: *Chaucerian and Other Pieces* (1899), 1–145.
——, *Testament of Love*, ed. Gary W. Shawver (Toronto: Toronto University Press, 2002).
Vincent of Beauvais, *Bibliotheca mundi: Vincentii bellovacensis speculum quadruplex; naturale, doctrinale, morale, historiale ...*, 4 vols (Douai: ptd B. Belleri, 1624).
Walsingham, Thomas, *The Chronica maiora of Thomas Walsingham 1376–1422*, trans. David Preest, ed. James G. Clark (Woodbridge: Boydell Press, 2005).
——, *Chronicon Angliae 1328–1388*, ed. E. M. Thompson, Rolls series, 64 (1874).
——, *Historia Anglicana*, ed. H. T. Riley, 2 vols, Rolls series, 28 (1864).
The Westminster Chronicle, ed. and trans. L. C. Hector and Barbara F. Harvey (Oxford: Clarendon Press, 1982).
Windeatt, B. A., ed. and trans., *Chaucer's Dream Poetry: Sources and Analogues*, Chaucer Studies, 8 (Woodbridge: Boydell and Brewer, 1982).
Witelo, *Perspectiva*, ed. Risner in *Opticae thesaurus ... 1572* (1972).
Wynnere and Wastoure, ed. Stephanie Trigg, EETS os 297 (1990).
Zupitza, J., ed., *Specimens of All the Accessible Unprinted Manuscripts of the Canterbury Tales: The Doctor-Pardoner Link, and Pardoner's Prologue and Tale*, Chaucer Society, first ser., 81 (1892; repr. New York: Johnson, 1967).

Secondary Works

Addy, Sidney Oldhall, *The Evolution of the English House*, rev. edn (London: George, Allen and Unwin, 1933).
Aers, David, 'Vox Populi and the Literature of 1381', in *Cambridge History*, ed. Wallace (1999), 432–53.
——, ed., *Culture and History 1350–1600: Essays on English Communities, Identities and Writing* (Hemel Hempstead: Harvester Wheatsheaf, 1992).
Aiken, Pauline, 'Arcite's Illness and Vincent of Beauvais', *PMLA* 51 (1936), 361–9.
——, 'The Summoner's Malady', *Studies in Philology* 33 (1936), 40–4.
——, 'Vincent of Beauvais and Chaucer's Knowledge of Alchemy', *Studies in Philology* 41 (1944), 371–89.
——, 'Vincent of Beauvais and Dame Pertelote's Knowledge of Medicine', *Speculum* 10 (1935), 281–7.
——, 'Vincent of Beauvais and the "Houres" of Chaucer's Physician', *Studies in Philology* 53 (1956), 22–4.
Albano, Robert A., *Middle English Historiography*, American University Studies, series 4; English Language and Literature, vol. 168 (New York: Lang, 1993).
Alford, John A., ed., *A Companion to 'Piers Plowman'* (Berkeley and Los Angeles: University of California Press, 1988).
Allen, Hope Emily, *Writings Ascribed to Richard Rolle, Hermit of Hampole, and Materials for His Biography*, Modern Language Association of America, Monograph series, 3 (New York: Modern Language Association of America, 1927), 47–9, 209–29.
Allen, Rosamund S., 'The *Siege of Thebes*: Lydgate's Canterbury Tale', in *Chaucer and Fifteenth-Century Poetry*, ed. Boffey and Cowen (1991), 122–42.
Anderson, Judith H., *The Growth of a Personal Voice: 'Piers Plowman' and 'The Faerie Queene'* (New Haven: Yale University Press, 1976).
Andreas, James R., 'Festive Limitiality in Chaucerian Comedy', *Chaucer Newsletter* 1:1 (1979), 3–6.
Antonelli, Roberto, 'The Birth of Criseyde – An Exemplary Triangle: "Classical" Troilus and the Question of Love at the Anglo-Norman Court', in *European Tragedy of Troilus*, ed. Boitani (1989), 21–48.
Ashley, Kathleen M., ed., *Victor Turner and the Construction of Cultural Criticism: Between Literature and Anthropology* (Bloomington: Indiana University Press, 1990).

Aston, Margaret, *England's Iconoclasts*, i: *Laws against Images* (Oxford: Clarendon Press, 1988).

——, 'Lollards and the Cross', in *Lollards and their Influence*, ed. Somerset, Havens and Pitard (2003), 99–113.

Baker, Peter and Howe, Nicholas, eds, *Words and Works: Studies in Medieval English Language and Literature in Honour of Fred C. Robinson* (Toronto: Toronto University Press, 1998).

Baldwin, R. G., 'The Yeoman's Canon's: A Conjecture', *JEGP* 61 (1962), 232–43.

Barney, Stephen A., 'Allegorical Visions', in *Companion to 'Piers Plowman'*, ed. Alford (1988), 117–33.

Barron, Caroline M., 'The Quarrel of Richard II with London 1392–7', in *Reign of Richard II*, ed. DuBoulay and Barron (1971), 173–201.

Bashe, E. J., 'The Prologue of the *Tale of Beryn*', *Philological Quarterly* 12 (1933), 1–16.

Baswell, Christopher, *Virgil in Medieval England: Figuring the 'Aeneid' from the Twelfth Century to Chaucer*, Cambridge Studies in Medieval Literature, 24 (Cambridge: Cambridge University Press, 1995).

Baugh, A. C., 'The Middle English Period (1100–1500)', in *A Literary History of England*, 2nd edn, ed. Baugh (1967), bk 1, pt 1.

——, ed., *A Literary History of England*, 2nd edn, 4 vols (London: Routledge and Kegan Paul, 1967).

Baum, Paull Franklin, 'The Canon's Yeoman's Tale', *Modern Language Notes* 40 (1925), 152–4.

Baumgartner, Emmanuèle. 'The Play of Temporalities; or, The Reported Dream of Guillaume de Lorris', in *Rethinking the 'Romance of the Rose'*, ed. Brownlee and Huot (1992), 21–38.

Beidler, Peter G., 'Chaucer's *Merchant's Tale* and the *Decameron*', *Italica* 50 (1973), 266–84.

Bennett, H. S., *Chaucer and the Fifteenth Century* [corrected edn], Oxford History of English Literature, vol. 2, pt 1 (Oxford: Clarendon Press, 1948).

Bennett, J. A. W., *Chaucer at Oxford and at Cambridge* (Oxford: Clarendon Press, 1974).

——, *Chaucer's 'Book of Fame': An Exposition of 'The House of Fame'* (Oxford: Clarendon Press, 1968).

Benson, David C., *The History of Troy in Middle English Literature* (Woodbridge: Boydell and Brewer, 1980).

Benson, Larry D., ed., *The Learned and the Lewed: Studies in Chaucer and Medieval Literature*, Harvard English Studies, 5 (Cambridge, Mass.: Harvard University Press, 1974).

Besserman, Lawrence and Storm, Melvin, 'Forum: Chaucer's Pardoner', *PMLA* 98 (1983), 405–6.
Biggs, Frederick M. and Howes, Laura L., 'Theophany in the Miller's Tale', *Medium Ævum* 65 (1996), 269–79.
Blake, N. F., 'Chaucer Manuscripts and Texts', *Review* 3 (1981), 219–32.
——, 'On Editing the *Canterbury Tales*', in *Medieval Studies*, ed. Heyworth (1981), 101–19.
——, 'The Relationship between the Hengwrt and the Ellesmere Manuscripts of the *Canterbury Tales*', *Essays and Studies* 32 (1979), 1–18.
——, *The Textual Tradition of the Canterbury Tales* (London: Arnold, 1985).
Blodgett, E. D., 'Chaucerian *Pryvetee* and the Opposition to Time', *Speculum* 51 (1976), 477–93.
Bodenham, C. H. L., 'The Nature of the Dream in Late Mediaeval French Literature', *Medium Ævum* 54 (1985), 74–86.
Boffey, Julia and Cowen, Janet, eds, *Chaucer and Fifteenth-Century Poetry*, King's College London Medieval Studies, 5 (London: King's College Centre for Late Antique and Medieval Studies, 1991).
—— and Edwards, A. S. G., 'Manuscripts and Audience', in *Concise Companion to Chaucer*, ed. Saunders (2006), 34–50.
Boitani, Piero, ed., *The European Tragedy of Troilus* (Oxford: Clarendon Press, 1989).
Bowers, John M., 'The *Tale of Beryn* and the *Siege of Thebes*: Alternative Ideas of the *Canterbury Tales*', *Studies in the Age of Chaucer* 7 (1985), 23–50.
Boyd, David Lorenzo, 'Seeking "Goddes pryvetee": Sodomy, Quitting and Desire in the Miller's Tale', in *Words and Works*, ed. Baker and Howe (1998), 243–60.
Brent, Cecil, 'Pilgrims' Signs', *Archaeologia Cantiana* 13 (1880), 111–15.
Brewer, Derek, 'Class Distinction in Chaucer', *Speculum* 43 (1968), 290–305.
——, 'Escape from the Mimetic Fallacy', in *Studies in Medieval English Romances*, ed. Brewer (1988), 1–10.
——, ed., *Geoffrey Chaucer* (London: Bell, 1974).
——, ed., *Studies in Medieval English Romances: Some New Approaches* (Cambridge: Brewer, 1988).
Brody, Saul N., 'Making a Play for Criseyde: The Staging of Pandarus's House in Chaucer's *Troilus and Criseyde*', *Speculum* 73 (1998), 115–40.
Brown, Peter, 'The Containment of Symkyn: The Function of Space in the Reeve's Tale', *Chaucer Review* 14 (1980), 226–36.
——, 'Higden's Britain', in *Medieval Europeans*, ed. Smyth (1998), 103–18.
——, 'Images', in *Companion to Medieval English Literature and Culture*, ed. Brown (2009), 307–21.
——, 'Is the Canon's Yeoman's Tale Apocryphal?', *English Studies* 64 (1983), 481–90.

—, 'Journey's End: The Prologue to the *Tale of Beryn*', in *Chaucer and Fifteenth-Century Poetry*, ed. Boffey and Cowen (1991), 143–74.
—, 'On the Borders of Middle English Dream Visions', in *Reading Dreams*, ed. Brown (1999), 22–50.
—, 'An Optical Theme in the Merchant's Tale', *Studies in the Age of Chaucer: Proceedings*, 1 (1985): *Reconstructing Chaucer*, ed. Paul Strohm and Thomas J. Heffernan, 231–43.
—, 'The Prison of Theseus and the Castle of *Jalousie*', *Chaucer Review* 26 (1991), 147–52.
—, '*Shot wyndowe* (Miller's Tale, I. 3358 and 3695): An Open and Shut Case?', *Medium Ævum* 69 (2000), 96–103.
—, ed., *A Companion to Chaucer* (Oxford: Blackwell, 2000).
—, ed., *A Companion to Medieval English Literature and Culture c.1350–c.1500* (Oxford: Blackwell, 2007).
—, ed., *Reading Dreams: The Interpretation of Dreams from Chaucer to Shakespeare* (Oxford: Oxford University Press, 1999).
Brownlee, Kevin, *Poetic Identity in Guillaume de Machaut* (Madison: University of Wisconsin Press, 1984).
—and Huot, Sylvia, eds, *Rethinking the 'Romance of the Rose': Text, Image, Reception* (Philadelphia: University of Pennsylvania Press, 1992).
— and Nichols, Stephen G., eds, *Images of Power: Medieval History/Discourse/Literature*, Yale French Studies, 70 (New Haven: Yale University Press 1986).
Bühler, Curt F., 'A Lollard Tract: On Translating the Bible into English', *Medium Ævum* 7 (1938), 167–83.
Burke, Peter, *The French Historical Revolution: The Annales School, 1929–89* (Cambridge: Polity Press, 1990).
Burlin, Robert B., *Chaucerian Fiction* (Princeton: Princeton University Press, 1977).
Burrow, J. A., 'Hoccleve and Chaucer', in *Chaucer Traditions*, ed. Morse and Windeatt (1990), 54–61.
—, *Thomas Hoccleve*, Authors of the Middle Ages, 4 (Aldershot: Variorum, 1994).
Butterfield, Ardis, 'French Culture and the Ricardian Court', in *Essays on Ricardian Literature*, ed. Minnis, Morse and Turville-Petre (1997), 82–120.
Calin, William, *A Poet at the Fountain: Essays on the Narrative Verse of Guillaume de Machaut* (Lexington: University Press of Kentucky, 1974).
Camille, Michael, *Image on the Edge: The Margins of Medieval Art* (London: Reaktion, 1992).
Carlson, David R., 'Thomas Hoccleve and the Chaucer Portrait', *Huntington Library Quarterly* 54 (1991), 283–300.

Catto, J. I., 'Citizens, Scholars and Masters', in *Early Oxford Schools*, ed. Catto (1984), 183–7.

——, ed., *The Early Oxford Schools*, The History of the University of Oxford, 1 (Oxford: Clarendon Press, 1984).

Caviness, Madeline Harrison, *The Early Stained Glass of Canterbury Cathedral: Circa 1175–1220* (Princeton: Princeton University Press, 1977).

——, *The Windows of Christ Church Cathedral, Canterbury*, Corpus vitrearum Medii Aevi, ii (Oxford: Oxford University Press for the British Academy, 1981).

Clark, David L., 'Optics for Preachers: The *De oculo morali* by Peter of Limoges', *Michigan Academician* 9 (1977), 329–43.

Clark, John, 'Trinovantum – The Evolution of a Legend', *Journal of Medieval History* 7 (1981), 135–51.

Collette, Carolyn P., *Performing Polity: Women and Agency in the Anglo-French Tradition 1385–1620* (Turnhout: Brepols, 2006).

Collingwood, R. G., *The Idea of History* (Oxford: Clarendon Press, 1946).

Copland, M., 'The Reeve's Tale: Harlotrie or Sermonying?' *Medium Ævum* 31 (1962), 14–32.

Crisp, Frank, *Mediaeval Gardens, 'Flowery Medes' and Other Arrangements of Herbs, Flowers and Shrubs Grown in the Middle Ages*, ed. Catherine Childs Paterson, 2 vols (London: Bodley Head, 1924).

Crossley, Paul, 'Bohemia Sacra: Liturgy and History in Prague Cathedral', in *Pierre, lumière, couleur*, ed. Joubert and Sandron (1999), 341–65.

——, 'The Politics of Presentation: The Architecture of Charles IV of Bohemia', in *Courts and Regions*, ed. Jones, Marks and Minnis (2000), 99–172.

Crow, Martin C. and Olson, Clair C., eds, *Chaucer Life-Records* (Oxford: Clarendon Press, 1966).

Cunningham, J. V., 'The Literary Form of the Prologue to the *Canterbury Tales*', *Modern Philology* 49 (1952), 172–81.

Curry, Walter Clyde, *Chaucer and the Mediaeval Sciences*, rev. edn (New York: Barnes and Noble, 1960).

Daiches, David and Thorlby, Anthony, eds, *The Mediaeval World*, Literature and Civilization, vol. 2 (London: Aldus, 1973).

Darjes, Bradley and Rendall, Thomas, 'A Fabliau in the Prologue to the *Tale of Beryn*', *Mediaeval Studies* 47 (1985), 416–31.

Davidoff, Judith M., *Beginning Well: Framing Fictions in Late Middle English Poetry* (London: Associated University Presses, 1988).

Davis, J. F., 'Lollards, Reformers and St Thomas of Canterbury', *University of Birmingham Historical Journal* 9 (1963), 1–15.

Dean, Christopher, *Arthur of England: English Attitudes to King Arthur and the Knights of the Round Table in the Middle Ages and the Renaissance* (Toronto: University of Toronto Press, 1987).
Dean, James M. and Zacher, Christian K., eds, *The Idea of Medieval Literature: New Essays on Chaucer and Medieval Culture in Honor of Donald R. Howard* (Newark, Del.: University of Delaware Press, 1992).
de Becker, Raymond, *The Understanding of Dreams, or the Machinations of the Night*, trans. Michael Heron (London: Allen and Unwin, 1968). [First published as *Les Machinations de la nuit* (Paris: Planète, 1965)].
Delany, Sheila, *Chaucer's House of Fame: The Poetics of Skeptical Fideism* (Chicago: University of Chicago Press, 1972).
de Looze, Laurence, *Pseudo-Autobiography in the Fourteenth Century: Juan Ruiz, Guillaume de Machaut, Jean Froissart and Geoffrey Chaucer* (Gainseville: University Press of Florida, 1997).
Dempster, Germaine, 'Manly's Conception of the Early History of the *Canterbury Tales*', *PMLA* 61 (1946), 379–415.
——, 'On the Source of the Deception Story in the Merchant's Tale', *Modern Philology* 34 (1936–7), 133–54.
Dimmick, Jeremy; Simpson, James; and Zeeman, Nicolette, eds, *Images, Idolatry, and Iconoclasm in Late Medieval England: Textuality and the Visual Image* (Oxford: Oxford University Press, 2002).
Doyle, A. I., 'English Books In and Out of Court from Edward III to Henry VII', in *English Court Culture*, ed. Scattergood and Sherborne (1983), 163–81.
—— and Parkes, M. B., 'Palaeographical Introduction', in *Chaucer, Canterbury Tales: Hengwrt Manuscript*, ed. Ruggiers (1979), xix–xlix.
——, 'The Production of Copies of the *Canterbury Tales* and the *Confessio Amantis* in the Early Fifteenth Century', in *Medieval Scribes*, ed. Parkes and Watson (1978), 163–210.
DuBoulay, F. R. H. and Barron, Caroline M., eds, *The Reign of Richard II* (London: Athlone Press, 1971).
Dufty, A. R., 'Review of *Castles and Cannon: A Study in Early Fortification in England*, by B. H. St J. O'Neil', *Archaeological Journal* 119 (1962), 367–70.
Dutton, Paul Edward, *The Politics of Dreaming in the Carolingian Empire* (Lincoln, NE: University of Nebraska Press, 1994).
Eade, John and Sallnow, Michael J., eds, *Contesting the Sacred: The Anthropology of Christian Pilgrimage* (London: Routledge, 1991).
Eberle, J., 'The Lovers' Glass: Nature's Discourse on Optics and the Optical Design of the *Romance of the Rose*', *University of Toronto Quarterly* 46 (1976–7), 241–62.

——, 'Richard II and the Literary Arts', in *Richard II*, ed. Goodman and Gillespie (1999), 231–53.

Echard, Siân, 'Gower's "bokes of Latin": Language, Politics and Poetry', *Studies in the Age of Chaucer* 25 (2003), 123–56.

Edwards, A. S. G., 'The Influence and Audience of the *Polychronicon*: Some Observations', *Proceedings of the Leeds Philosophical and Literary Society* (Literary and Historical Section), 17:6 (1980) 113–19.

——, 'John Trevisa', in *Middle English Prose*, ed. Edwards (1984), 133–46.

——, ed., *Middle English Prose: A Critical Guide to Major Authors and Genres* (New Brunswick: Rutgers University Press, 1984).

Edwards, J. G., 'Ranulph, Monk of Chester', *English Historical Review*, 47 (1932), 94.

Edwards, Robert R. *The Dream of Chaucer: Representation and Reflection in the Early Narratives* (Durham, NC: Duke University Press, 1989).

Eliason, Norman E., *The Language of Chaucer's Poetry: An Appraisal of the Verse, Style, and Structure*, Anglistica, 17 (Copenhagen: Rosenkilde and Bagger, 1972).

Erickson, Carolly, *The Medieval Vision: Essays in History and Perception* (New York: Oxford University Press, 1976).

Farrell, Thomas J., 'Privacy and the Boundaries of Fabliau in the Miller's Tale', *ELH* 56 (1989), 773–95.

Federico, Sylvia, *New Troy: Fantasies of Empire in the Late Middle Ages*, Medieval Cultures, 36 (Minneapolis: University of Minnesota Press, 2003).

Fein, Susanna Greer; Raybin, David; and Braeger, Peter C., eds, *Rebels and Rivals: The Contestive Spirit in 'The Canterbury Tales'*, Studies in Medieval Culture, 29 (Kalamazoo, Mich.: Medieval Institute Publications, 1991).

Fentress, James and Wickham, Chris, *Social Memory* (Oxford: Blackwell, 1992).

Ferster, Judith, *Fictions of Advice: The Literature and Politics of Counsel in Late Medieval England* (Philadelphia: University of Pennsylvania Press, 1996).

Fisher, J. H., *John Gower: Moral Philosopher and Friend of Chaucer* (London: Methuen, 1965).

Fleming, John V., 'Chaucer and Erasmus on the Pilgrimage to Canterbury: An Iconographical Speculation', in *Popular Literature of Medieval England*, ed. Heffernan (1985), 148–66.

Foreville, Raymonde, *Le Jubilé de saint Thomas Becket du XIIIe au XVe siècle (1220–1470): étude et documents* (Paris: S.E.V.P.E.N., 1958).

Fowler, David C., *John Trevisa*, Authors of the Middle Ages, 2 (Aldershot: Variorum, 1993).

Frye, Northrop, *The Secular Scripture: A Study of the Structure of Romance* (Cambridge, Mass.: Harvard University Press, 1976).

Galbraith, V. H., 'An Autograph MS of Ranulph Higden's *Polychronicon*', *Huntington Library Quarterly* 23 (1959–60), 1–18.
——, *Historical Research in Medieval England*, The Creighton Lecture in History, 1949 (London: Athlone Press, 1951).
——, 'Nationality and Language in Medieval England', *Transactions of the Royal Historical Society*, 4th series, 23 (1941), 113–28.
Galloway, Andrew, 'Gower in his Most Learned Role and the Peasants' Revolt of 1381', *Mediaevalia* 16 (1993), 329–47.
Gardiner, F. C., *The Pilgrimage of Desire: A Study of Theme and Genre in Medieval Literature* (Leiden: Brill, 1971).
Gaylord, Alan T., 'Portrait of a Poet', in *The Ellesmere Chaucer* ed. Stevens and Woodward (1995), 121–42.
Gellrich, Jesse M. *The Idea of the Book in the Middle Ages: Language Theory, Mythology and Fiction* (Ithaca, NY: Cornell University Press, 1985).
Geremek, Bronislaw, 'The Marginal Man', in *Medieval Callings*, ed. le Goff (1987), 347–73.
Given-Wilson, Chris, *The Royal Household and the King's Affinity: Service, Politics and Finance in England 1360–1413* (New Haven: Yale University Press, 1986).
Goodman, Anthony and Gillespie, James, eds, *Richard II: The Art of Kingship* (Oxford: Clarendon Press, 1999).
Gordon, Dillian; Monnas, Lisa; and Elam, Caroline, *Regal Image of Richard II and the Wilton Diptych* (London: Harvey Miller, 1997).
Gransden, Antonia, *Historical Writing in England*, ii: *c.1307 to the Early Sixteenth Century* (London: Routledge and Kegan Paul, 1982).
——, 'Silent Meanings in Ranulf Higden's *Polychronicon* and in Thomas Elmham's *Liber Metricus de Henrico Quinto*', *Medium Ævum* 46 (1977), 231–40.
Green, Richard Firth, *Poets and Princepleasers: Literature and the English Court in the Late Middle Ages* (Toronto: University of Toronto Press, 1980).
——, 'The *Familia Regis* and the *Familia Cupidinis*', in *English Court Culture*, ed. Scattergood and Sherborne (1983), 87–108.
Grennen, Joseph Edward, 'The Canon's Yeoman and the Cosmic Furnace: Language and Meaning in the Canon's Yeoman's Tale', *Criticism* 4 (1962), 225–40.
——, 'Chaucer and the Commonplaces of Alchemy', *Classica Mediaevale* 26 (1965), 306–33.
——, 'Jargon Transmuted: Alchemy in Chaucer's Canon's Yeoman's Tale', Diss. Fordham Univ., 1960.
——, 'Saint Cecilia's "Chemical Wedding": The Unity of the *Canterbury Tales*, Fragment VIII', *JEGP* 65 (1966), 466–81.

Gunn, Alan M. F., *The Mirror of Love: A Reinterpretation of the 'Romance of the Rose'* (Lubbock: Texas Tech Press, 1951).

Gurevich, Aaron, *Historical Anthropology of the Middle Ages*, ed. Jana Howlett (Cambridge: Polity Press, 1992).

Hagen, Susan K. *Allegorical Remembrance: A Study of 'The Pilgrimage of the Life of Man' as a Medieval Treatise on Seeing and Remembering* (Athens, Ga.: University of Georgia Press, 1990).

Hale, David G., 'Dreams, Stress, and Interpretation in Chaucer and his Contemporaries', *Journal of the Rocky Mountain Medieval and Renaissance Association* 9 (1988), 47–61.

Hanks, D. Thomas, Jr., '"Goddes pryvetee" and Chaucer's Miller's Tale', *Christianity and Literature*, 33.2 (1984), 7–12.

Hanning, R. W., 'Telling the Private Parts: "pryvetee" and Poetry in Chaucer's Canterbury Tales', in *The Idea of Medieval Literature*, ed. Dean and Zacher (1992), 108–25.

Hansen, Elaine Tuttle, *Chaucer and the Fictions of Gender* (Berkeley: University of California Press, 1992).

Hanna, Ralph, III, 'Producing Manuscripts and Editions', in *Crux and Controversy*, ed. Minnis and Brewer (1992), 109–30.

Harbert, Bruce, 'Lessons from the Great Clerk: Ovid and John Gower', in *Ovid Renewed*, ed. Martindale (1988), 83–97.

Harris, Mollie, *Privies Galore* (Stroud: Sutton, 1990).

Hartung, Albert E., 'The Non-Comic Merchant's Tale, Maximianus, and the Sources', *Mediaeval Studies* 29 (1967), 1–25.

——, '"Pars secunda" and the Development of the Canon's Yeoman's Tale', *Chaucer Review* 12 (1977), 111–28.

Harvey, John H., *Henry Yevele c.1320 to 1400: The Life of an English Architect* (London: Batsford, 1944).

——, 'Henry Yeveley and the Nave of Canterbury Cathedral', *Canterbury Cathedral Chronicle*, No. 79 (1985), 20–32.

Heffernan, Thomas J., ed., *The Popular Literature of Medieval England*, Tennessee Studies in Literature, 28 (Knoxville: University of Tennessee Press, 1985).

Hermann, John P. and Burke, John J., eds, *Signs and Symbols in Chaucer's Poetry* (University: University of Alabama Press, 1981).

Heyworth, P. L., ed., *Medieval Studies for J. A. W. Bennett* (Oxford: Clarendon Press, 1981).

Hieatt, Constance B., '*Un Autre Forme*: Guillaume de Machaut and the Dream Vision Form', *Chaucer Review* 14 (1979), 97–115.

——, *The Realism of Dream Visions: The Poetic Exploitation of the Dream-Experience in Chaucer and his Contemporaries*, De Proprieraribus Litterarum, series practica 2 (The Hague: Mouton, 1967).
Housman, John E., 'Higden, Trevisa, Caxton and the Beginnings of Arthurian Criticism', *Review of English Studies* 23 (1947), 209–17.
Hudson, Anne, *The Premature Reformation: Wycliffite Texts and Lollard History* (Oxford: Clarendon Press, 1988).
Hult, David F., *Self-Fulfilling Prophecies: Readership and Authority in the First 'Roman de la rose'* (Cambridge: Cambridge University Press, 1986).
Huppé, Bernard F., *A Reading of the Canterbury Tales* (Albany, NY: State University of New York, 1964).
Ingledew, Francis, 'The Book of Troy and the Genealogical Construction of History: The Case of Geoffrey of Monmouth's *Historia regum Britanniae*', *Speculum* 69 (1994), 665–704.
Jacob, E. F., *Archbishop Henry Chichele* (London: Nelson, 1967).
Jonassen, Frederick B., 'The Inn, the Cathedral and the Pilgrimage of *The Canterbury Tales*', in *Rebels and Rivals*, ed. Fein, Raybin and Braeger (1991), 1–35.
Jones, Sarah Rees; Marks, Richard; and Minnis, A. J., eds, *Courts and Regions in Medieval Europe* (York: York Medieval Press, 2000).
Jones, W. R., 'Lollards and Images: The Defense of Religious Art in Later Medieval England', *Journal of the History of Ideas* 34 (1973), 27–50.
Joseph, Gerhard, 'Chaucerian "Game" – "Earnest" and the "Argument of Herbergage" in the *Canterbury Tales*', *Chaucer Review* 5 (1970), 83–96.
Joubert, Fabienne and Sandron, Dany, eds, *Pierre, lumière, couleur: études d'histoire du Moyen Age en l'honneur d'Anne Prache*, Cultures et Civilisations Médiévales, 20 (Paris: Presses de l'Université de Paris-Sorbonne, 1999).
Jusserand, J. J., *English Wayfaring Life in the Middle Ages (XIVth Century)*, trans. Lucy Toulmin Smith, 3rd edn (London: Unwin, 1925).
Justice, Steven, *Writing and Rebellion: England in 1381*, New Historicism, 27 (Berkeley and Los Angeles: University of California Press, 1994).
Kamerick, Kathleen, *Popular Piety and Art in the Later Middle Ages: Image Worship and Idolatry in England, 1350–1500* (New York: Palgrave, 2002).
Keen, M. H., *England in the Later Middle Ages: A Political History* (London: Routledge, 1973).
——, 'Mediaeval Ideas of History' in *The Mediaeval World*, ed. Daiches and Thorlby (1973), 285–314.
Kellogg, Alfred L. and Haselmayer, Louis A., 'Chaucer's Satire of the Pardoner', *PMLA* 66 (1951), 251–77.

Kelly, Douglas, *Medieval Imagination: Rhetoric and the Poetry of Courtly Love* (Madison: University of Wisconsin Press, 1978).

Kibre, Pearl and Siraisi, Nancy G., 'The Institutional Setting: The Universities', in *Science in the Middle Ages*, ed. Lindberg (1978), 120–44.

Kingsford, C. L., 'A London Merchant's House and Its Owners, 1360–1614', *Archaeologia* 74 (1923–4), 137–58.

Kiser, Lisa, *Telling Classical Tales: Chaucer and the 'Legend of Good Women'* (Ithaca, NY: Cornell University Press, 1983).

Kittredge, G. L., *Chaucer and His Poetry* (Cambridge, Mass.: Harvard University Press, 1915).

Knapp, Daniel, 'The Relyk of a Seint: A Gloss on Chaucer's Pilgrimage', *ELH* 39 (1972), 1–26.

Knapp, Ethan, *The Bureaucratic Muse: Thomas Hoccleve and the Literature of Late Medieval England* (University Park: Pennsylvania State University Press, 2001).

——, 'Eulogies and Usurpations: Hoccleve and Chaucer Revisited', *Studies in the Age of Chaucer* 21 (1999), 247–73.

Kohl, S., 'Chaucer's Pilgrims in Fifteenth-Century Literature', *Fifteenth-Century Studies* 7 (1983), 221–36.

Kolve, V. A., *Chaucer and the Imagery of Narrative: The First Five Canterbury Tales* (London: Arnold, 1984).

——, 'From Cleopatra to Alceste: An Iconographic Study of the *Legend of Good Women*', in *Signs and Symbols*, ed. Hermann and Burke (1981), 130–78.

Krochalis, Jeanne E., 'Hoccleve's Chaucer Portrait', *Chaucer Review* 21 (1986), 234–45.

Kruger, Steven F., *Dreaming in the Middle Ages*, Cambridge Studies in Medieval Literature, 14 (Cambridge: Cambridge University Press, 1992).

——, 'Medical and Moral Authority in the Late Medieval Dream', in *Reading Dreams*, ed. Brown (1999), 51–83.

——, 'Mirrors and the Trajectory of Vision in *Piers Plowman*', *Speculum* 66 (1991), 74–95.

Ladner, Gerhart B. '*Homo Viator*: Mediaeval Ideas on Alienation and Order', *Speculum* 42 (1967), 233–59.

Leach, Edmund, *Culture and Communication: The Logic by which Symbols are Connected: An Introduction to the Use of Structuralist Analysis in Social Anthropology* (Cambridge: Cambridge University Press, 1976).

le Goff, Jacques, 'Dreams in the Culture and Collective Psychology of the Medieval West', in his *Time, Work and Culture* (1980), 201–4. [First published as 'Les Rêves dans la culture et la psychologie collective de l'Occident médiéval', *Scolies* 1 (1971), 123–30].

—, *Medieval Callings*, trans. Lydia G. Cochrane (Chicago: University of Chicago Press, 1987). [First published as *L'uomo medieval* (Roma-Bari: Laterza, 1987)].

—, *Time, Work and Culture in the Middle Ages*, trans. Arthur Goldhammer (Chicago: University of Chicago Press, 1980). [First published as *Pour un autre Moyen Age: temps, travail et culture en Occident* (Paris: Gallimard, 1977)].

Lerer, Seth, *Chaucer and His Readers: Imagining the Author in Late-Medieval England* (Princeton: Princeton University Press, 1993).

Lewis, Dulcie, *Kent Privies* (Newbury: Countryside Books, 1996).

Leyerle, John, 'The Heart and the Chain', in *The Learned and the Lewed*, ed. Benson (1974), 113–45.

Lincoln, Jackson Steward, *The Dream in Primitive Cultures* (London: Cresset Press, 1935).

Lindberg, David C., *Theories of Vision from Al-Kindi to Kepler* (Chicago: University of Chicago Press, 1976).

—, ed., *Science in the Middle Ages* (Chicago: University of Chicago Press, 1978).

Lindley, Philip, 'Absolutism and Regal Image in Ricardian Sculpture', in *Regal Image of Richard II*, ed. Gordon, Monnas and Elam (1997), 61–83.

Loftin, Alice Cornelia, 'Visions', in *Dictionary of the Middle Ages*, ed. Strayer (1989), xii, 475–8.

Lynch, Kathryn L. *The High Medieval Dream Vision: Poetry, Philosophy, and Literary Form* (Stanford: Stanford University Press, 1988).

McDonald, Nicola F., 'Chaucer's *Legend of Good Women*, Ladies at Court and the Female Reader', *Chaucer Review* 35 (2000), 22–42.

McGregor, James H., 'The Iconography of Chaucer in Hoccleve's *De Regimine Principum* and in the *Troilus* Frontispiece', *Chaucer Review* 11 (1977), 338–50.

McIntosh, H. M., 'The Literary Background of the *Tale of Beryn*', Diss. University of Chicago, 1931.

McKisack, May, *The Fourteenth Century, 1307–1399*, The Oxford History of England, v (Oxford: Clarendon Press, 1959).

McNiven, Peter, *Heresy and Politics in the Reign of Henry IV: The Burning of John Badby* (Woodbridge: Boydell Press, 1987).

Mahoney, J. and Keller, J. E., eds, *Mediaeval Studies in Honor of Urban Tigner Holmes, Jr.*, University of North Carolina Studies in the Romance Languages and Literatures, 56 (Chapel Hill, NC: University of North Carolina Press, 1965).

Manly, John M. and Rickert, Edith, 'The "Hengwrt" Manuscript of Chaucer's *Canterbury Tales*', *National Library of Wales Journal* 1 (1939), 59–75.

Mann, Jill, *Chaucer and Medieval Estates Satire: The Literature of Social Classes and the General Prologue to the 'Canterbury Tales'* (Cambridge: Cambridge University Press, 1973).

Manzalaoui, M., 'Chaucer and Science', in *Geoffrey Chaucer*, ed. Brewer (1974), 224–61.
Martindale, Charles, ed., *Ovid Renewed: Ovidian Influences on Literature and Art from the Middle Ages to the Twentieth Century* (Cambridge: Cambridge University Press, 1988).
Matheson, Lister M. 'Historical Prose', in *Middle English Prose*, ed. Edwards, 209–48.
——, 'Printer and Scribe: The *Polychronicon*, and the *Brut*', *Speculum* 60 (1985), 593–614.
Miller, Paul, 'John Gower, Satiric Poet', in *Gower's 'Confessio Amantis'*, ed. Minnis (1983), 79–105.
Minnis, A. J., ed., *Gower's 'Confessio Amantis': Responses and Reassessments* (Cambridge: Brewer, 1983).
——, *Medieval Theory of Authorship: Scholastic Literary Attitudes in the Later Middle Ages*, 2nd edn (London: Scolar Press, 1988).
—— and Brewer, Charlotte, eds, *Crux and Controversy in Middle English Textual Criticism* (Cambridge: Brewer, 1992).
——; Morse, Charlotte; and Turville-Petre, Thorlac, eds, *Essays on Ricardian Literature: In Honour of J. A. Burrow* (Oxford: Clarendon Press, 1997).
Mitchiner, M., *Medieval Pilgrim and Secular Badges* (London: Hawkins, 1986).
Morgan, Philip, *War and Society in Medieval Cheshire, 1277–1403*, Remains Historical and Literary Connected with the Palatine Counties of Lancaster and Cheshire, vol. 34, 3rd series (Manchester: Chetham Society, 1987).
Morse, Charlotte and Windeatt, Barry, eds, *Chaucer Traditions: Studies in Honour of Derek Brewer* (Cambridge: Cambridge University Press, 1990).
Muir, Lynette R., *Literature and Society in Medieval France: The Mirror and Its Image 1100–1500* (Basingstoke: Macmillan, 1985).
Munby, Julian, '126 High Street: The Archaeology and History of an Oxford House', *Oxoniensia* 40 (1975), 254–308.
Muscatine, Charles, *Chaucer and the French Tradition: A Study in Style and Meaning* (Berkeley and Los Angeles: University of California Press, 1957).
——, *The Old French Fabliaux* (New Haven: Yale University Press, 1986).
——, *Poetry and Crisis in the Age of Chaucer*, University of Notre Dame Ward-Phillips Lectures in English Language and Literature, 4 (Notre Dame: University of Notre Dame Press, 1972).
Nagera, Humberto, et al., *Basic Psychoanalytic Concepts on the Theory of Dreams*, Hampstead Clinic Psychoanalytic Library, 2 (London: George, Allen and Unwin, 1969).
Neuss, Paula, '*Double-entendre* in the Miller's Tale', *Essays in Criticism* 24 (1974), 325–40.
Nicholson, Ranald, *Edward III and the Scots: The Formative Years of a Military Career, 1327–1335* (London: Oxford University Press, 1965).

Nissé, Ruth, '"Oure Fadres Olde and Modres": Gender, Heresy, and Hoccleve's Literary Politics', *Studies in the Age of Chaucer* 21 (1999), 275–99.
Nolan, Barbara, *The Gothic Visionary Perspective* (Princeton: Princeton University Press, 1977).
Olmert, K. Michael, 'The Canon's Yeoman's Tale: An Interpretation', *Annuale Medievale* 8 (1967), 70–94.
Olsson, Kurt, 'John Gower's *Vox clamantis* and the Medieval Idea of Place', *Studies in Philology* 84 (1987), 134–58.
Ormrod, W. M., 'The Personal Religion of Edward III', *Speculum* 64 (1989), 849–77.
——, *The Reign of Edward III: Crown and Political Society in England 1327–1377* (New Haven: Yale University Press, 1990).
Owen, Charles A., 'Forum: Chaucer's Pardoner', *PMLA* 98 (1983), 254.
Pantin, W. A., 'The Development of Domestic Architecture in Oxford', *Antiquaries' Journal*, 27 (1947), 120–50.
——, 'Medieval English Town-House Plans', *Medieval Archaeology*, 6–7 (1962–3), 202–39.
Parkes, M. B. and Watson, Andrew G., eds, *Medieval Scribes, Manuscripts and Libraries: Essays Presented to N. R. Ker* (London: Scolar Press, 1978).
Parr, Johnstone, 'Astronomical Dating for Some of Lydgate's Poems', *PMLA* 67 (1952), 251–8.
Patterson, Lee, 'Court Politics and the Invention of Literature: The Case of Sir John Clanvowe', in *Culture and History*, ed. Aers (1992), 7–41.
——, '"What is me?": Self and Society in the Poetry of Thomas Hoccleve', *Studies in the Age of Chaucer* 23 (2001), 437–70.
——, ed., *Literary Practice and Social Change in Britain 1380–1530* (Berkeley and Los Angeles: University of California Press, 1990).
Pearsall, Derek, 'Hoccleve's *Regement of Princes*: The Poetics of Royal Self-Representation', *Speculum* 69 (1994), 386–410.
——, *The Life of Geoffrey Chaucer: A Critical Biography*, Blackwell Critical Biographies, 1 (Oxford: Blackwell, 1992).
——, *Old English and Middle English Poetry*, Routledge History of English Poetry, 1 (London: Routledge and Kegan Paul, 1977).
Peden, Alison M., 'Macrobins and Mediaeval Dream Literature', *Medium Ævum* 54 (1985), 59–73.
Pelen, Marc M. 'Machaut's Court of Love Narratives and Chaucer's *Book of the Duchess*', *Chaucer Review* 11 (1976), 128–55.
Percival, Florence, *Chaucer's Legendary Good Women* (Cambridge: Cambridge University Press, 1998).

Perkins, Nicholas, *Hoccleve's 'Regiment of Princes': Counsel and Constraint* (Cambridge: Brewer, 2001).
Petersen, Kate Oelzner, *On the Sources of the 'Nonne Prestes Tale'*, Radcliffe College Monographs, 10 (Boston: Ginn, 1898).
Piehler, Paul, *The Visionary Landscape: A Study in Medieval Allegory* (London: Arnold, 1971).
Pison, Thomas, 'Liminality in *The Canterbury Tales*', *Genre* 10 (1977), 157–71.
Pratt, Robert A., 'Some Latin Sources of the Nonnes Preest on Dreams', *Speculum* 52 (1977), 538–70.
Pugh, Ralph B., *Imprisonment in Medieval England* (Cambridge: Cambridge University Press, 1968).
Quinn, William A., *Chaucer's 'Rehersynges': The Performability of the 'Legend of Good Women'* (Washington DC: Catholic University of America Press, 1994).
Reyburn, Wallace, *Flushed with Pride: The Story of Thomas Crapper* (London: Macdonald, 1969).
Robbins, R. H., 'The English Fabliau: Before and After Chaucer', *Moderna Språk* 64 (1970), 231–44.
Robertson, W. A. Scott, 'The Crypt of Canterbury Cathedral', Part 2, *Archaeologia Cantiana* 13 (1880), 500–51.
Rose, Christine, 'Woman's "pryvetee", May and the Privy: Fissures in the Narrative Voice in the Merchant's Tale, 1944–86', *Chaucer Yearbook* 4 (1997), 61–77.
Rosenberg, Bruce A., 'The Contrary Tales of the Second Nun and the Canon's Yeoman', *Chaucer Review* 2 (1968), 278–91.
——, 'Reason and Revelation in the *Canterbury Tales*', Diss. Ohio State University, 1965.
Rowland, Beryl, 'What Chaucer Did to the Fabliau', *Studia Neophilologica* 51 (1979), 205–13.
Russell, J. Stephen, *The English Dream Vision: Anatomy of a Form* (Columbus: Ohio State University Press, 1988).
Russell-Smith, Joy H., 'Walter Hilton and a Tract in Defence of the Veneration of Images', *Dominican Studies* 7 (1954), 180–214.
Ryan, Lawrence V., 'The Canon's Yeoman's Desperate Confession', *Chaucer Review* 8 (1974), 297–310.
Sabine, Ernest L., 'Latrines and Cesspools of Mediaeval London', *Speculum* 9 (1934), 303–21.
Saintsbury, George, 'The English Chaucerians', in *Cambridge History*, ed. Ward and Waller, vol. 2 (1908), 197–222.
Salzman, L. F., *Building in England down to 1540: A Documentary History* (Oxford: Clarendon Press, 1952).

Sargent-Baur, Barbara N., ed., *Journeys Toward God: Pilgrimage and Crusade*, Studies in Medieval Culture, 30 (Kalamazoo: Medieval Institute Publications, 1992).
Saunders, Corinne, ed., *A Concise Companion to Chaucer* (Oxford: Blackwell, 2006).
Saul, Nigel. *Richard II* (New Haven: Yale University Press, 1997).
Scanlon, Larry, 'The King's Two Voices: Narrative and Power in Hoccleve's *Regement of Princes*', in *Literary Practice and Social Change*, ed. Patterson (1990), 216–47.
Scattergood, V. J., 'Literary Culture at the Court of Richard II' in *English Court Culture*, ed. Scattergood and Sherborne (1983), 29–43.
—— and Sherborne, J. W., eds, *English Court Culture in the Later Middle Ages* (London: Duckworth, 1983).
Scheifele, Eleanor, 'Richard II and the Visual Arts', in *Richard II*, ed. Goodman and Gillespie (1999), 255–71.
Schleusener-Eichholz, Gudrun, 'Naturwissenschaft und Allegorese: der *Traaatus de oculo morali* des Petrus von Limoges', *Frühmittelalterliche Studien* 12 (1978), 258–309.
Schmidt, A. V. C., 'The Inner Dreams in *Piers Plowman*', *Medium Ævum* 55 (1986), 24–40.
Schofield, John, *Medieval London Houses* (New Haven: Yale University Press for the Paul Mellon Centre for Studies in British Art, 1994).
Seward, D., *Henry as Warlord* (London: Sidgwick and Jackson, 1987).
Seymour, M. C., 'The Manuscripts of Hoccleve's *Regiment of Princes*', *Transactions of the Edinburgh Bibliographical Society* 4 (1974), 253–97.
Shippey, T. A., 'Between Ellesmere and Hengwrt', *Times Literary Supplement* (16 January 1981), 60.
Simpson, James, *Reform and Cultural Revolution*, Oxford English Literary History, ii: *1350–1547* (Oxford: Oxford University Press, 2002).
Skeat, Walter W., *The Chaucer Canon, with a Discussion of the Works Associated with the Name of Geoffrey Chaucer* (Oxford: Clarendon Press, 1900).
——, *The Evolution of the 'Canterbury Tales'*, Chaucer Society, 2nd ser., 38 (1907; repr. New York: Haskell House, 1968).
Smalley, Beryl, *English Friars and Antiquity in the Early Fourteenth Century* (Oxford: Blackwell, 1960).
Smyser, H. M., 'The Domestic Background of *Troilus and Criseyde*', *Speculum* 31 (1956), 297–315.
Smyth, Alfred P., ed., *Medieval Europeans: Studies in Ethnic Identity and National Perspectives in Medieval Europe* (Houndmills: Macmillan, 1998).
Somerset, Fiona; Havens, Jill C.; and Pitard, Derrick G., eds, *Lollards and their Influence in Late Medieval England* (Woodbridge: Boydell Press, 2003).

Southern, R. W., 'Aspects of the European Tradition of Historical Writing: 2. Hugh of St Victor and the Idea of Historical Development', *Transactions of the Royal Historical Society*, 5th series, 21 (1971), 159–79.
Spearing, A. C., 'Lydgate's Canterbury Tale: The *Siege of Thebes* and Fifteenth-Century Chaucerianism', in *Fifteenth-Century Studies*, ed. Yeager (1984), 333–64.
——, *Medieval Dream-Poetry* (Cambridge: Cambridge University Press, 1976).
——, *Medieval to Renaissance in English Poetry* (Cambridge: Cambridge University Press, 1985).
Spiegel, Gabrielle M., *Romancing the Past: The Rise of Vernacular Prose Historiography in Thirteenth-Century France*, The New Historicism: Studies in Cultural Poetics, 23 (Berkeley, Los Angeles and Oxford: University of California Press, 1993).
Stakel, Susan, 'Structural Convergence of Pilgrimage and Dream-Vision in Christine de Pizan', in *Journeys Toward God*, ed. Sargent-Baur (1992), 195–203.
Stanbury, Sarah, *Seeing the 'Gawain'-Poet: Description and the Act of Perception* (Philadelphia: University of Pennsylvania Press, 1991).
——, 'Visualizing', in *Companion to Chaucer*, ed. Brown (2000), 457–79.
——, 'The Vivacity of Images: St Katharine, Knighton's Lollards, and the Breaking of Idols', in *Images, Idolatry, and Iconoclasm*, ed. Dimmick, Simpson and Zeeman (2002), 131–50.
Stanley, A. P., *Historical Memorials of Canterbury*, 11th edn (London: Murray, 1912).
Stevens, Martin and Woodward, Daniel, eds, *The Ellesmere Chaucer: Essays in Interpretation* (San Marino: Huntington Library, 1995).
Storm, Melvin, '"A Culpa et a Poena": Christ's Pardon and the Pardoner's', *Neuplologische Mitteilungen* 83 (1982), 439–42.
——, 'The Pardoners Invitation: Quaestor's Bag or Becket's Shrine?', *PMLA* 97 (1982), 810–18.
Strohm, Paul, 'Chaucer's Fifteenth-Century Audience and the Narrowing of the "Chaucer Tradition"', *Studies in the Age of Chaucer* 4 (1982), 3–32.
——, *England's Empty Throne: Usurpation and the Language of Legitimation 1399–1422* (New Haven: Yale University Press, 1998).
——, 'Hoccleve, Lydgate and the Lancastrian Court', in *Cambridge History*, ed. Wallace (1999), 640–61.
——, *Hochon's Arrow: The Social Imagination of Fourteenth-Century Texts* (Princeton: Princeton University Press, 1992).
——, 'Politics and Poetics: Usk and Chaucer in the 1380s', in *Literary Practice and Social Change*, ed. Patterson (1990), 83–112.
Sumption, Jonathan, *Pilgrimage: An Image of Mediaeval Religion* (London: Faber, 1975).

Tanner, Marie, *The Last Descendant of Aeneas: The Hapsburgs and the Mythic Image of the Emperor* (New Haven: Yale University Press, 1993).
Tatlock, J. S. P., 'The Canterbury Tales in 1400', *PMLA* 50 (1935), 100–39.
Tatton-Brown, T., *Medieval Inns in Canterbury* (Canterbury: Canterbury Archaeological Trust, 1987).
Taylor, Andrew. 'Anne of Bohemia and the Making of Chaucer', *Studies in the Age of Chaucer* 19 (1997), 95–119.
Taylor, John, *English Historical Literature in the Fourteenth Century* (Oxford: Clarendon Press, 1987).
——, *The 'Universal Chronicle' of Ranulf Higden* (Oxford: Clarendon Press, 1966).
Tedlock, Barbara, ed., *Dreaming: Anthropological and Psychological Interpretations* (Cambridge: Cambridge University Press, 1987).
——, 'Zuni and Quiché Dream Sharing and Interpreting', in *Dreaming*, ed. Tedlock (1987), 105–31.
Thomas, Alfred, *A Blessed Shore: England and Bohemia from Chaucer to Shakespeare* (Ithaca, NY: Cornell University Press, 2007).
Thomson, S. Harrison, 'Learning at the Court of Charles IV', *Speculum* 25 (1950), 1–20.
Thorndike, Lynn, *A History of Magic and Experimental Science*, ii: *During the First Thirteen Centuries of Our Era* (New York: Columbia University Press, 1923).
Tolmie, Sarah, 'The *Prive Scilence* of Thomas Hoccleve', *Studies in the Age of Chaucer* 22 (2000), 281–309.
Torti, Anna, *The Glass of Form: Mirroring Structures from Chaucer to Skelton* (Cambridge: Brewer, 1991).
Tuck, J. Anthony, 'Carthusian Monks and Lollard Knights: Religious Attitudes at the Court of Richard II', *Studies in the Age of Chaucer: Proceedings*, 1 (1984): *Reconstructing Chaucer*, ed. Paul Strohm and Thomas J. Heffernan, 149–61.
——, 'Richard II and the House of Luxembourg', in *Richard II*, ed. Goodman and Gillespie (1999), 205–29.
Tupper, Frederick, 'The Pardoner's Tavern', *JEGP* 13 (1914), 553–65.
Turner, D. H., 'The Customary of the Shrine of St Thomas Becket', *Canterbury Cathedral Chronicle*, No. 70 (1976), 16–22.
Turner, Edith, 'The Literary Roots of Victor Turner's Anthropology', in *Victor Turner*, ed. Ashley (1990), 163–9.
Turner, Hilary L., *Town Defences in England and Wales: An Architectural and Documentary Study AD 900–1500* (London: Baker, 1971).
Turner, Victor, 'Betwixt and Between: The Liminal Period in *Rites de Passage*', in his *Forest of Symbols* (1967), 93–111.
——, *Dramas, Fields, and Metaphors: Symbolic Action in Human Society* (Ithaca, NY: Cornell University Press, 1974).

——, *The Forest of Symbols: Aspects of Ndembu Ritual* (Ithaca, NY: Cornell University Press, 1967).
——, *From Ritual to Theatre: The Human Seriousness of Play* (New York: Performing Arts Journal Publications, 1982).
——, 'Liminal to Liminoid, in Play, Flow, and Ritual: An Essay in Comparative Symbology', in his *From Ritual to Theatre* (1982), 20–60.
——, 'Pilgrimage and Communitas', *Studia Missionalia* 23 (1974), 305–27.
——, *The Ritual Process: Structure and Anti-Structure*, The Lewis Henry Morgan Lectures, 1966 (Chicago: Aldine, 1969).
—— and Turner, E., *Image and Pilgrimage in Christian Culture: Anthropological Perspectives*, Lectures on the History of Religions Sponsored by the American Council of Learned Societies, NS, 2 (New York: Columbia University Press, 1978).
Turville-Petre, Thorlac, *England the Nation: Language, Literature, and National Identity, 1290–1340* (Oxford: Clarendon Press, 1996).
Tuve, Rosemond, *Seasons and Months: Studies in a Tradition of Middle English Poetry* (1933; repr. Cambridge: Brewer, 1974).
Vale, Juliet, *Edward III and Chivalry: Chivalric Society and Its Context 1270–1350* (Woodbridge: Boydell Press, 1982).
van Gennep, Arnold, *The Rites of Passage*, trans. Monika B. Vizedom and Gabrielle L. Caffee (Chicago: University of Chicago Pess, 1960). [First published 1908.]
van Dussen, Michael, *From England to Bohemia: Heresy and Communication in the Later Middle Ages* (Cambridge: Cambridge University Press, 2012).
——, 'Three Verse Eulogies for Anne of Bohemia', *Medium Ævum* 78 (2009), 231–60.
Wakelin, Martin, 'Go, Litel Book', *Times Educational Supplement* (7 November 1980), 23.
Waldron, Ronald, 'The Manuscripts of Trevisa's Translation of the *Polychronicon*: Towards a New Edition', *Modern Language Quarterly* 51(1990), 281–317.
Walker, Simon, *The Lancastrian Affinity, 1361–1399* (Oxford: Clarendon Press, 1990).
Wallace, David, 'Anne of Bohemia, Queen of England, and Chaucer's *Emperice*', *Litteraria Pragensia* 5 (1995), 1–16.
——, *Chaucerian Polity: Absolutist Lineages and Associational Forms in England and Italy* (Stanford: Stanford University Press, 1997).
——, '"Whan She Translated Was": A Chaucerian Critique of the Petrarchan Academy', in *Literary Practice and Social Change*, ed. Patterson (1990), 156–215.
——, ed., *The Cambridge History of Medieval English Literature* (Cambridge: Cambridge University Press 1999).
Ward, A. W. and Waller, A. R., eds, *Cambridge History of English Literature*, 15 vols (Cambridge: Cambridge University Press, 1867–1922).

Ward, Benedicta, *Miracles and the Medieval Mind: Theory, Record and Event 1000–1215* (London: Scolar Press, 1982).
Warton, Thomas, *The History of English Poetry, from the Close of the Eleventh Century to the Commencement of the Eighteenth Century*, 2 vols (London: 1774–8).
Watkins, Charles A., 'Modern Irish Variants of the Enchanted Pear Tree', *Southern Folklore Quarterly* 30 (1966), 202–13.
Watson, Nicholas, '"Et que est huius ydoli materia? Tuipse": Idols and Images in Walter Hilton', in *Images, Idolatry and Iconoclasm*, ed. Dimmick, Simpson and Zeeman (2002), 95–111.
Weisheipl, James A., 'Curriculum of the Faculty of Arts at Oxford in the Early Fourteenth Century', *Mediaeval Studies* 26 (1964), 143–85.
Wentersdorf, Karl P., 'Chaucer's *Merchant's Tale* and Its Irish Analogues', *Studies in Philology* 63 (1966), 604–29.
———, 'A Spanish Analogue of the Pear-Tree Episode in the Merchant's Tale', *Modern Philology* 64 (1967), 320–1.
Wilkins, Nigel, 'A Pattern of Patronage: Machaut, Froissart and the Houses of Luxembourg and Bohemia in the Fourteenth Century', *French Studies* 37 (1983), 257–84.
Williams, A., 'Some Documents on English Pardoners, 1350–1400', in *Mediaeval Studies* ed. Mahoney and Keller (1965), 197–207.
Wimsatt, James I., *Chaucer and His French Contemporaries: Natural Music in the Fourteenth Centuries* (Toronto: University of Toronto Press, 1991).
Windeatt, Barry, 'Master Copy', *Times Higher Education Supplement* (20 March 1981), 19.
Winstead, Karen A., 'The *Beryn*-Writer as a Reader of Chaucer', *Chaucer Review* 22 (1988), 225–33.
Wood, Margaret, *The English Mediaeval House* (London: Bracken Books, 1983).
Woodruff, C. Eveleigh, 'A Monastic Chronicle Lately Discovered at Christ Church, Canterbury: With Introduction and Notes', *Archaeologia Cantiana* 29 (1911), 47–84.
———, 'The Financial Aspect of the Cult of St Thomas of Canterbury as Revealed by a Study of the Monastic Records', *Archaeologia Cantiana* 44 (1932), 13–32.
Woods, William F., 'Private and Public Space in the Miller's Tale', *Chaucer Review* 29 (1994), 166–78.
Wolff, Werner, *The Dream – Mirror of Conscience: A History of Dream Interpretation from 2000 B.C. and a New Theory of Dream Synthesis* (New York: Grune and Stratton, 1952).
Wright, Lawrence, *Clean and Decent: The Fascinating History of the Bathroom and Water Closet* (London: Routledge and Kegan Paul, 1960).

Wright, Steven, 'Deguileville's *Pèlerinage de Vie Humaine* as "Contrepartie Edifiante" of the *Roman de la Rose*', *Philological Quarterly* 68 (1989), 399–422.

Wylie, James Hamilton and Waugh, William Templeton, *The Reign of Henry the Fifth*, iii: *1415–1422* (Cambridge: Cambridge University Press, 1929).

Yeager, Robert F., ed., *Fifteenth-Century Studies: Recent Essays* (Hamden, Conn.: Archon Books, 1984).

Zacher, Christian K., *Curiosity and Pilgrimage: The Literature of Discovery in Fourteenth-Century England* (Baltimore: Johns Hopkins, 1976).

Zeeman, Nicolette, 'The Idol of the Text', in *Images, Idolatry, and Iconocalsm*, ed. Dimmick, Simpson and Zeeman (2002), 43–62.

Zink, Michael, 'The Allegorical Poem as Interior Memoir', in *Images of Power*, ed. Brownlee and Nichols (1986), 100–26.

Index

Footnotes are indicated by the page number followed by 'n' and the note number.

Addy, Sidney Oldhall 102n17
Aeneas 83
Aers, David 163n17
Agnes of Lancecrona 59
Aiken 131n12, 149n16
Albano, R. A. 10n19, 129
Alceste 64, 65, 67–8
alchemy 127, 147–8, 150, 151–2
Alhazen 129, 137
  De aspectibus 128
Allen, R. S. 194n63
altered consciousness 41–2, 45, 50–1, 164
Anderson, J. H. 37n43
Anderson, R. 187
  Poets of Great Britain 181
Andreas, J. R. 5180
Anne of Bohemia 4
  as Alceste 64–5, 66–7
  alleged heresy 73–4
  arrival and reception in England 58–9
  command of English 73
  as Criseyde 67, 73, 78
  death 59
  influence on Clanvowe 64
  intercessory role 59, 60, 65–6, 78
  letter writing to Richard 74
  linguistic abilities 73–4
  marriage to Richard II 60
  patronage of Queen's College, Oxford 74
  as recipient of *Troilus and Criseyde* 66, 73, 84
  religious attitudes 82–3

Antonelli, Roberto 75n49
'anxiety of influence' 215
Apocalypse (N. T.) 27–8, 46
Aristotle 129
Arnold of Villanova 153
Arthurian legend 5–6, 11–12, 21
Arundel, Thomas 73, 163
Aston, Margaret 159n6,7, 160n9
audience
  Anne of Bohemia as 66, 84
  appeal for tolerance 61–2
  of *Beryn* 155, 187, 197–8, 200, 215
  courtly audience of *Troilus and Criseyde* 61, 74
  'curtesy' and 'gentilnes' 198
  for dream visions 26, 29, 42, 47
  for Higden 8, 11
  intelligence of 197–8
  and reception of *Canterbury Tales* 215–16
  relationship with narrator 72–3, 74–5
  social groups 200
  textual awareness of 74–5, 215
  women 200
Augustine, St, *City of God* 7

Babington, C. and Lumby, J. R. 6n3, 9
Bacon, Roger 127
Badby, John 172
Bado Aureo, Johannis de 74
Baldwin, R. G. 152n23
Barney, S. A. 52n81
Barron, Caroline M. 78n56

Bashe, E. J. 184n26, 190n47
Baswell, Christopher 66n36
Bartholomew the Englishman, *De proprietatibus rerum* 131–2, 137
Baugh, A. C. 184n27
Baum, Paull Franklin 155n25
Baumgartner, E. 28n14
Becker, R. de 37n41
Becket, Thomas, shrine of 142, 189, 190–1, 205, 206
  income 190–1
  and indulgences 204
bedchambers 30–1, 102–3
Bede 12, 20
Beidler, Peter G. 124n2
Bell, J., *Poets of Great Britain* 181, 181n8
Bennett, H. S. 180n3, 192
Bennett, J. A. W. 41n54, 101n14
Benson, David C. 75n49
Bernabó Visconti, duke of Milan 57, 58
Beryn see Tale of Beryn
Besserman, Lawrence and Storm, Melvin 204n79, 206n87
Bible 6, 23
  dreams 38
  images in 177
  translations 73–4
Blake, N. F. 143, 145–6, 145n9, 146n10, 147, 149–50, 154, 182n18
blind husband stories 123–5, 136
blindness 88, 123, 126, 131–2, 133
  inner/spiritual 133, 134, 135, 136–7, 148
  moral 152–3
Blodgett, E. D. 106n34
Boccaccio, Giovanni
  Il Filostrato 62, 64, 74
  Teseida 89, 90
Bodenham, C. H. L. 23n2
Boethius, *Consolation of Philosophy* 33, 34–5, 39, 64, 81

Boffey, Julia and Edwards, A. S. G. 65n30
Bohemians
  arrival and reception in England 58–9
  court in Prague 76–7
  'impoverishing the king' 59
  influence on English court 60
  marriage into English nobility 59
Bowers, John M. 179n1
Boyd, David Lorenzo 107n31
Brent, Cecil 191n50, 198n75
Brewer, D. 49n76
Britain 6
  in Higden's *Polychronicon* 10–21
  myths of national identity 11–12, 21, 77–8
  political/social conditions 33, 49–50
  see also England; Scotland; Wales
Brody, Saul N. 105n31
Browne, Sir Thomas 36n39
Brownlee, K. 37n43
Brownlee, K. and Huot, S. 28n14
Brut 11, 21
Brutus 77, 78
Bryan, W. F. and Dempster, G. 111n2
Burke, P. 10n19
Burley, Sir Simon 57, 59
Burlin, Robert B. 134n22
Burrow, J. A. 168n32, 171n38
Butterfield, Ardis 59n12

Calin, W. A. 35n36, 43n61
Camille, Michael 105n33
Canterbury
  the Cheker of the hope 193, 212
  Christ Church 142, 188, 190, 193, 211
  defences 193–4
  jubilee celebrations 196
  St Augustine's abbey 188–9
  shrine of St Thomas Becket 189, 190–1, 195, 205, 206
  The Sun 193

Canzoniere, Il see Petrarch
Carlson, David R. 169n33
Carthusians 82–3
Catto, J. I. 98n4
Caviness, Madeline Harrison 191n51
Caxton 9
Cecilia, St. 147–8
Ceyx and Alcyone 36
Chalmers, *Works of the English Poets* 181
chansons d'aventure 44
Charles IV, Emperor 4, 57, 76–7
Chaucer, Geoffrey
  audience 66–7, 216, 217
    interaction with 72–3
    textual awareness of 74–5
  Boece 33, 81
  Book of the Duchess 3, 31, 32, 35, 38, 39, 41, 46
    Ceyx and Alcione and the Black Knight 36–7
    influence of Froissart 63–4
    influence of Machaut 63
    Mercury and Morpheus 175
  Canterbury Tales 23, 55, 87
    authenticity debates 143–55
    Canon Yeoman's Prologue and Tale 141, 147–55
      alchemy 127, 147–8, 151–2
      Almachius 153
      Cecilia, St. 147–8, 153
      moral blindness 152–3
      pars secunda 152–3, 154, 155
      and Second Nun's Tale 148–9
    Clerk's Prologue and Tale 145
    Cook's Tale 211
    Ellesmere manuscript 97
    fellowship 214
    Franklin's Tale 145
    Hengwrt manuscript 97, 141, 143–4, 145, 146–7, 154
    Host 150
    Knight's Tale 87, 89–95, 109, 149, 215
      Arcite 90, 93, 94, 95, 109
      Emelye 93, 94, 105
      mimetic and iconographic meaning 90–1, 95
      Palamon 90, 93, 94, 95, 109
      prison of love tradition 91
      prison tower of Theseus 89–91, 92, 93–4, 105
      and *Roman de la rose*: castle of *Jalousie* 93–4
      tournament 95
    Merchant's Tale 88, 104–5, 123–37
      Damian 104, 123, 124, 129, 132, 136
      deception stories: Optical-Illusion and Blind-Husband blend 123–4, 136
      defective vision 131–2
      inner blindness 134–6
      January 124, 125–6, 127, 128, 130, 132, 134, 135–6
      Justinus 134
      May 88, 104, 123, 124, 125–6, 127, 132, 134, 135, 136
      Nature 130
      Placebo 134
      Pluto 124
      ruler of Pavye 133, 136
      sources 136–7
      visual deception 123, 130
    Miller's Tale 87, 97–107, 109, 149
      Absolon 99, 100, 101–2, 103, 105, 106, 208–9
      Alisoun 95, 99, 100, 101–2, 103, 105, 106, 109
      jealousy 95, 106
      John 95, 101, 106
      Nicholas 95, 99, 103, 105, 109
      privy 104, 105, 106, 107
      shot wyndowe 87, 97–107

Chaucer, Geoffrey *(continued)*
  'Nonne' 145, 146
  Pardoner 206
  Pardoner's Prologue 151
  Parson 109
  positioning of tales 148–9
  reception of 215–16
  Reeve's Tale 88, 109–21, 210–11
    Aleyn 113, 114, 115, 116, 117–18, 119, 120
    compared with *Meunier et les .II. clers* 110–12
    John 113, 114, 115, 117–18, 119, 120, 210
    Malyn 113, 114, 115
    perception of objects 115–16
    space 109–10, 113, 117
      bedchamber scene 113–17, 120
      house 118
      movements 114
    Symkyn 88, 113, 114, 115–16, 117–18, 119–20, 209–10, 211
      social pretensions 120–1
    Symkyn's wife 112, 113, 114, 115, 116, 119, 121
  Second Nun's Tale 144–5, 146, 148–9, 153, 154
  space, use of 109–13
  Squire's Tale 127
  Tabard Inn 109
  Wife of Bath's Prologue 151
  see also Tale of Beryn
Chaucer's life at court 60–1
dream visions
  altered consciousness 42–3
  authority in dreams 38
  dream boundary 45
  insomnia 31
  intensified sensual experience 41
  literary possibilities 46
  melancholy in love 35
  'middle vision' 24
  numbness and preoccupation 32, 33
  release of spirit 39
  setting 27, 28, 29
  wakefulness and sleep 36–7
Gamelyn 150
and Hoccleve, *Regiment of Princes*
  the old man 174–5
  portrait 167, 168, 169–70
House of Fame 27, 30, 35
journeys to France and Italy 57, 61
knowledge of Bohemia 62–3
Legend of Good Women 28, 29, 32, 45
  Anne of Bohemia as Alceste 64–5, 66–7
  Anne of Bohemia as recipient 66
natural and spiritual world 147–8
Parliament of Fowls 33, 37, 47, 64
qualities admired by Hoccleve 168–9, 173
realism 102, 112–13
Romaunt of the Rose 29, 36, 38, 41
science, use of 127, 130–4
Troilus and Criseyde
  Anne of Bohemia
    as Criseyde 6, 7, 73, 78
    as recipient 66, 73, 84
  appeal for tolerance of foreign ways 61–2
  audience, textual awareness of 74–5
  audience-narrator interaction 72–3
  Calkas 79
  Canticus Troili 75–6, 81
  Cassandra 67–8
  choice of Troy as setting 77–8
  circulation of books and documents 69–72
  courtly milieu 66
  Criseyde
    alleged infidelity 67–8
    anxiety about the war 69

Index

beauty of 67
  spiritual dimension of 83–4
Deiphebus 70
Diomede 67–8, 80
Helena 70
influences 64
letter writing 70–2, 74
Lollius as source 74–6
love ('fire of') 79–83
narrator as translator and transmittor 72–3
Pandarus 68, 70–1, 79–80
reading *Siege of Thebes* 69–70
sign interpretation 69
sources of 74–6
Troilus
  dream 67–8
  and fire of love 79–83
  funeral rites 79
  pilgrimage through love 82
  response to Criseyde's letters 71–2
  Richard II as 78
  spirituality 83–4
Troy 69, 79
Chaucer Society 181
Chester 19, 21
Chichele, Archbishop 205, 206
Chillenden, Prior 193
Christ 45, 48
  and Cross 159, 161
  God made flesh 176
  love of 81, 82
Christ Church, Canterbury 142, 188, 190, 193, 211
Christianity 159, 176
  see also Bible; Christ; God; pilgrimage
Chronicon Anglie 160
Cicero, *De republica* 36
Clanvowe, Sir John 30n22, 31, 64
Clark, David L. 133n19

Collingwood, R. G. 7n6
Condé, Jean de 34
Confessio Amantis see Gower, John
Copland, M. 117n10
Corpus Christi 166
Coventry Charterhouse 83
Crisp, Frank 212n96
Crow, Martin C. and Olson, Clair C. 57n1
Cunningham, J. V. 23n1
Curry, W. C. 41n53, 117n10
'curtesy' 198, 199–200

Dante, *Inferno* 32
Darjes, Bradley and Rendell, Thomas 186, 186n32
Darton 181
Davidoff, J. M. 26
Davis, J. F. 195n67
Davis, Norman et al 98n9
De proprietatibus rerum see Bartholomew the Englishman
Dean, C. 6n2
deception stories 123–4
Deguileville, G. de 51n81
Delany, S. 27n9
Dempster, Germaine 123, 123n1, 124, 137n24, 144n4
Deschamps, E.
  Elegiae Maximiniani 137
  Lay de franchise, Le 43–4
  Miroir de mariages 137
Diomede 67–8
Dit de la fonteinne amoureuse see Guillaume de Machaut
Dit de la panthère d'Amours see Nicole de Margival
Dit dou lyon see Guillaume de Machaut
Dives and Pauper 36, 47
Douglas, Gavin, *Aeneid* 97
Doyle, A. I. 73n41, 192

Doyle, A. I. and Parkes, M. B. 144, 145, 147, 192n56
dream visions 3, 23–56
  14th century revival 24–5
  advantages as rhetorical device 26–7, 49
  afterlife of dreams 46–9
  altered consciousness 41–2, 45, 50–1, 164
  anxiety 32
  authority in dreams 38–9
  bedchamber as setting 30–1
  betweenness 24, 50–1, 53–4
  and *chansons d'aventure* 44
  divine inspiration 42
  enchantment 42–3
  historical context 25–6, 49–50
  insomnia 31
  intensified sensual experience 41
  literary possibilities 46–7
  love 34–5, 47–8
  paradisal settings 29–30, 41–2, 45
  pilgrimage 51, 52–3
  recent studies of 24–5
  receptivity of narrator 35
  release of spirit 39–40
  and rites of passage 53–4
  sadness 33–4
  searching or wandering 35–6
  sense of death 32
  and social/political conditions 49–50
  solitude 30–1
  transformations 40–1
  wakefulness-dream boundary 36–8, 39–40, 43–5
Dufty, A. R. 194n62
Dussen, Michael van 60n15, 74n46, 83
Dutton, P. E. 50n78

Eade, J. and Sallnow, M. J. 56n90
Early English Text Society 181

Eberle, Patricia J. 130n11
Echard, Siân 167n26
Edward III 5–6, 21, 63
Edwards, A. S. G. 8n12, 9n13, 11n23, 64n30
Edwards, J. G. 5, 5n1
Edwards, R. R. 27n10
Effled, Queen of Mercia 19
England 16
  Anglo-Bohemian treaty 57
  and characteristics of English 17–18
  origins of name (Higden) 20
Erickson, C. 23n2
Ernest of Pardubice 76
etymology 19–20
Euclid 128
Eye Priory 83
Ezekiel (O. T.) 27, 39

Fablel dou Dieu d'amors, Li 43
fabliaux 198, 212–13
faery forces 42
Farrell, Thomas J. 103n24
Federico, Sylvia 77n52
fellowship 54, 214
Fentress, J. and Wickham, C. 19n53
Ferster, Judith 163n19
Filostrato, Il see Boccaccio, Giovanni
Fischer, S. R. 44n64
Fisher, John H. 147n11, 161n13
Fleming, John V. 191n50
Foreville, Raymonde 191n50
Fowler, D. C. 9n13
fragmentation of society 49–50
French, W. H. and Hale, C. B. 182, 182n15
Frere, S. S. and Bennett, P. 194n60
friars 190, 199
Froissart, J. 30n23, 31, 63–4, 77–8
  Méliador 63–4
  Paradys d'Amours 35, 63
  Prison amoureuse 91

Index

Frye, N. 42n57
Furnivall, F. J. and Stone, W. G. 181, 183–4, 188

Galbraith, V. H. 6n4, 7n6, 10n20, 12n28
Galloway, Andrew 164n20
garderobes 103
Gardiner, F. C. 52n82
Gawain 3
Gaylord, Alan T. 169n33
Gellrich, J. M. 45n65
Gennep, Arnold van 53, 53n85
genres 25
'gentil' behaviour 198–9
Geoffrey of Monmouth 11
Geremek, B. 51n80
Given-Wilson, C. 60n16
God
 emanating love 80–1
 worship 158–9
 see also Christ
Gower, John 157–8
 Confessio Amantis 23
 Vox clamantis 77, 141, 158–67
  choice of dream vision genre 164
  contradictory attitudes 163, 164
  dedication 163
  distraction of religious images 158–9
  Gower's hostility to religious imagery 159–60
  inversion of hierarchical order 165–6
  and peasants' rebellion 163–5
  sign of the cross as permissible 159, 165
Grandson, Oton de, *Le Songe Saint Valentin* 47
Gransden, A. 5n1, 7n7, 8n9, 9
Gray, Douglas, *Riverside Chaucer* 98

Green, Richard Firth 66n33, 74n48, 216n103
Gregory, St. 20
Grennen, J. E. 148, 148n13, 149n16
Grosseteste, Robert 127
Guillaume de Lorris and Jean de Meun, *Roman de la rose*
 Bialacoil 92
 castle of *Jalousie* 87, 91–3
 influence of as dream vision 23, 24, 29, 36, 38
 paradisal setting 41
 science of optics 129–30
Guillaume de Machaut 24, 62
 Dit de la fonteinne amoureuse 31, 35
 Dit dou lyon 43
 Jugement dou roy de Behaigne 63, 64
Gunn, Alan M. F. 130n11
Gurevich, A. 10n19

Hagen, S. K. 52n81
Hale, David G. 32n29, 48n73
Hanks, D. Thomas Jr. 103n24
Hanna, Ralph III 9n13
Hanning, R. W. 106n34
Hansen, Elaine Tuttle 106n34
Harbert, Bruce 166n25
Harris, Mollie 104n28
Hartung, Albert E. 137n24, 155, 155n25
Harvey, John H. 194n60
Hawkwood, Sir John 57
Hengwrt manuscript 97, 141, 143–4, 145, 146–7, 154
Henry IV, King 170
Henry, Prince 170, 176
herbergage 109, 119–20, 210
Hereford, Nicholas 74
heresy 50, 66, 205–6
 of Anne of Bohemia 73
 and images 161, 162
Hieatt, C. B. 38n44, 43n59

Higden, Ranulph, *Polychronicon* 5–21
  Britain
    characteristics of English 17–18
    cohesion and diversity 13–15
    cultural/political divisions 16–18
    geographical identity 12–13
    history and customs 19
    liminality/otherness 15–16
    linguistic divisions 16–17
    as main subject 10–11
    myths of national identity 11–12, 21
    national identity and etymology 19–20
    national identity and sense of the past 18–20
    origins of name 20
    positive features 13–14, 15
    role of monarchy 14
  collation and selection of materials 11–12
  contents 7–8
  death of Higden 21
  English translations 8–9
  modern studies on 9
  objective 6
  success and dissemination 8–9
  writing process 6
Hilton, Walter 160
history
  and national identity 18–19
Hoccleve, Thomas
  admiration of Chaucer 168–9
  and Gower 157–8
  The Regiment of Princes 42n57, 141, 167–77
    illustration of Geoffrey Chaucer 167, 168, 169–70, 171–2
    the old man 173–5
    success of poem 171
Holkot, Robert 133–4, 137
Holy Church 38

Housman, J. E. 12n25
Hudson, Anne 159n6
Hult, D. F. 38n44
Huntington Library 6
Huppé, Bernard F. 106n34

images 141
  aiding memory 169–70
  attribution of magical powers to 161–2
  books for the unlettered 165
  distraction from true worship 158–9, 172
  hostility to 159–62
  image of God in human beings 159, 161, 165
  leading into error 162
  Lollard views on 160, 161–2, 172
    see also Gower, John, *Vox clamantis*
  and magic 162
  need to substitute living counterparts 162–3
  possessed internally 171
  and power of dream images 164
  prohibition of to Moses 158–9
  secular and religious 157
  sign of the cross 159, 161
  as signa 164
  as stimulus to devotion 171
  and symbols 90–1
  used for exploitation 162
  views of 'tretyse of ymagis' (British Library) 161–3
indulgences 195, 196, 204–5, 206
Ingledew, F. 11n24
Italian language 75

Jacob, E. F. 196n69, 205n84
Jauss and Fowler 25
jealousy
  and castle of *Jalousie* (*Roman de la Rose*) 87, 91–3

Index

in Miller's Tale 95, 106
as prison (Knight's Tale) 91–5
Jean de Meun *see* Guillaume de Lorris and Jean de Meun, *Roman de la rose*
Jean l'Aveugle 63, 77
John of Gaunt 3, 61
John of Newmarket 76
Jonassen, F. B. 51n80
Jones, W. R. 160n9
Joseph, Gerhard 109–10, 109n1
jubilees 195
Jugement dou roy de Behaigne see Guillaume de Machaut
Julius Caesar 19
Jusserand, J. J. 204n81
Justice, Steven 163n19

Kaiser, R., *Medieval English* 182, 182n17
Kamerick, Kathleen 160n7
Keen, M. H. 6n2, 7n6, 18n49
Kellogg, Alfred L. and Haselmayer, Louis A. 205n85
Kelly, Douglas 157n2
Kibre, Pearl and Siraisi, Nancy G. 128n6
Kingsford, C. L. 103n20
Kiser, Lisa 65n31
Kittredge, G. L. 184, 184n25
Knapp, Daniel 189n44
Knapp, Ethan 171n36, 175n44
Knighton, Henry, *Chronicle* 159
Kohl, S. 185–6, 186n31
Kolve, V. A. 65n32, 87, 89n1
  Chaucer and the Imagery of Narrative 89–95
Krochalis, E. 169n33
Kruger, S. F. 24, 24n4, 25, 35, 35n36, 46n68, 50
Kyngyston, Edmund 189

Ladner, G. B. 52n82

Langland, William, *Piers Plowman* 3, 23, 24, 32
  confusion after the dream 48
  divine inspiration of dreams 42
  dreams within a dream 45, 46
  effects of dream 48–9
  exploring individual identity 3, 37
  motif of pilgrimage 55
  receptivity of narrator 35–6
  revelation of Christ 45
  setting 28
  taking dreams seriously 47
  tree of Charity 45, 46
  Truth 48
  vision of the universe 40
law of sanctuary 14
le Goff, J. 35, 35n35
Leach, E. 53n86
Lerer, Seth 78n54
Lewis, Dulcie 104n28
Leyerle, John 105n33
Liber de oculo morali see Peter of Limoges
liminality 51, 53–4
  and pilgrimage 54, 56
  social context 56
Lincoln, J. S. 31n26
Lindberg, David C. 127, 127n5
Lindley, Philip 60n18
Loftin, A. C. 23n2
Lollards 55, 73–4, 141, 158
  uprising 205–6
  views on images 160, 161–3, 172
Lollius 74–5
London 4, 69
  British Library
    castle of *Jalousie* 93
    MS Additional 24202 'tretyse of ymagis' 161–3
    MS Harley 4866: Hoccleve 167–8
  as New Troy 77–8, 166
Long, Thomas 179

Loomis, Roger Sherman and Willard, Rudolph 182, 182n16
Looze, Laurence de 64n26
love 79–84
  carnal and spiritual 81–2, 202
  of Christ 81, 82
  delights of spiritual love 81–2
  in dream visions 34–5, 47–8
  emanating from God 80–1
  'fire of' 79–83
  as improving force 80
  as key ingredient of the universe 80–1
  as life-force 80
  longing for good 81
  transforming power of 81
Luxembourgs 62–4, 77
Lydgate, John, *Siege of Thebes* 181, 185, 194–5, 215
Lynch, K. L. 23n2, 24–5, 51, 53

McGregor, James H. 169n33
McIntosh, H. M. 188, 188n40
McKisack, May 18n49
Macrobius 23, 24, 36, 38, 39, 42, 46
magic
  and images 162
  and science 125, 127
Manly, John M. and Rickert, Edith 97n2, 143, 143n2, 144, 188, 192
Mann, Jill 209, 209n93
Manzaloui, M. 127n4
Mars 130
Martin V, Pope 195–6, 206
Matheson, L. M. 9n15, 11n24
Méliador see Froissart, J.
Meunier et les .II. clers 110–12
Miller, Paul 163n19
Minnis, A. J. 12n27
mirrors 130
mistaken identity 129

Mitchiner, M. 191n50
Montague, Sir John 160
moral blindness 152–3
Morgan, P. 21n57
Moses 158
Muir, L. R. 51n81
Munby, Julian 103n18
Muscatine, C. 50n77, 102n16, 198n74
  Chaucer and the French Tradition 147–8, 154

Nagera, H. et al 37n41, 49n76
Neuss, Paula 106n34
Nicholson, R. 18n49
Nicole de Margival, *Dit de la panthère d'Amours* 30–1, 41, 47
Nissé, Ruth 175n44
Nolan, B. 27n11
Northumberland, Duke of 179
Northumbrians 19
Numbers (O. T.) 38

Olmert, K. M. 148, 148n15, 150n18
Olsson, Kurt 165n21
optics 127–9, 131–3
Order of the Garter 6
Ormrod, W. M. 6n2, 198n76
Owen, Charles A. 206n87

Palmer, R. B. 43n61
Pantin, W. A. 100n12, 103n18
paradisal settings 29–30, 41–2, 45
Paradys d'Amours see Froissart, J.
Parlement of Thre Ages 28, 29, 32
Parr, Johnstone 195n64
Patterson, Lee 175n43
Pearl
  authenticity 42
  circumstances of dream 27
  closeness to death 32, 36, 39
  grief of poet 33

Index

transformation of reality 40
use of dream vision 23
Pearsall, D. 23n1, 57n2, 61n20, 170n34, 192, 193n57
Peden, A. M. 23n2
Pelen, M. M. 24n3
Percival, Florence 65n32
Perkins, Nicholas 167n29
perspectiva 127–8
Peter of Limoges, *Liber de oculo morali* 133
Peterson, Kate Oelzner 133n20
Petrarch
  Canzoniere 75
  and Charles IV 76
Philippa of Hainault, Queen 63
Piaget, A. 48n72
Picts 16
Piehler, P. 30n22
Piers Plowman see Langland, William
pilgrimage 51–6
  in Christian tradition 52
  dream visions 51, 52–3
  false piety of 195
  and indulgences 204
  intensifying piety 54
  and liminality 54, 56
  self-awareness and reconstruction 54–5
  sense of *communitas* 54
  and visions 52
Pison, T. 51n80
Plantagenets 62
Polychronicon see Higden, Ranulph
Porphyry 39
Prague 77, 83
Pratt, Robert A. 133n20
pride 121, 133, 162
Prison amoureuse see Froissart, J.
privacy 87, 88, 106
privies 102–3, 103–4, 104
Pugh, Ralph B. 90n3

Quinn, William A. 65n32

Regiment of Princes, The see Hoccleve, Thomas
relics 189, 191, 195, 206
  true and false 204, 205
Reyburn, Wallace 104n28
Richard II, King 4, 57–8, 78
  love for Anne of Bohemia 60
  marriage 60
  as Troilus 78
Richard of Maidstone 83
  Concordia 78
rites of passage 53–4
Ritson 183, 183n22
Robbins, R. H. 185n29
Robert de Vere 59
Robertson, W. A. Scott 191n49
Robinson, F. N. 98
Roët, Philippa 60
Rolle, Richard, *Incendium Amoris* 81–3
Roman de la rose see Guillaume de Lorris and Jean de Meun
Roman de Troie 75
Rose, Christine 105n31
Rosenberg, Bruce A. 148, 148n14
Rowland, Beryl 211n95
Russell, J. S. 23n2, 24, 24n5, 25
Russell-Smith, Joy H. 160n8
Ryan, Lawrence V. 150n18

Sabine, Ernest L. 102n17
saints 13, 141, 161, 176
  and relics 204, 205
  see also Becket, Thomas, shrine of
Saintsbury, George 184, 184n24, 188
Salzman, L. F. 102n17
Saul, Nigel 58n4
Saxons 20
Scanlon, Larry 168n30
Scheusener-Eichholz, Gudrun 133n19

Schmidt, A. V. C. 45n66
Schofield, John 103n19
science
  and magic 125, 127
  mis/application 127
  optics 123, 127, 129–30
  see also alchemy
Scipio 38, 42, 46, 47
Scotland 16
  Franco-Scottish alliance 18n49
Scots 16
Seneca: letter to Lucilius 133
Senior 153
sermon literature 133
seven deadly sins 133
Seward, D. 198n76
Seymour, M. C. 171n39
Shaner, M. C. E. and Edwards, A. S. G. 65n32
Sheen: manor house 60
Shippey, T. A. 147n11
Siege of Thebes see Lydgate, John
sign of the cross 159, 161
Simpson, James 157n2
Sir Orfeo 42
six ages of the world 7
Skeat, W. W. 98, 117n10, 146n10, 155, 180n7, 187
Smalley, B. 10n21
Smith, William 159
Smyser, H. M. 103n20
Southern, R. W. 7n6
Spearing, A. C. 29n20, 175n44, 194n63, 215
Spiegel, G. M. 10n19
Stakel, S. 53n84
Stanbury, S. 52n84, 160n7, 160n12
Stanley, A. P. 191n50, 193n58
Stonehenge 14–15
Storm, Melvin 204n80, 206n87
Stow, John 180

Strohm, Paul 60n15, 61n19, 66n34, 158n3, 171n37, 216, 216n102, 217
Sudbury, Simon 194
Sumption, J. 52n83
Swynford, Catherine 60
symbolism 90

Tale of Beryn 142, 179–217
  audience 198, 216–17
  author's antagonism towards the Pope 206–7
  author's knowledge of Chaucer 192
  authorship 188–92
  body language 213
  borrowing from Chaucer 209, 210–11, 215
  chosen genre 197–8, 212
  compared with Chaucer 184–6, 201–3, 211–12
  critical reception 183–5
  'curtesy' 198, 199–200
  date 192–5
  detailed descriptions of places 211–12
  dramatic element 213
  editions 181–2
  fellowship, threat to 214
  Friar 190, 199
  Host 191, 195, 199, 201, 203, 204, 206, 214
  Jak the innkeeper 210
  Jenkyn Harpour 201, 202, 213
  Knight 193, 194, 199
  Miller 184, 191, 199
  Monk 189–90
  MS 445 Alnwick 179
  Nun 190
  Pardoner and Kitt 183, 191, 198–9, 200–10, 213, 214–15
    and Miller's Tale 208–9
    and Reeve's Tale 210–11

Index

Parson 189, 190
pilgrims/pilgrimages 190–2, 204–5
Prioress 186, 207
relationship to *Canterbury Tales* 186–7, 200–1, 215
title 182–3
treatment of monks and friars 189–90
Urry's text 180
Wife of Bath 186, 207, 208
Tamanini 182, 185, 193
Tanner, Marie 77n52
Tatlock, J. S. P. 145n9
Tatton-Brown, T. 193n59
Taylor, Andrew 58n6
Taylor, J. 5n1, 8n8, 9
Tedlock, B. 31n26
Theseus 92
Thomas, Alfred 63n23
Thomas, Timothy 180
Thorndike, Lynn 38n44
Tolmie, Sarah 176n45
Torti, Anna 168n30
Trevisa, John 8–9, 74
Troy 4, 77
Trumpington 211, 212
Tuck, J. Anthony 83n61
Tupper, Frederick 203n78
Turner, D. H. 189n45, 191n48
Turner, E. 51n80
Turner, Hilary L. 194n60
Turner, V. 53n87, 54, 54n89, 55, 56, 56n90
Turner, V. and Turner, E. 51, 52n84, 54n89
Turville-Petrie, T. 11n23
Tuve, R. 28n15
Tyrwhitt, Thomas 98

'universal history' 7
Urry, John 180, 187
Usk, Thomas 34n31, 65n34

Vale, J. 6n2
Venus 80–1, 83, 130
Vincent of Beavais, *Speculum maius* 130–1, 137
vision (eyesight) 128–9
defects 130–1, 131–3, 153
and seven sins 133
visions 26
see also dream visions
visual deception 128–9
Vox Clamantis see Gower, John
Vulcan 130
Vyel, John 189

wakefulness-dream boundary 36–8, 39–40, 43–5
Wakelin, Martin 147n11
Waldron, R. 9n14
Wales 16, 19
Walker, S. 21n57
Wallace, David 60n15, 62
Wallace, Reyburn 104n28
Walsingham, Thomas 58, 60
Ward, B. 52n83
Warton, Thomas 183, 183n21, 187
Watkins, Charles A. 124n2
Watson, Nicholas 160n10
Weisheipl, James A. 128n6
Wenceslas of Brabant 63–4
Wentersdorf, Karl P. 124n2
Westminster Chronicle 58, 59
Weytestathe, Richard 159
Williams, A. 204n81
Wimsatt, James I. 63n24
Windeatt, B. A. 26n7, 147n11
windows 100
in Knight's Tale and Miller's Tale 105
shot wyndowe (Miller's Tale) 87, 97–107
etymology of *shot* 97–9, 103–4

Winstead, Karen A. 183n19, 186
Witelo 128, 129, 137
Witelo, Perspectiva 128–9
Wodnesburgh, Prior 206
Wolff, W. 31n26
Wood, Margaret 100n12
Woodruff, Eveleigh 191n49, 193n58, 195n66
Woods, William F. 106n34
world as prison 109
Wright, Lawrence 102n17
Wright, S. 52n81
Wright, Thomas 97
Wyclif, John 73, 74, 141, 158, 160
Wylie, James Hamilton and Waugh, William Templeton 198n76
Wynnere and Wastoure 32, 33
  setting 28, 29, 31, 40

Zacher, Christian K. 205n82
Zeeman, Nicolette 157n2
Zink, M. 40n51